PRODUCING MUSICALS

PRODUCING MUSICALS

John Gardyne

The Crowood Press

First published in 2004 by
The Crowood Press Ltd
Ramsbury, Marlborough
Wiltshire SN8 2HR

www.crowood.com

British Library Cataloguing-in-Publication Data
A catalogue record for this book is available from the British Library.

ISBN 1 86126 627 8

All photographs by the author, unless otherwise stated.
Line illustrations by Keith Field.

Front cover: *Cabaret* produced by GSA Conservatoire at the Yvonne Arnaud Theatre, Guildford. Director, Peter Barlow; choreographer, Gerry Tebbutt; designer, Roger Ness; lighting designer, Richard Jones. Photograph by Mark Dean.
Back cover: *Calamity Jane* produced by GSA Conservatoire at the Yvonne Arnaud Theatre, Guildford. Director, John Gardyne; designer, Janey Gardiner; lighting designer, Alex Rails. Photograph by Mark Dean.

Typeset by Jean Cussons Typesetting, Diss, Norfolk

Printed and bound in Great Britain by Biddles, King's Lynn

CONTENTS

INTRODUCTION

'Producing a musical': the phrase conjures up a flood of images. The composer picking out the hit tune, note by note, on his grand piano at 3am. The producer chomping on a fat cigar at the back of the auditorium. The harassed director pleading with the leading lady who has locked herself in her dressing room. The choreographer screaming at the chorus girls as they pound through a production number for the fiftieth time. The last-minute backstage crisis. The hush of expectation as the house lights dim. The conductor raising his baton to begin the overture.

In an age when the bulk of our entertainment is provided electronically, stage musicals are more popular than ever. Every night in towns and cities all over the world, thousands of people go out to the theatre to share the unique buzz that only live performance can provide. The musical's fusion of song, music, drama, dance and spectacle creates an experience that can be intoxicating and even overwhelming for performers and audience alike. There is, literally, no business like show business.

It is therefore not surprising that many people in many different circumstances – in schools, colleges, community groups, amateur drama societies or small professional companies – wish to stage a musical themselves. It is also not surprising that they often find the sheer scale and complexity of musical theatre daunting in the extreme. Co-ordinating the numerous elements that come together to make a musical, and moulding them into an entertaining and aesthetically rewarding performance, can appear at the outset an impossibly difficult and complex task.

In this book I have sought to de-mystify that process, and provide the reader with a step-by-step guide through it, from the earliest planning stages to the final performance. It doesn't matter whether your show is large or small, amateur or professional, by Gilbert and Sullivan or Stephen Sondheim: the same basic principles of budgeting, organization and scheduling will always apply. The wardrobe department of a West End production may consist of dozens of buyers, cutters, dressmakers and dressers working seven days a week; the 'wardrobe department' of a school production may be two mothers sewing on a Saturday afternoon. Either way, somebody somewhere has to make the costumes, check that they fit, and get them ready in time for the opening night.

There are, however, some significant differences between professional and amateur theatre practice, and these are outlined in each chapter. I have also drawn attention to the ways in which staging a musical differs from staging a straight play.

A whole book could be written – indeed, whole books *have* been written – on each of the individual components that make up musical theatre, from set-building to vocal technique, choreography to sound design. Readers seeking more information than I have space to provide here should refer to the 'Further Reading' section at the back of this book.

All practical examples are taken from musicals that I have directed or worked on myself, or which are generally well known. There are, of course, thousands of other shows out there to be discovered and enjoyed, and potential producers, directors, performers, designers and technicians should read, watch and listen to as many of them as they can.

John Gardyne
August 2003

www.johngardyne.biz

The way in. Entering a theatre by the stage door for the first time is an unforgettable experience.

Acknowledgements

I always knew that producing a show was a collaborative effort: now I have found out that writing a book is one as well. I would like to thank the numerous writers, composers, producers, actors, designers, musicians and technicians that I have worked with on plays, musicals and operas over the years for their enthusiasm, support, skills and ideas.

I would like to thank the following for allowing me to photograph their work: Carol Metcalfe and the staff at the Bridewell Theatre, London; Gillian Thorpe and the staff of the Orange Tree Theatre, Richmond; Peter Barlow, Gerry Tebbutt, Caroline Heale, Jaqui George, Roger Ness, Carol Dean and the staff and students at GSA Conservatoire; Nicholas Barter, Neil Fraser and the students at RADA; Ian Watt-Smith, Paul Chant and the staff and students at the School of Musical Theatre, Arts Educational School, London; and Sammy Lam and Susanna Chan at the Hong Kong Academy for Performing Arts (www.hkapa.edu).

For their advice and assistance on individual chapters, my grateful thanks are also due to producers Rosemary Richards, Mark Watty and Richard Jordan; composers Carl Davis, Nick Bicât and Matthew Miller; musical directors Robert Lamont, Jon Laird, Ian Smith, Peter Roberts and Martin Waddington; designers Alison Cartledge, Alison Chitty, Tina Bicât, Janey Gardiner, Jesse Schwenk and Roger Ness; directors Tim Flavin, David Flaten and Robin Tebbutt; choreographers Jill Francis, Mark Bruce, Tracey Collier, Aidan Treays and Ayse Tashkiran; and lighting and sound designers Neil Fraser, Kim Hanson, Roger Frith, Simon Baxter and Mark Dymock. Also to Amanda Smith and Geoff Saunders at Samuel French Ltd, John Sinfield at Musicscope, Seán Grey at Josef Weinberger and Kathryn Oswald and Martin Kingsbury at Faber Music; to Professor Ken Pickering and Dr Margaret McAliskey at Trinity College, London; to Mark Dean, Paul Thompson (paulthomps@aol.com) and Chris Honeywell (chris@working-images.co.uk) for photography; to Tanya Lees at Dress Circle; to Peter Jennison for computer equipment, Andrew Taylor for scanning and Ian Finlay for photographic equipment; to Jan Warringon for proof-reading; and to Sam Walters at the Orange Tree for giving me my first job in the theatre.

Extracts from *Bernice Bobs Her Hair* (music by Matthew Miller, book and lyrics by John Gardyne) are reproduced by permission of the authors. For further information about the work, contact: info@johngardyne.biz.

Extracts from *The Mermaid* (music by Carl Davis, book and lyrics by Hiawyn Oram) are reproduced by permission of the publisher Faber Music Ltd. For further information about the work contact Performance Promotion Department, Faber Music Ltd, 3 Queen Square, London WC1N 3AU, England. Tel +44(0)20 7833 7911/2, Fax +44 (0)20 7833 7939, email: promotion@fabermusic.com.

1 THE PRODUCER

We've all seen the old movies. Mickey Rooney sticks out his chin and shouts, 'Heck, we'll do the show right here in the barn!' Judy Garland clasps her hands and gazes at him lovingly, their friends cheer, Mickey gives that goofy grin, and they're off. They're putting on a show. Just a couple of weeks later Mickey and Judy, exhausted but triumphant, hug each other as the packed audience rise as one to give them a standing ovation on opening night.

Well, that's the Hollywood version. Simplistic, dated, idealized, incredible? Of course. But the thing that is absolutely spot on is Mickey's attitude: his steely-eyed determination, his boundless energy and optimism, his willingness to take on anybody who gets in his way, his utterly unshakeable belief that, despite all the obstacles that lie before him, the show will go on.

You see, Mickey may be the show's star, author, composer, choreographer and director, but first and foremost he's something else: he's the producer.

The Palace Theatre in the West End of London. Home to Les Misérables, *one of the most successful musicals of all time.*

GETTING STARTED

It doesn't matter whether it's a primary school Christmas play, a late-night revue, a college musical, a large-scale community opera or a West End show: every musical production begins life in the same way. One fine morning somebody takes the decision to make it happen, and at that moment, that person becomes the show's producer.

It is not a job for the faint-hearted. When you first mention that you are thinking about producing a show, expect to meet a lot of resistance. Initially nobody – *nobody* – will believe that it will ever happen. Everyone will raise objections: they will say that there isn't enough money, or time or resources, nobody will want to be in it, it's too risky, it's too much effort, it'll never work, and there is no point in even trying.

As a producer, you need huge reserves of resilience, self-belief, energy and persuasiveness to combat this. You will spend months raising money, planning, finding a theatre, negotiating rights, recruiting a creative team, scheduling, helping to cast performers, balancing budgets, raising more money, promoting the show, doing deals on ticket sales, raising yet more money, monitoring rehearsals – and you may end up selling ice creams in the interval.

You must take responsibility for recruiting and motivating a team of dozens – even hundreds – of disparate individuals over a period of weeks or months; for resolving artistic disagreements and personality clashes; for dealing with sponsors, bankers, politicians, public officials, journalists, actors, designers, musicians, advertising executives – and of course the general public who make up the audience. In addition you will be the business manager of the whole undertaking, and as such will be ultimately responsible for all the financial aspects of the show, from paying the wages to buying the champagne for the first night party.

It's a tough and scary job. Don't ever think it'll be easy.

INDIVIDUALS AND ORGANIZATIONS

If your production is very small scale – a one-off cabaret evening, say – it may be just about possible for you to work as a private individual, to pay the costs from your personal bank account, and to pocket the takings after the performance (although this may then lead to some awkward questions from the taxman). However, it is preferable to set up a separate bank account and put the whole operation on a proper business footing; even a short musical revue with two performers should operate as a business partnership. Banks and businesses – and indeed individuals – are far more willing to deal with an organization that has proper financial accountability than with a single person. Grant-awarding and funding bodies are extremely unlikely to accept applications for public money from a private individual for a theatre project.

If you are producing a show for a school, college or existing theatre company – amateur or professional – some sort of organizational structure will already exist. You may have a company bank account, available premises, an existing pool of potential participants, even some money earmarked for the budget. On the other hand, you may be starting from scratch.

PROFIT-MAKING AND NON-PROFIT-MAKING ORGANIZATIONS

If your production is a commercial enterprise and you intend to attract investors and to make profits, you will need to create a limited company with a managing director, a

The Questors Theatre in West London, an amateur theatre equipped to professional standards.

company secretary and a board of directors. Obviously the legal and financial implications of business law vary from country to country, and you would be well advised to seek professional advice if you need to set up a limited company.

If your production is not intended to make a profit, you can set up a voluntary or not-for-profit organization, which may then make you eligible for grant aid from national and local government and/or various funding bodies. Again, specific legal requirements will vary, but in most cases you will need to draw up a constitution with an agreed managerial structure, define a statement of intent, and assemble a committee to be responsible for running it. Most public funding bodies will require your organization to state its general aims and intentions as well as the aims of the project you are undertaking, and to demonstrate that this will have good effects within the community in which you live and work. Even private sponsors will need a summary of your organization and project aims, so it is as well to get your plans and proposals on paper before you start applying for funds.

Depending on the organization's circumstances, it may also be possible to register it as a charity, and benefit from tax breaks and other concessions.

Try and recruit someone with an accounting or legal background onto your management committee. The better the organization of your legal and financial affairs, and the greater your credibility, the more likely you will be to raise the money you need. Even a not-for-profit organization is sometimes well advised to become a limited company, so that individuals do not become personally responsible for its finances.

Types of theatre

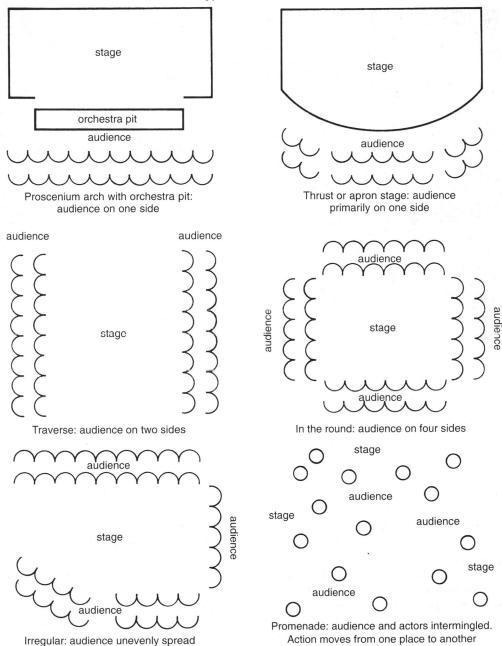

Proscenium arch with orchestra pit:
audience on one side

Thrust or apron stage: audience
primarily on one side

Traverse: audience on two sides

In the round: audience on four sides

Irregular: audience unevenly spread

Promenade: audience and actors intermingled.
Action moves from one place to another

The layout of the theatre dictates the relationship between the actors and audience. Always consider where the piano or orchestra will be placed.

Equal Oportunities

It is becoming common practice for companies and voluntary organizations to undertake and adhere to equal opportunities policies, and to ensure that employment by, and/or participation in, their activities will, as far as possible, not be influenced by considerations of gender, age, religious persuasion, sexual persuasion or ethnic origin.

In some countries, adherence to an equal opportunities policy may be a prerequisite for grant aid and central and/or local government funding. You may also be required to monitor your activities and provide evidence of the effectiveness of your policy if required.

FINDING A THEATRE

The next question is, where will the performance take place? Of course, if you are producing the show at a school or college you may already have access to a purpose-built theatre. Many amateur groups now have their own theatres, some equipped to professional standards. If you are not in this fortunate situation you will have to hire a venue.

Apart from a few repertory theatres that produce their own work fifty-two weeks of the year, most theatre managements will consider renting their premises to a visiting production. But be warned: this may be expensive. Any theatre is a business, and there is no reason why their owners should be willing to take a financial risk on the success of your show. Normally they will charge a weekly hire rate, payable in advance.

The Orange Tree Theatre in Richmond-upon-Thames. A purpose-built theatre-in-the-round.

Site-specific productions can be extraordinary events. A performance of Sondheim's **The Frogs** *at Brentford swimming pool. Director, John Gardyne; designer, Alison Heffernan; lighting designer, Chris Jones.*

Visit the theatres in your area, and see if any of them suit your requirements. Phone around to get some hire charges – and be prepared to be shocked. At the time of writing, even a small fringe theatre in a room above a pub in London can cost in excess of £1,000 a week. Large, purpose-built theatres may cost ten times that. Hire charges usually include the use of some technical equipment and support, front-of-house staff and ushers, box-office services, and some advertising. When you phone around, find out exactly what is included in the price, as these extras can make a big difference to your bottom line.

Even if you can afford it, there is no guarantee that the management of the venue will agree to rent it to you. They need to safeguard their artistic reputation and maintain their core audience. If you are a new company without a track record of successful production, they may doubt your credibility. On the other hand, if you are already known to the management and/or extremely persuasive and/or very lucky (probably all three), you may be able to pay a reduced rent or negotiate a box-office split with the venue.

ALTERNATIVE PERFORMANCE SPACES

If you cannot find a purpose-built public theatre to meet your needs, try other options.

Investigate school halls, college and university facilities, church halls, scout huts, assembly rooms, community centres, rooms in pubs, barns, warehouses, factories. They may not be as grand as a 'proper' theatre, but they will almost certainly be a lot cheaper.

Be positive, and consider what you would need to make such places into a viable performance space: a raised stage area? Extra seating? Lighting and sound equipment? Be creative, too: maybe you could put the audience on four sides and stage the show 'in the round'? Or put them on two sides and stage it in traverse? Sometimes a non-theatre venue can provide the ideal setting for a particular show. How about *Seven Brides for Seven Brothers* in a barn, *Grease* in a high-school gym, or *The Pyjama Game* in a disused factory?

In recent years the author has directed Gilbert and Sullivan's *Trial by Jury* in a courtroom, *The King and I* in London's Freemasons' Temple, and Sondheim's *The Frogs* in a swimming pool. In each case the setting lent the production a unique excitement and resonance that would have been impossible to create in a traditional proscenium-arch theatre. A word of warning, however: when looking at alternative venues it is sometimes easy to get carried away with excitement about the atmosphere and performance opportunities offered by the space, and completely ignore the fact that the musicians will have to go somewhere. Don't forget the band.

PERFORMING LICENCES

By law, all theatres, concert halls and performance venues must meet certain minimum health and safety conditions before they can be licensed for public entertainment. If you plan to present a public performance in a non-licensed venue, you must acquire a performance licence from the local authority. When you apply for this a safety officer will visit the venue and calculate the maximum audience numbers permitted to attend per performance.

Don't assume that a licence will be granted automatically. The licensing authority will have a stringent set of criteria that must be met concerning access, fire exits, electricity supply, facilities and audience safety. So contact the local authority as soon as possible, and find out exactly what their requirements are likely to be. Be as co-operative as you can with the safety officer, and be conscientious about meeting any additional conditions that may be required. If you fail to do so you can be closed down before the curtain goes up.

THE PRODUCER'S SCHEDULE

How far ahead should you plan? The two vital commodities that a producer needs are money and time. If money is limited – and when isn't it? – at least give yourself plenty of time. Consider how much you have to do: for instance, do you have to set up a company or find premises? Do you have a director in mind? How many people will you have to recruit? How long will it take to find them?

The Frogs involved nearly one hundred people and took over a year to produce. *Oomf!* – an open-air music and theatre spectacular mounted in Oxford to celebrate the millennium – used 3,000 performers and 250 musicians, and was two-and-a-half-years in the making. At the other end of the scale, a friend of the author recently decided to put together a one-woman cabaret of songs to showcase her repertoire. She booked a small London theatre for three nights, hired a pianist, rehearsed, advertised the show, and sold out all performances. The whole process took less than two months.

A producer starting from scratch will obviously need more time than one who is working within an existing organization or company. Remember that most public theatres are

OOMF! Oxfordshire's Own Millennium Festival: two-and-a-half years in the making, one performance only. Musical theatre events do not get much bolder or more spectacular than this. Photo: Chris Honeywell

scheduled between six and twelve months ahead, and you may not be able to get a slot in the theatre you want for over a year.

More importantly, give yourself a realistic chance of raising the money. Funding bodies work to yearly budgets, and applications for any kind of grant must usually be submitted well in advance. The closing date for applications for funding in the financial year starting 1 April may well be in the previous September. If you plan to recoup all your expenditure costs from ticket sales – or even make a profit –

remember that you will not see this money for a long time.

If you are not working within an existing organization, give yourself at least twelve months, and longer if it is a big show involving a large cast. Nine months is ambitious, especially if you are expecting people to give their time and services for free. If you are working within a school, college or existing company, even six months may be tight, and to try and stage a musical in less than this is foolhardy.

Trial by Jury Master Schedule				
Weeks To Open/ Week Commencing	Production Schedule	Actors Calls	Design Schedule	Venue Schedule
18 9/1/95	approach 94 Designer approach 94 Cast approach 94 MD approach 94 CSM illustration to Nicky Webb in kind credits to Nicky Webb		confirm Design sponsors	
17 16/1/95				
16 23/1/95				
15 30/1/95	book rehearsal hall book audition venue book audition pianist finalize all creative team confirm 94 cast returning		confirm Designer	
14 6/2/95	confirmed bios to Ben C.			
13 13/2/95	press conference mlw away from 16th to 12th			
12 20/2/95	mlw away			
11 27/2/95	mlw away			
10 6/3/95	mlw away			
9 13/3/95	mlw returns! mlw theatre royal hanley			
8 20/3/95	arrange final auditions			
7 27/3/95	hold final auditions			
6 3/4/95	finalize cast production brief		final designs agreed	
5 10/4/95				
4 17/4/95			props/costumes assembly	
3 24/4/95			props/costumes assembly	
2 1/5/95			props/costumes assembly fittings	
1 8/5/95	start rehearsals	rehearse	final fittings	
9/5/95		rehearse pm venue		pm rehearsal

10/5/95		rehearse	
11/5/95		rehearse	get in
		perform pm	performance pm
12/5/95		perform pm	performance pm
13/5/95		warmup rehearsal hall	performance pm
		4pm platform	
		perform pm	
0			
17/5/95		perform pm	performance pm
18/5/95		perform pm	performance pm
19/5/95		perform pm	performance pm
20/5/95		warmup rehearsal hall	
		2pm platform	performance pm
		perform pm	get out

Producer Mark Watty's schedule for a revival of Gilbert and Sullivan's Trial by Jury. *With a running time of thirty-five minutes, this production only needed to be rehearsed for one week – but note that planning began eighteen weeks in advance.*

The producer's desk. Note the year planner on the wall.

SETTING THE DATE

The theatre is booked, and the date of the first night is set. There is no such thing as late delivery in the theatre: everything *has* to be ready for that performance. So get a big chart and start planning.

Some producers like to designate the week the show opens as 'week 0'. The previous week – the last week of rehearsals – is 'week minus one' (week −1), the week before that 'week minus two' (week −2) and so on, right up to the present, which may be 'week −48'. They feel that 'counting down' helps to focus the mind.

Work backwards from the opening night. If you plan to rehearse for two months, then you should aim to have a complete cast no later than week −10. (Scheduling rehearsals is dealt with in detail in Chapter 7.) The designer and director will need to have agreed the set design before rehearsals start. Say they need four weeks to do their work (and this may be ambitious, depending on their experience and ability). The director will usually have been appointed first, so the designer has to be on board by week −13 at the latest. The director may wish to consider several designers, which will take more time. Let's give him three weeks to find the right person: that takes us to week −16.

The theatre requires a deposit of £1,000 six months in advance, so the producer needs to have raised this money by (at least!) week −27. A vital funding application has to be submitted six months before the end of the tax year – that is, no later than week −35. And so on ...

Don't underestimate how long things will take, and build as much leeway into the schedule as you can. Once the producer has set the clock ticking, it can't be stopped.

2 CHOOSING A SHOW

If you have decided to produce a musical it is quite likely that you will already have a particular show in mind. If you haven't, then it's time to get researching.

SEEKING INSPIRATION

Start by flicking through as many books on musical theatre history as you can find. This should not be a chore: enjoy yourself! Immerse yourself in the world of show business and your research will be as entertaining as it is illuminating. Be open – the oddest fact, the tiniest detail about a show may catch your eye: a photo, a line from a song, an anecdote, a review. Don't worry about going down blind alleys, and don't edit your research, since you don't know what you're looking for yet.

If you find yourself intrigued by a particular composer, writer, show, director, choreographer or star, then give yourself time to read round the subject. Look at biographies and autobiographies, contemporary reviews and critical analyses; cross-index with other books and check out the footnotes.

Detailed summaries and critiques of shows can be found in Kurt Gänzl's *Gänzl's Book of the Broadway Musical*, Stanley Green's *Broadway Musicals Show by Show* and Rexton S. Bunnett's *Guide to Musicals*. *Let's Put On a Musical* by Peter Filichia categorizes shows by their casting and production requirements, while Ken Mandelbaum's *Not Since Carrie* provides a fascinating overview of shows that for one reason or another flopped on their opening. *The Virgin Encylopedia of Stage and Film Musicals* edited by Colin Larkin is well worth a look, too.

Using the Internet

In recent years the Internet has changed all our lives by providing instant, cheap and easy access to unimaginable volumes of information. Research has never been easier.

Currently there are several excellent web sites devoted to musical theatre, and more will no doubt appear in the future. These can prove invaluable in your search for the right show. Try visiting www.musicalstages. co.uk, www.musicalheaven.com, www. musicalshows.me.uk and www.nodanw.com. John Kendrick's wonderful *Cyber Encyclopaedia of Musical Theatre, TV and Film* at www. Musicals101.com is also highly recommended. As well as providing access to a wealth of reference material, these sites offer newsletters, bulletin boards, chatrooms, download services and links to related sites worldwide: use them all. Surf for an hour, and you will know what is happening in musical theatre this week in Adelaide and Edinburgh, New York and Berlin, Vancouver and London, Stockholm and Zagreb. Make a note of anything that sounds interesting, and start following up leads.

If you find yourself chasing a particularly obscure show and your researches are getting nowhere, try posting a question on the net. Musical theatre buffs love to share their

Samuel French's Theatre Bookshop in central London.

Browsing through CDs at Dress Circle.

knowledge: somebody, somewhere, will have the answer.

Listening to the Music

Finding the music is the fun part. Browse through the CDs in the 'Stage and Screen' sections of music shops and libraries: who knows what you will find amongst all those film soundtracks?

If you can get to London, go to Dress Circle in Covent Garden (57–59 Monmouth Street, WC2H 9DG), the self-styled 'greatest showbiz shop in the world', which specializes in recordings, sheet music, books and memorabilia. The enthusiastic, friendly staff will astound you with their encyclopaedic knowledge of musical theatre. And if you can't get there in person, browse their web site at www.dresscircle.com. Ten minutes' walk away is French's Theatre Bookshop at 52 Fitzroy Street, W1T 5JR (www.samuelfrench-london.co.uk).

In New York the place to go is Footlight at 113 East 12th Street. They also have a website at www.footlight.com where you can buy material online and use their information service to keep up with the latest theatre news and gossip. There are two other excellent shops in New York: Drama Book Shop at 250 West 40th Street (www.dramabookshop.com), and Applause at 211 West 71st Street.

Beg, borrow or buy as many cast recordings as you can (or can afford). Put some time aside to listen to them carefully, without distractions, on headphones if you have them. Then read the liner notes for a summary of the plot, scenes and characters. How much of this information did you glean from the soundtrack? Do the songs help to tell the story, or do they seem to be irrelevant? Do the characters appear likeable and fresh, or clichéd and dull?

How about the music? Did it make you tap your feet? Did it make you smile? Did it make you laugh? Did it make the hairs on the back of your neck stand on end? If the answer to this last question is 'yes', then listen to it again immediately because you may be on to something.

Films and Videos

Find out if there is a movie of any of the shows in which you are interested, then track them down through libraries and video shops. You may be able to find them at specialist musical theatre suppliers such as Dress Circle and Footlight, or you can order them on video or DVD online through www.amazon.com or cult film web sites such as www.blackstar.co.uk.

Again, set time aside and watch them carefully. Enjoy the performances, the editing, the location and the design, but be analytical, too. Ask yourself what is the basic story? Who are the main characters? Do you care about them? Does the music move you, or leave you cold?

Stage versus Screen

A word of warning: stage and screen are very different media, and original theatre scripts are often substantially rewritten for film versions. Songs, characters and scenes may have been added or cut during the adaptation process. For instance, *Showboat* has been filmed on three occasions, each time with substantial changes in dialogue, score and lyrics: John O'Hara's hard-edged, cynical script for Rodgers and Hart's *Pal Joey* was bowdlerized for the 1957 movie starring Frank Sinatra; and the original stage script for *Grease* was significantly re-worked for the hit 1978 film in order to showcase the talents of John Travolta and Olivia Newton-John.

What you see is not necessarily what you will get.

Printed Music and Scores

Sooner or later you will need to lay hands on the printed music and script. You may be able to find scores of some of the older shows and operettas in music shops and libraries. The

Cabaret

The musical *Cabaret* underwent a series of radical changes in its transformation from Tony-winning stage show to multi-Oscar-winning movie. The nationality of Sally Bowles was changed from English to American to accommodate the casting of Liza Minelli; several songs were cut, and others added; and the subplot was completely rewritten. In limiting the songs in the film almost entirely to the numbers performed in The Kit Kat Klub and filming them for the most part in close-up, director Bob Fosse found a brilliant method of blending the conventions of stage performance with the more naturalistic demands of cinema.

It is a rare example of a musical that exists in two very different versions, each of which remains a perennial favourite: even people who claim to hate movie musicals love *Cabaret*.

complete scores are expensive, but include all vocal parts, plus underscoring, incidental and scene-change music.

Watch out for printed 'Vocal Selections': these are collections of sheet music of individual songs from a show, usually solos. However, they will not normally be sufficient to make a proper assessment of the whole work.

MUSIC PUBLISHERS AND AGENTS

While many bookshops have a whole section dedicated to the printed scripts of straight plays, the script of a musical (often referred to as its libretto, or 'book') may be harder to get hold of. Worldwide performance rights to musicals are controlled by music publishing companies such as Samuel French, Josef Weinberger, Musicscope, Tams Witmark and Music Theater International. They act as agents for the writers and protect their interests.

A selection of publishers' catalogues and other research material.

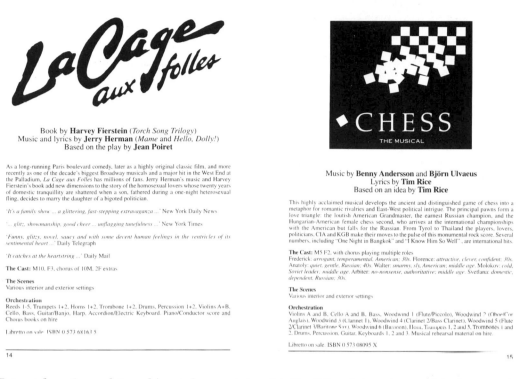

Catalogue of Musical Plays

Full Scale Musicals

Book by **Harvey Fierstein** (*Torch Song Trilogy*)
Music and lyrics by **Jerry Herman** (*Mame* and *Hello, Dolly!*)
Based on the play by **Jean Poiret**

As a long-running Paris boulevard comedy, later as a highly original classic film, and more recently as one of the decade's biggest Broadway musicals and a major hit in the West End at the Palladium, *La Cage aux Folles* has millions of fans. Jerry Herman's music and Harvey Fierstein's book add new dimensions to the story of the homosexual lovers whose twenty years of domestic tranquillity are shattered when a son, fathered during a one-night heterosexual fling, decides to marry the daughter of a bigoted politician.

'It's a family show ... a glittering, fast-stepping extravaganza ...' New York Daily News

'... glitz, showmanship, good cheer ... unflagging tunefulness ...' New York Times

'Funny, glitzy, novel, saucy and with some decent human feelings in the ventricles of its sentimental heart ...' Daily Telegraph

'It catches at the heartstring ...' Daily Mail

The Cast: M10, F3, chorus of 10M, 2F extras

The Scenes
Various interior and exterior settings

Orchestration
Reeds 1-5, Trumpets 1+2, Horns 1+2, Trombone 1+2, Drums, Percussion 1+2, Violins A+B, Cello, Bass, Guitar/Banjo, Harp, Accordion/Electric Keyboard. Piano/Conductor score and Chorus books on hire

Libretto on sale. ISBN 0 573 68163 5

14

Music by **Benny Andersson** and **Björn Ulvaeus**
Lyrics by **Tim Rice**
Based on an idea by **Tim Rice**

This highly acclaimed musical develops the ancient and distinguished game of chess into a metaphor for romantic rivalries and East-West political intrigue. The principal pawns form a love triangle: the loutish American Grandmaster, the earnest Russian champion, and the Hungarian-American female chess second, who arrives at the international championships with the American but falls for the Russian. From Tyrol to Thailand the players, lovers, politicians, CIA and KGB make their moves to the pulse of this monumental rock score. Several numbers, including "One Night in Bangkok" and "I Know Him So Well", are international hits.

The Cast: M5 F2, with chorus playing multiple roles
Frederick: *arrogant, temperamental, American; 30s.* Florence: *attractive, clever, confident; 30s.* Anatoly: *quiet, gentle, Russian; 40s.* Walter: *smarmy, sly, American; middle age.* Molokov: *cold, Soviet leader; middle age.* Arbiter: *no-nonsense, authoritative; middle age.* Svetlana: *domestic, dependent, Russian; 30s.*

The Scenes
Various interior and exterior settings

Orchestration
Violins A and B, Cello A and B, Bass, Woodwind 1 (Flute/Piccolo), Woodwind 2 (Oboe/Cor Anglais), Woodwind 3 (Clarinet 1), Woodwind 4 (Clarinet 2/Bass Clarinet), Woodwind 5 (Flute 2/Clarinet 3/Baritone Sax), Woodwind 6 (Bassoon), Horn, Trumpets 1, 2 and 3, Trombones 1 and 2, Drums, Percussion, Guitar, Keyboards 1, 2 and 3. Musical rehearsal material on hire.

Libretto on sale. ISBN 0 573 08095 X

15

Extract from Samuel French's catalogue, giving details of the plot, cast, scenes and orchestration for each show.

A musical is a very valuable commodity, the fruit of many months and years of hard work by the writer. As with all copyright material, there is a constant threat of piracy and unlicensed performance. For this reason the agents maintain a tight hold over all the essential printed material: libretti, scores, instrumental arrangements, band parts and so on.

Publishers' Catalogues
Each company publishes a catalogue of the shows it controls; this will typically include the outline of the plot, lists of musical numbers, a breakdown of the main characters and scenes, and instrumental requirements. Find out which company controls the performance rights in your country for the show or shows in which you are interested. You can find directories of licensing agents at many of the larger theatre web sites, including www.Musicals101.com, and www.musicalheaven.com.

You should then apply in writing to the agent for a 'perusal copy' of the printed copy of the show. If the show is available for production (*see* the section on 'Availability', below) the agent will send you this, on loan, for an agreed period of time, usually one month. (You may be asked to pay a small charge for this service.)

Perusal Form

To: Josef Weinberger Ltd.
12-14 Mortimer Street
London W1N 7RD
Fax: (0044)+(0)171-436 9616

Date *14 July 2002*

Please Use Block Capitals

Please send me perusal material of the shows listed below:

1 *GUYS & DOLLS* . . . .

2 *HOW TO SUCCEED IN BUSINESS* . . . .

3 . . . .

Name *A. PRODUCER* . . . .

Organization *A. COMPANY LTD* . . . .

Address *57 MAIN STREET* . . . .

. . . . . *TOWN* . . . .

. . . . . *COUNTY, POSTCODE* . . . .

Telephone *1234-56789* . . . .

Conventional stages are traditionally divided into nine areas for the purposes of rehearsal, and abbreviations such as 'UR' or 'DSL' often appear in libretti.

upstage right U.R. or U.S.R.	up centre U.C.	upstage left U.L. or U.S.L.
stage right R. or S.R.	centre C.	stage left L. or S.L.
downstage right D.R. or D.S.R.	down centre D.C.	downstage left D.L. or D.S.L.

audience

Perusal Material

Perusal material usually consists of a full libretto of the show and a piano score. If a full score is not available a 'vocal book', with vocal lines and simple song arrangements, may be provided. Demo tapes of songs are occasionally supplied for lesser known musicals and children's shows.

Sometimes the piano score has instrumental band cues marked so it can be used to conduct the show from the piano or conductor's podium. This is known as the 'piano conductor'. Full orchestral scores such as exist for classical operas and oratorios are not usually available for modern musicals.

Note that the perusal copy is supplied in good faith and should not be photocopied or

scanned in any way. To do this is a breach of the writer's copyright.

Reading the Script/Playing the Music
When you receive the perusal material, read right through the show from the top, aloud. How do the words sound when spoken? Can you follow the plot?

Even if you can read music well, it is worth getting someone to play the score as you go. Often the full power of a vital scene is only truly revealed by the emotional subtext of the underscoring. You may be surprised – pleasantly or otherwise – to discover additional songs that never made it onto the original cast albums.

Persuade a couple of friends to sing the numbers for you. If you have heard only a single cast recording up to this point, these new vocal performances will provide you with a fresh perspective on the music.

OPPOSITE: *Perusal material request form from Josef Weinberger Ltd.*

Look into your heart and tell me that she's your true mate ...

(The Prince looks over at Oriana. She turns her head away proudly. The Prince is torn for a moment. Then looks back at Ingrid and assents.)

PRINCE   Yes ...

MUSIC 27   Betrayed

MERSISTERS, MR DOLPHIN & SEA CREATURES *(a rising wail)*

Betrayed, betrayed, betrayed!

(FX of a storm brewing in distance as Grandmother Mer and Sea King exit and the Bishop marries the Prince and Ingrid. The Prince lifts her veil and kisses her.)

(The Queen kisses Ingrid and the Prince and they exit with Guests following.)

(Wind FX increase. Oriana remains alone on Deck. She looks down at her legs. She takes a few steps and then as if suddenly overcome by the wonder of them, she dances, glorying in what they can do.)

(Lights dim on the Deck area and rise in the Ocean Area. The Mersisters and Mr Dolphin have not yet seen the Sea Witch though she's seen them.)

RADEGUND   I'm not giving up. There's still time before dawn. We must bargain with the Sea Witch.

ANCHORET   We wouldn't dare.

RADEGUND   We have to.

(The Sea Witch reveals herself.)

SEA WITCH   Looking for something are we? A lost life perhaps? Well, if you're that desperate to save your little sister, persuade your father to give me what I ask .... and emphasise the private army!

RADGEUND   You're wasting your time, Witch. Our Father will never give in to your demands. But when this is over, and Oriana is gone forever, who do you think he'll turn on to avenge his pain?

ESMERALDA and ANCHORET   You!
(they point at her)

You, Witch!

RADEGUND   Unless you find it in yourself to help us save her, your life will not be worth living.

SEA WITCH   Hmmm ... I see you're not just pretty heads.

RADEGUND   Negotiate with us.

(The Sea Witch takes out a glinting knife. She holds it up and caresses their long hair.)

SEA WITCH   Well, since you mention it, there is one chance to save your sister's life. But it will cost you ... such pretty pretty hair ...

(Lights black on the Ocean Area as the Sea Witch leads the Mersisters off. Lights rise on the Deck as the Prince enters looking for Oriana. He sees Oriana on a pile of fishing nets, quietly unravelling them and approaches.)

PRINCE   Mysterious one, without a name, a past, a voice to explain yourself.

(She looks at him then away.)

PRINCE   O ... you must listen ...

LEFT: *Extract from the libretto of* The Mermaid. *Book and lyrics copyright 2003 by Hiawyn Oram.*

ABOVE: *Matching page from the score of* The Mermaid, *showing how the two interrelate. Music copyright 2003 by Carl Davis. Book and lyrics copyright 2003 by Hiawyn Oram.*

Conventions

The libretti and scores of musicals use a number of conventions that may not be familiar to actors and directors who have previously worked only on straight plays.

In the libretto, all song lyrics are printed as verse, and may be in capital letters. When different lyrics are sung simultaneously they are printed side by side. Underscored passages – passages of spoken dialogue that are accompanied by music – are often indicated by a continuous vertical line in the left-hand margin. Songs and musical passages are identified by numbers that relate to numbers in the score and band parts.

The libretti of older musicals are often littered with stage directions and technical instructions. These describe the original staging and need not be followed. (*See* Chapter 9 for further information on this.)

In the score or piano conductor, the cue for each musical number is marked at the top of the page. Key dialogue cues are marked where appropriate. When key pieces of action are timed to the music, this is indicated.

French's Acting Editions

Libretti of the older musicals published by Samuel French Ltd often appear in 'acting editions', which include lengthy and detailed blocking instructions such as 'moves DC', 'crosses L', 'picks up handkerchief', and so on. These are usually reproduced from the prompt copy of the original production. Although these sometimes make the libretti difficult to read, try not to be intimidated by them; there is no obligation for actors, directors and choreographers to follow these moves, so your production will not be straightjacketed by them.

In libretti of newer musicals these weighty stage directions do not appear, mainly because directors are now much more careful about protecting the copyright on what is essentially their work. It is also true that in recent years producing companies, both amateur and professional, have become much more inventive and rehearse for longer, and are therefore more inclined to create their own blocking and choreography.

French's acting editions may also include groundplans of sets, lighting plots, props lists, costume breakdowns, and a list of cues for each staging department. Use this information sparingly, however, and do not rely on it, because it may be irrelevant to the design and staging of your production.

Availability

You should be aware that there is a possibility that the show you have set your heart on is not available for production. A professional producer may already have acquired the exclusive rights to performance in your country or region for a certain period. During this time, any rival production – on whatever scale – can represent a potential threat to ticket sales, and thus to the producer's profits and the writer's royalties. So the show becomes 'unavailable' for a time, during which applications for smaller professional or amateur productions will be automatically refused.

Musicals will not usually be made available to amateurs until the writer's agent feels that the market for professional productions has been fully exploited. The original West End or Broadway run may be followed by a tour, or by regional theatre productions, and the show remain unavailable for years. *The Rocky Horror Show* – now over thirty years old – has never been made available for amateur production, and is unlikely to be while professional productions continue to play to packed houses worldwide.

If a show is unavailable, it is unavailable. The agent may suggest an alternative, or he may ask you to re-apply at a later date.

Do not attempt to go ahead with an unlicensed production. Such an action will severely compromise your credibility as a producer, and probably lead to legal action.

SOME PRACTICAL CONSIDERATIONS

Before making your final choice of show, it would be as well to double-check certain practical considerations. For instance, is it suitable for the venue? In theory, any show can be performed anywhere: *Into the Woods, Calamity Jane, The King and I, The Sound of Music* and *Seven Brides for Seven Brothers* have all been performed in recent years in London in tiny fringe theatres.

However, just be aware that each show will have certain minimum requirements that you will have to be able to meet. The central image of *A Chorus Line* is just that: a line of sixteen dancers standing staring out into a deserted auditorium. This would be tricky in the round. *Little Shop of Horrors* depends on complex puppetry to operate Audrey II, the man-eating alien plant: will your venue be able to accommodate it? Rock musicals such as *Tommy, Godspell* and *Hair* are loud: if your venue is small, can you be sure that the audience won't be deafened by pounding drums and a thumping bass guitar?

Don't get scared off too easily: anything – well, nearly anything – is possible. Just remember that a large-scale musical with lots of choreography may feel cramped in a small venue, while a pocket-sized show like *Starting Here, Starting Now* may get lost on a huge stage.

Ask yourself if it is suitable for the potential cast: if actors are to be drawn from a limited group of people (for instance, students from

your school or college), consider the general suitability of the show for those available.

A show may require dazzling jazz dance (*A Chorus Line, West Side Story*) or red-hot tap (*42nd Street, Crazy for You*): do you have enough performers with these skills? The musicals of Stephen Sondheim require such skilful and accurate singing that even professionals find them extremely challenging. Will your cast be up to it?

Publishers' Websites

Most publishers now post their catalogues on the Internet. The following web sites may well prove useful:

Samuel French Ltd
www.samuelfrench-london.co.uk (UK)
www.samuelfrench.com (International)

Josef Weinberger Ltd
www.josef-weinberger.com (UK and international)

Broadway Play Publishing Inc
www.broadwayplaypubl.com (US and internatonal)

Music Theater International
www.musictheaterinternational.com (US and international)

Dramatists' Play Service
www.dramatists.com (US and international)

Tams Witmark
www.tamswitmark.com (US and international)

Rodgers and Hammerstein Musical Library
www.rnh.com (US and international)

MEMORANDUM OF AGREEMENT made this   day of
BETWEEN SAMUEL FRENCH LTD., hereinafter called the Agents, of 52 Fitzroy Street, London, W1T 5JR of the one part and

(hereinafter called the Society) of the other part
WHEREBY IT IS AGREED:-
THAT the said Agents grant to the said Society permission to perform

for   nights and   matinees

commencing

and terminating on

at

on the following terms and conditions:

THAT the Society will pay to the said Agents whichever is the greater of the following

A Minimum Fee for   performances of £   **PLUS VAT**

or   % of the Gross Box Office Receipts, PLUS VAT, in the calculation of which the following shall be taken into account

> Any tickets issued or any Seats occupied either personally or vicariously by any person who shall be entitled to buy tickets at a reduced price or to receive free seats by virtue of being an Honorary Member of the Society or having made a donation or paid a periodic or one-time subscription shall be deemed to have been sold at the full price (or at an agreed discounted price) and the number and face value (or agreed discounted price) of the tickets for any such seats shall be included as part of the Gross Box Office Receipts
> All other tickets issued free or at a reduced price shall be declared and the Agents reserve the rights to apply the above mentioned percentage to the face value of all or a portion of any such tickets

THAT the said society will deliver to the said Agents within TWENTY ONE DAYS of the last performance a Certified Statement of the Gross Box Office Receipts as defined above and one copy of the Programme and will pay the performing fee to the said Agents on receipt of a Statement of Account submitted by them.

THAT the said Agents will supply one set of Band Parts and will despatch these ONE MONTH prior to the first performance, subject to the payment of £   for the hire of the same having been received in advance

THAT the said society will return all such Rental Material to the said Agents in good condition, without any damage, defacement and erasure not later than SEVEN DAYS after the final performance or in the event of damage pay the cost of making good.

THAT the said Agents will then issue an invoice showing all Royalty Fees plus VAT if applicable.

THAT the said Society will undertake to pay in full the said invoice within FOURTEEN DAYS of receipt thereof.

Sample contract from Samuel French Ltd granting license for an amateur production in the UK. Details may alter from country to country.

THAT all Advertising Matter shall be printed in such a manner to make it clear that the audience will witness a production by a company of amateurs

THAT equal credit must be given to the Authors and Composers by printing their names in the same size type on all programmes, posters and other advertising matter and the musical announced as being

AN AMATEUR PRODUCTION BY ARRANGEMENT WITH SAMUEL FRENCH LIMITED

THAT no Alterations or Additions are made to the Libretto described above or to the Music.

Signed on behalf of SAMUEL FRENCH LTD.	Signed _____ (Office)_____ on behalf of (Society)_____ Name_____ Address_____ _____ _____
Managing Director	Tel. No. (Day)_____

Fancy doing *Oliver?* Where are all those little boys going to come from? How about *The King and I?* Where are you going to find the Siamese children (and the King of Siam, for that matter)?

Be as ambitious as you can – but be realistic, too.

Another important consideration is whether you can cast the lead role. Several popular musicals were written to showcase the unique talents of a star performer such as Ethel Merman, Danny Kaye, Carol Channing or Chita Rivera. Some leading characters hardly ever leave the stage, and are said to 'carry' the show – Tevye in *Fiddler on the Roof*, Rose in *Gypsy*, Barnum, Sweet Charity. Performers who can carry a show are rare: do you have anyone within your group who has a realistic attempt of meeting such a challenge?

Will you be able to afford it? Again, there is virtually no limit to what an imaginative production team may produce on a tiny budget. But be aware that a small cast show will nearly always be cheaper than one with a large cast, and that any musical set in a historical period

will generally be more expensive than one set in the present day. *DuBarry Was A Lady*, set partly in the court of Louis XV, is never going to be cheap.

Finally, you need to believe in it, and this is really the acid test. As the producer, you will be living and breathing this show for months to come, and you will have to convince dozens of people that it is worth them giving up their time, money and effort to make this production succeed, and hundreds more that it is worth buying a ticket to see it. If you don't believe in it, how can you expect other people to?

If you're not sure, then keep looking. If you are, take a deep breath and contact the agent.

APPLYING FOR PERFORMANCE RIGHTS

Once you have decided on the show you want to do, apply to the agent for a licence to perform it. (This is quite different from the performance licence for the venue as discussed in Chapter 1.) The agent will require certain key information: the dates and location of the performance, the size of the auditorium, ticket prices, the maximum potential value of ticket sales, and so on. They may also want to know certain practical details of your production – for instance, whether you are intending to use an orchestra, or just a solo piano.

Permission may be refused because another production – professional or amateur – has already been licensed in your area. Again, you may wish to find an alternative, or to apply at a later time.

It can be extremely frustrating to have rights refused because someone else has got in before you. Just remember that this works both ways: once you have been granted the rights, the agent will protect your production in the same way as they are now protecting your rivals'.

For amateur productions, permission is granted on the basis that you pay the agent either a set fee per performance, or a certain percentage of gross ticket sales, usually between 7.5 per cent and 12.5 per cent, whichever is the greater. If you are planning to produce the show professionally you may have to conduct protracted negotiations with the agent regarding the casting, creative team, venue and financial credibility of the production before the rights are granted to you.

THE CONTRACT

Once the agent has agreed to award you the rights, you will be sent a contract enumerating certain conditions. Depending on the scale and nature of your production, the details will vary from country to country, but will typically include the following information:

* The name of the performing company, venue, dates and number of performances.

* An undertaking to perform the work in its entirety without cuts or amendments.
* Fees for royalties and rental of performance material.
* Authors' and rights owners' credits to appear on publicity and programme matter.
* Time scale within which fees are to be paid and performing material returned to the rights owner.
* Reservation of two tickets per performance for the rights owner.
* An exclusion clause specifying what rights are not included in the licence, for example recording, broadcasting, television.
* A clause covering the rights owners' right to charge fees in the event of cancellation.

Signing the Contract

You will normally be asked to make a part-payment at this stage. In return, the agent will undertake to supply you with sufficient copies of libretti, vocal books and scores for your cast and production team.

Depending on which agent you are dealing with, libretti may be bought or hired. Scores are nearly always for hire only, and remain the property of the agent. Rental material is usually booked for a period of three months: as they have to be returned at the end of the production, all hired scores and libretti should only ever be marked in pencil, and any annotations rubbed out before they are returned. Instrumental parts if required are usually hired separately and for a much shorter period (usually one month on an amateur production).

It's a great day when you sign the contract and send it off. Scary too, because you have now made a legal undertaking that you will produce the show.

3 THE CREATIVE TEAM

S taging a musical is a collaborative enterprise. A group of individuals – each with a specific area of expertise – comes together to pool their ideas and skills. Their task is to agree a practical and aesthetically coherent approach to the work that the composer, librettist and lyricist have written, and then to realize that on the stage within an agreed budget.

THE DIRECTOR

While the producer controls the business and financial aspects of the production, overall responsibility for all artistic considerations lies with the director.

It is the director's job to lead the creative team and cast, and to drive the production and rehearsal process through to the opening

Director Ian Watt-Smith watching a run-through of **The Secret Garden** *at the Arts Educational School, London.*

night. The director must collaborate with the other members of the team, allow them to make their respective contributions, and respond to and act upon their suggestions and ideas, while ensuring that at all times the overall focus of the production is maintained. Ultimately the director is responsible for everything – *everything* – that appears on the stage.

Directing requires a rare combination of artistic vision, openness, excellent communication skills, tact, diplomacy, hard-headed practicality, technical awareness and mental toughness. Most of the major American directors of musicals of recent years started out as performers: Bob Fosse, Jerome Robbins, Gower Champion, Tommy Tune, Michael Bennett. In contrast, many of the top British directors who emerged in the eighties and nineties, such as Trevor Nunn, Nicholas Hyntner, Stephen Pimlott and Sam Mendes, first learned their trade directing classical drama and opera.

To be a successful director of a musical, at whatever level, it is essential to have an extensive knowledge and experience of as many areas of theatre as possible – and the wider the better.

Finding a Director

If you are working within a school, college or existing organization there may be an obvious candidate for the job who has just the experience and personal qualities required. Directors are typically self-motivated individuals, and often the impetus to mount a production in the first place comes from someone's desire to direct a particular show.

If, on the other hand, you are going out to recruit a director, be careful. Many people like the idea of being a director: it sounds important and dynamic, and offers a heady combination of power and glamour. 'What I really want to do is direct' is one of the great clichés of the theatre profession. An advertisement in the press seeking a director for even the

---

Job Specification: Director

The director has the following responsibilities:

- Working with the producer to put the creative team together.
- Collaborating with the set, costume, lighting and sound designers in realizing a visual and auditory style for the production.
- Auditioning actors and casting the show with the producer, musical director and choreographer.
- Supervising the rehearsal period, scheduling an appropriate proportion of rehearsals for musical and dance rehearsals, and directing the cast in all dialogue scenes.
- Liaising with the lighting, sound and other technical departments in the latter stages of rehearsal, and ensuring the show is artistically coherent and technically secure for the first performance.
- Watching the show from time to time during the run, monitoring actors' performances and ensuring that artistic standards are maintained.

---

humblest production will attract a mountain of replies.

Before advertising, try to narrow down the search by asking around for personal recommendations. Local theatre companies – amateur or professional – may come up with suggestions, as may actors and musicians. Contact the production offices of drama schools and colleges: they will be able to put you in touch with professionals who have experience of working with small budgets and inexperienced actors.

Check up on the directors of shows that you have seen and enjoyed recently; you will

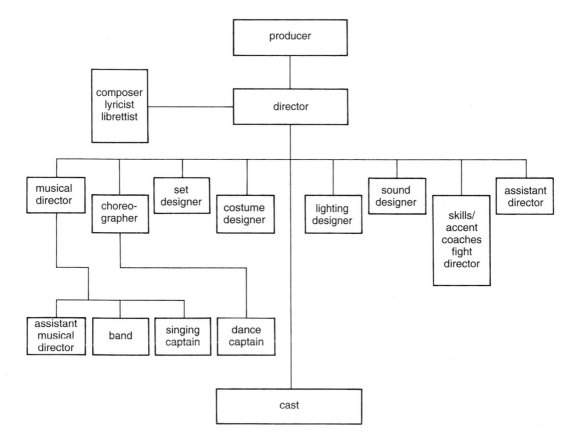

Organizational chart of the creative team required for production of a musical.

almost certainly be able to contact them through the theatre companies for whom they have worked. Even if they themselves are unable to help, they may be able to give you other recommendations. The theatre is a close-knit community, and on the whole its members like to help one another find work.

No matter whom you are talking to, be honest about what you are hoping to achieve and the scale of your production. Do not make promises you will not be able to keep. If you are offering payment, make it clear from the start how much money – or how little – is involved.

Make a shortlist of prospective candidates and ask them to send you a CV or resumé. If they have a show on at the time, go and see it; and even if it is wonderful, it is worth making discreet enquiries to find out how the actors and management found the experience of working with the director.

Meet your most promising candidates for an informal chat over a cup of coffee or a drink; also, it may be worth taking a friend along to get a second opinion. Ask yourself if you trust this person; do you like them? And do they share your enthusiasm for the production? Remember, you will be entrusting the success of the show to the person you choose, not to mention a significant proportion of the money that you are still sweating to raise. In the months ahead the director will be your closest colleague, ally and confidante. Choosing a director is like choosing a person to marry.

Your final choice should be based on a balance of experience and commitment. If you can only offer a small fee, a hungry young director eager to get another credit may be a better choice than the seasoned pro with a CV as long as your arm, who will almost certainly be looking around for a better paid job elsewhere.

Watch out for old hands who have directed the show twice already and tell you exactly how they did it last time. Obviously experience is important, but directors almost invariably work best when they are discovering the show for the first time and responding to new challenges imposed by the budget, cast and venue, rather than re-creating work they did under different circumstances in the past.

The Producer/Director

It is possible – just – to produce a show and direct it yourself. People have done it: they rarely do it more than once. 'Never again!' is the cry.

If you are considering doing this, be aware that each job makes enormous and unreasonable demands in time, energy and effort. In

Helen Porter, musical director of **The Frogs,** *running a solo music rehearsal.*

addition, the roles of producer and director can frequently come into conflict with each other. Trying to do both can take a considerable toll on your health and general well-being.

You have been warned.

PUTTING A CREATIVE TEAM TOGETHER

The director is usually the first member of the creative team to be appointed. Amateur or professional, they will probably suggest people for the creative team, usually colleagues with whom they have worked on other productions.

The producer may also have people in mind – a specific designer or choreographer, say. Respect each other's suggestions, and be prepared to work together to make the best choice of person for each role. It is worth noting that while directors will usually favour people they have worked with successfully in the past, they often work more effectively with a team that includes at least some new faces.

For the producer, assembling a successful creative team can be one of the most satisfying aspects of the job. It is also reassuring to have in the director a lasting ally.

The Musical Director

The musical director (usually known as the 'MD') is responsible for all musical aspects of the show, including conducting the band or orchestra. The MD needs to be an excellent musician, with a finely tuned ear and an ability to understand and accommodate singers' strengths and weaknesses.

Although piano accompanists may be brought in to play at auditions (budget allowing), many MDs prefer to play the piano themselves, especially in the early stages of rehearsal. They need to be well organized, confident, and have the ability to control and motivate groups of twenty, thirty or forty people at

---

Job Specification: Musical Director

The musical director has the following responsibilities:

- Working through the score with the director to identify musical issues that may arise.
- Attending auditions, assessing the singing ability of performers, and assisting the director in casting.
- Teaching the cast their music, and giving group and individual coaching and assistance where required.
- Supervising the organization of band or orchestra, and rehearsing with them both before they integrate with the cast, and afterwards.
- Collaborating with the sound designer to create a good sound balance in the auditorium.
- Conducting the show either from the keyboard or the podium, and/or recruiting a deputy to do this if required.

---

once. They also have to be confident performers with considerable stamina, as they may be playing for up to six hours a day during rehearsals and matinée days.

Depending on the scale of your show, it may be necessary to have an assistant MD to run rehearsals when the MD is absent, to play the piano for dance rehearsals, give extra coaching, and possibly conduct the show on occasions. Sometimes the assistant MD is referred to as the 'repetiteur', the term used for a similar role in the opera world.

The MD may also wish to appoint a singing captain from the company (usually a chorus member or actor in a smallish role) to lead cast warm-ups and add additional support during the run.

Choreographer Jill Francis working with a large group in a small space.

The Choreographer

The choreographer is responsible for the dance and movement aspects of the show. The precise nature of his contribution varies from one musical to another, depending on the material and the director. Some shows are virtually non-stop dance, others may have just one or two short featured numbers or a brief social dance. It is not uncommon for directors who have trained in dance to choreograph their own shows.

Choreographers need to be – or to have been – excellent dancers with an imaginative and creative response to music. They need a comprehensive technical understanding of the

Job Specification: Choreographer

The choreographer has the following responsibilities:

- Working through the score with the director to identify areas where choreography is required, and agreeing on dance style and approach.
- Attending auditions, assessing the dance ability of performers, and assisting the director in casting.
- Devising dance routines as required, and teaching them to the cast.
- Rehearsing with groups and individuals.
- Coaching, and giving assistance where required with dance technique.

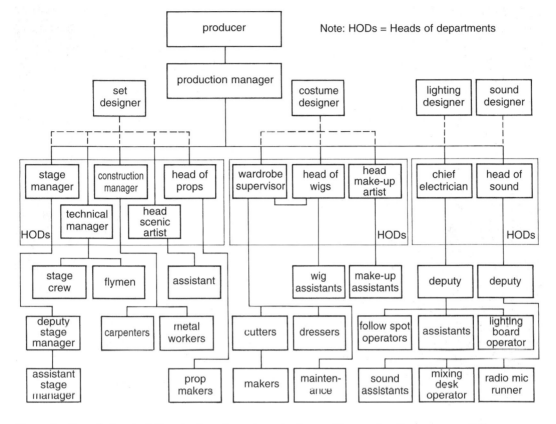

Organizational chart of the staging departments. In smaller productions many of these functions are often amalgamated, or may even be unnecessary.

relevant dance style required for the show (jazz, tap, ballet and so on), and in general, the wider range of experience they have, the better. In addition, they need to be able to deal with large groups of actors, and to identify from moment to moment areas and individuals that need more work.

It is worth noting that many non-professional performers (and some professionals, too) are extremely self-conscious about their bodies, and feel inhibited regarding their ability to express themselves through dance and movement. Choreographers working with untrained dancers may therefore need to be extremely patient and supportive.

The choreographer should appoint a member of the cast as dance captain, ideally someone with sufficient experience to learn the routines quickly and provide additional coaching for the rest of the cast during rehearsals. The dance captain will usually be responsible for dance warm-ups before rehearsals and performances, and for 'brushing up' dance numbers during the run as required.

Physically dancing can be risky, and injuries are frequent. In the professional world the dance captain may be employed as a 'swing' – that is, a performer who knows all the dance roles in all the numbers, and can deputize if any dancer is unable to perform.

THE DESIGN TEAM AND THE PRODUCTION MANAGER

While the director, MD and choreographer will spend most of their time in the rehearsal room with the cast, other members of the creative team will see much less of them. A team of specialist designers works with the director to create unique and specific designs for the set, costumes, lighting and sound, and the task of actually building, making, installing and operating these aspects of the show is undertaken by a series of staging departments.

The production manager is in overall charge of costing and co-ordinating this work, and liaises with the heads of each department (the 'HODs') to ensure that it is being carried out satisfactorily, according to the schedule, and within budget. The production manager plays a pivotal role in making the designers' ideas a reality; this role is discussed more fully in subsequent chapters.

Set Designer

The set designer is responsible for creating a visual setting in which the musical can be presented.

Designing a set is an extremely complex job, which requires artistic vision and a very high degree of technical expertise. Most set designers in the professional world have a background in the visual arts, and have trained on a specialized design course.

The Costume Designer

The costume designer is responsible for designing all the clothes that the actors wear on stage. Sometimes both set and costume design is undertaken by one person, sometimes by a

---

Job Specification: Set Designer

The set designer has the following responsibilities:

- Working with the director on the script and score to discuss the practical staging requirements of the musical.
- Visiting the venue to assess the physical possibilities and limitations of the performance space.
- Creating a scale model of the set, which both reflects the director's artistic vision for the show and is achievable within the technical specifications of the theatre.
- Working with the production manager to ensure that the set can be built within the production budget, and modifying it as appropriate.
- Working with the stage manager to design, source and build any props that may be required.
- Producing a full set of technical drawings from which the set can be built.
- Liaising with scenic painters to ensure the scenery is painted according to the original designs.
- Attending the 'fit-up' of the set in the venue, and dealing with any problems that may arise before the opening performance.

---

team who work together to ensure aesthetic and practical coherence.

Most costume designers in the professional world have a background in fashion or textiles, which may be followed by practical experience in a wardrobe department and/or training on a specialized design course.

Lighting Designer

Unprecedented technical developments over the past thirty years have meant that effective

Job Specification: Costume Designer

The costume designer has the following responsibilities:

- Working with the director on the script to assess the number and type of costumes the show requires.
- Maintaining an ongoing liaison with the set designer to ensure thematic coherence in the overall visual effect.
- Creating a full set of costume drawings for every character in the show.
- Working with the wardrobe supervisor to source fabric and materials required.
- Working with the production manager to ensure that the costumes can be made within the production budget, and modifying it as appropriate.
- Overseeing the hiring or acquisition of costumes that will not be specially made for the show.
- Liaising with the wardrobe supervisor to ensure that the costumes are made according to the original designs.
- Attending and supervising all costume fittings with the actors.
- Attending all dress rehearsals, and dealing with any problems that may arise before the opening performance.

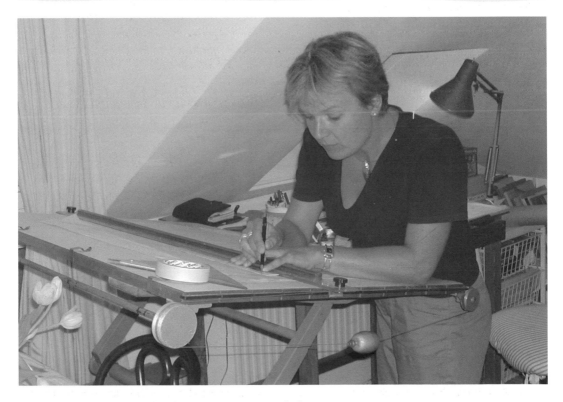

Designer Alison Cartledge drawing up a ground plan.

Skilful lighting design by Jesse Schwenk gives this dramatic moment from **Bernice Bobs Her Hair** *an almost cinematic intensity. Photo: Paul Thompson*

stage lighting has developed into a specialist craft – some would say an art – of its own. The lighting designer is responsible for producing and implementing a dramatic and effective lighting plot for the show, which will both support and enhance the work of the set and costume designers.

The lighting designer must combine a keen visual sense with a strong technical ability. Professionals often start as technical assistants in theatre or industry electrical departments, and/or specialize in lighting on stage management or specialist courses.

The Sound Designer

This is a relatively new role that has developed in recent years alongside developments in microphone, amplification and sound-balance technology. Just as the lighting designer is responsible for letting the audience see clearly, the sound designer is responsible for letting them hear.

Sound designers working in musicals must have a keen and critical ear, a creative and imaginative response to music and live performance, and a strong understanding of the theory and practice of audio science. Professionals

Job Specification: Lighting Designer

The lighting designer is responsible for:

- Working with the director, set and costume designers to understand the artistic and visual concept of the show.
- Agreeing a light cue synopsis, identifying when lighting changes will be required during performance.
- Visiting the venue to assess the existing technical set-up; this may involve close liaison with the resident chief electrician and other staff.
- Drawing up a lighting plan on a technical plan of the theatre's lighting rig.
- Identifying any lighting equipment that may have to be hired.
- Working with the production manager to ensure that the lighting expenses stay within the production budget, and modifying it as appropriate.
- Liaising with the chief electrician of the venue when the lighting is rigged and focused.
- Attending lighting rehearsals with the director to agree on all lighting states and transitions.
- Attending all dress rehearsals, and dealing with any lighting issues that may arise before the opening performance.

may have a background in the music industry or technical theatre, and/or specialize in sound on stage management or specialist courses.

These are the key members of the creative team who will realize the musical on stage during the pre-production and rehearsal period. Depending on the circumstances of your production, the creative team may also include a writer/composer, an assistant director and a fight director, a language coach and special skills tutors.

The Writer/Composer

If you are producing a new show, the writers will almost certainly be present for at least some rehearsals. Every new musical goes through some rewriting during its initial rehearsal period. 'Musicals are not written,' it has often been said, 'they are rewritten.'

Job Specification: Sound Designer

The sound designer has the following responsibilities:

- Working with the director to identify what sound effects may be required in the show, agreeing a sound cue synopsis, and sourcing or recording effects as appropriate.
- Visiting the venue to assess the existing technical set-up and acoustics, and working with the director and musical director to decide to what degree the show may need to be microphoned and amplified.
- Designing and drawing up a technical plan of an appropriate sound rig.
- Identifying any equipment that may have to be hired.
- Working with the production manager to ensure that the sound expenses stay within the production budget, and modifying it as appropriate.
- Liaising with resident technicians of the venue when the sound equipment is rigged and tested.
- Attending sound and technical rehearsals as required.
- Running sound checks with the director, musical director, cast and orchestra, and agreeing volume, mixing and balance levels.
- Supervising sound cueing and live mixing during all dress rehearsals, and dealing with any sound issues that may arise before the opening performance.

When working on a new musical the director will often collaborate closely with the writers prior to rehearsals. Here, the author discusses an early draft of Pilgrim's Progress *with composer Carl Davis.*

Be aware though, that excessive rewriting during a limited rehearsal period can be unsettling for an inexperienced cast, and can waste a lot of time. The director and the producer have to keep a tight control over this, and know when to say enough is enough.

The Assistant Director

If the show you are rehearsing has many crowd scenes with a large number of smaller roles or chorus members, an assistant director may be required, especially if time is limited. The assistant may be asked to stage elements of the background action while the director deals with principal actors, to help schedule rehearsals, and to assist in taking notes.

Assistants are especially useful in shows such as *Annie*, *Oliver* or *The King and I* in which there are large numbers of children, as they often have to be rehearsed separately from the adult cast. In the professional world, assistants arc also responsible for understudy rehearsals, and monitoring the show once the run is under way.

The Fight Director

Putting together a good stage fight that is both convincing to the audience and safe for the participants is a skilled job. Whether it's a large-scale, full-on bar-room brawl or a single blow, you need someone who knows what they are doing.

Many countries, including Australia, Great Britain, Canada and the USA, have their own fight director associations: use the Internet to research the services they offer. Alternatively, contact local theatres, drama schools or colleges to find out the names of qualified fight directors in your area. If you aren't trained in stage fighting, don't try and do it yourself. Someone will almost certainly get hurt, and you may end up on the wrong end of a legal action.

The Dialect/Language Coach

Many musicals require actors to adopt an accent, usually American. If you don't have the money for a trained dialect coach, try and find someone from the country or area in question who has the genuine accent. Get them to read some lines out loud, and tape them. Agree on some general rules of pronunciation and stick to them. Even if the accents are not 100 per cent accurate, you are more likely to get away with it if everybody sounds more or less the same.

Special Skills Tutors

Certain shows require actors to demonstrate special skills, for instance circus skills and tumbling in *Barnum*, playing (or appearing to play) the cello in *A Little Night Music*, roller skating in *The Rink*. If actors have to acquire such skills, it is highly advisable to employ someone who can teach them as soon as possible.

WORKING AS A TEAM

Staging a show is therefore a collective undertaking, and members of the creative team must collaborate in the fullest sense of the word. It only takes one person to start being uncooperative, obstructive or selfish to unbalance the whole delicate process. There is nothing better than working within a team with a strong collective self-belief, a sense of mutual support and respect – and nothing worse than trying to hold together a team that is divided and unfocused.

Picking each member of the team is a big responsibility. Be careful.

4 DRAFTING THE BUDGET

usicals are expensive. They involve the participation of large numbers of people, at least some of whom will almost certainly have to be paid. Even if everybody is providing their services free of charge, you will still have to pay out substantial amounts of money on the premises, equipment, materials, publicity and administrative back-up necessary to get your show on to the stage.

It is vital that the producer drafts an expenditure and income budget as early as possible. If you are working within an existing organization, this may have to be submitted to, and agreed by, the management committee or board of directors before the pre-production process can begin. If you are working independently, it will give you an early indication of the production's financial viability.

The scale and details of your budget will, of

Producers spend many days and many nights trying to get the budget to balance.

course, depend on your circumstances. However, whether you are producing a one-man for-one-night-only cabaret, or an extended run of *Oklahoma!* with a company of fifty, the same basic principle applies. You need to identify all possible sources of income, estimate your potential expenditure, and then try and find ways of making the former greater than the latter.

Many independent producers, Mickey Rooney-like, start off with a vision of the show they want to produce, work out how much it is likely to cost, and then set about finding ways of raising that amount of money. Alternatively you may start by calculating how much money you are likely to make from ticket sales and other sources of income, and then plan expenditure accordingly. Whatever your starting point, remember this: a successful producer needs to be both a visionary and a businessman. Too much wild, unfocused artistic ambition and you will go bust; too much financial caution and the show will never get beyond the planning stages. Every producer is caught between these two opposing forces, and sometimes you will feel torn apart by their conflicting demands.

CREATING A SPREADSHEET

Make a list of all the major expenditure and income categories and, using this chapter as a guide, work through them one by one, putting in the best estimates you can. Creating a spreadsheet on a PC will save you a lot of time later on.

Some of the expenditure categories dealt with below may not apply to your particular circumstances. In an amateur theatre group the wages bill will be minimal; a school production may have access to free rehearsal rooms; a music college may have an orchestra on hand; a theatre group may already have a van – or their own theatre, come to that.

Expenditure and Income

Expenditure will include some, or all, of the following:

Wages:
> Creative team; cast; musicians; crew; administrative staff; theatre staff

Premises hire:
> Theatre; rehearsal rooms; office space

Administrative costs:
> Telephone; computers; photocopying; post

Publicity/PR:
> Design; printing; advertising; distribution; PR

Production costs:
> Set; props; costume; lighting; sound; transport; miscellaneous; hire or purchase of scores and libretti

Performance rights

Contingency fund

Income can be classified as either 'unearned' or 'earned' as follows:

Unearned income:
> Grants and awards; sponsorship; investors; donations

Earned income:
> Ticket and programme sales; refreshment and bar sales; other fund-raising activities

---

If this is the case, do not leave those categories off your spreadsheet, but give them a notional cost of zero. Do not forget about them, and do not take it for granted that they will continue to be free. Circumstances may change: your volunteer rehearsal pianist may get ill, leaving you no choice but to employ a professional at short notice; an informal arrangement may break down and you find

TOTAL FEES/ WAGES CALCULATION SHEET

Creative team fees

Director
MD (may be paid weekly if playing/conducting)
Choreographer
Set designer
Costume designer
Lighting designer
Sound designer
Fight director

Performers

Actors

__ adults × __ weeks @ £__/ week =
Plus holiday pay
__ children × __ weeks @ £__/ week =
Plus holiday pay

Musicians

__ musicians × __ weeks @ £__/ week

Production staff

Production Manager*

Stage Manager: __ weeks @ £__/week
Deputy Stage Manager: __ weeks @ £__/week
Assistant Stage Manager: __ weeks @ £__/week

Technical Manager: __ weeks @ £__/week
Permanent stage crew: __ weeks @ £__/week
Casual staff for production week: __ days @ £__/day

Master carpenter: __ weeks @ £__/week
Assistant carpenters: __ days @ £__/day

Head scenic artist: __ days @ £__/day
Assistant scenic artists: __ days @ £__/day

Chief electrician: __ weeks @ £__/week
Assistant electricians: __ weeks @ £__/week
Lighting board operator: __ weeks @ £__/week

Sound board operator: __ weeks @ £__/week
Sound assistant/ mic runner: __ weeks @ £__/week

Costume supervisor*:
Wardrobe mistress: __ weeks @ £__/week
Costume makers: __ days @ £__/day
Dressers: __ weeks @ £__/week

Administrative staff

Administrator/ office manager: __ weeks @ £__/week
Press and publicity officer*:
Box office staff: __ people × __ weeks @ £__/week

Front of house manager: __ weeks @ £__/week
Ushers: ___ ushers × __ days @ £__/day

*Staff that may be paid a set fee.

Once you start paying everybody, costs go through the roof.

yourself having to pay for rehearsal rooms after all. The golden rule is, *don't underestimate*. If in doubt, put it in the budget – you can always take it out later.

Initially some of your figures may be wild guesses. Identify the areas you are unsure of, and start researching. Get quotes from suppliers. Find out about hire and rental costs. Phone up trade unions for details of current scales of pay. Speak to experienced designers, production managers and other theatre professionals – especially those who may have worked in the venue before – to get a broad idea of what it may be possible to achieve on certain sums of money. If you are producing a show within an organization, ask for a copy of the balance sheet from previous productions. Keep updating and modifying your budget, and it will gradually become more accurate.

To begin with, the whole undertaking will seem utterly impossible, since the potential costs always exceed the income, often by a vast amount. However, *this is perfectly normal*.

Don't give up. Start working out ways to maximize the income while cutting expenditure. Think laterally, be creative, do research into funding bodies and charitable trusts, drum up support from your family and friends and get their suggestions and help. To produce a show successfully you need a sound business brain, but you also need a huge amount of self-belief and faith. Yes, it may seem impossible, *but you will find a way of making it happen*.

Production Costs and Running Costs
If you are planning a long or open-ended run, you should make a clear distinction in the budget between production costs and running costs.

The production costs cover everything required to get the show on the stage for the first night, including the fees for the creative team, actors' payment for rehearsal, building the set, making the costumes, and any capital expenditure on equipment.

51

The running costs are the costs of performing the show for each subsequent week, and include the hire of the theatre and equipment, wages for performers, musicians and crew, and set, costume and prop maintenance.

In commercial theatre, the production costs are in effect an investment: a product is developed that has a retail value. As long as the weekly income from ticket sales exceeds the running costs, the show will continue to be performed and the production costs gradually recouped, eventually generating a profit.

That's the theory, anyway. In practice many theatre productions fail to recoup their original investment, and the statistics for musicals are even more depressing.

EXPENDITURE

Wages

Who, if anyone, is going to get paid? In the amateur world, nobody does – or that is the theory. People may pay a membership subscription to a club or society, effectively subsidizing the show out of their own pockets. Theatre is their hobby and passion, and they are happy to give their time for free.

However, in some areas a musical may demand a level of ability beyond the range of the amateur. For example, musicians who are capable of playing to a sufficient standard are likely to have had training, and may expect payment, if only to cover their expenses. Modern theatres need experienced staff to operate safely and effectively: you might find a qualified electrician who will work for free, but don't count on it.

As the standard of amateur productions has risen, the boundaries with the professional world have become increasingly blurred. Some amateur companies employ a professional director for large musicals. While this will raise the standard of individual performances to an extent, remember that any director is largely dependent on the skills of the people working around them. They may feel that they can only do their job properly when working alongside a professional musical director, set designer, costume designer and so on, and wish to bring in other professionals. And once you pay some members of the creative team it is difficult not to pay all of them, even if the fees involved are nominal.

Performing on stage is an extremely popular ambition for many people, and it is a fact of life that there will always be large numbers of actors, singers and dancers – including trained professionals – willing to work for no payment just so they can be part of a production. If your actors are not to be paid, make that very clear when you post your audition notices. Don't pay some of the cast and not others: that is a recipe for disaster.

The actors' union Equity has agreed minimum rates of pay for directors, choreographers, designers, dancers, actors and stage managers. Rates for musicians and technicians are set by their own unions, and are renegotiated annually. The current rates are available on application to the relevant organization in your country. Only producers that belong to the appropriate theatre managers' and producers' trade associations are obliged to pay these rates. Many small-scale and fringe productions only get off the ground because the creative team, cast and crew agree to work for far below the going rate on a co-operative or 'profit share' basis.

Royalties from successful shows have made some directors and designers multi-millionaires; others struggle along on the breadline. Some actors can command star salaries of thousands of pounds a week; others barely make a living wage from one year to the next.

That's showbiz.

Premises

The cost of hiring a public theatre can be

Methods of Payment to Professionals

In the professional world, most members of the creative team work on a freelance basis and negotiate a fee for their services, which is paid in three instalments: a third on signing the contract, a third on the first day of rehearsals, and a third on press night. In commercial productions they would also seek to negotiate royalty payments – additional weekly or monthly payments calculated on a certain percentage of the box office receipts.

Professional actors, musicians, stage man-agement staff and technicians sign up for short-term contracts depending on the expected run of the show, and are paid weekly. In some cases the production company may be liable for paying NI or other employer's insurance payments, making deductions for tax and paying holiday pay at agreed union rates.

Rehearsal pianists and musical deputies are paid per session worked; casual technical staff per day.

Paper, office space, photocopying... It all costs money.

substantial, and rates are normally fixed and non-negotiable. Before signing a contract, check exactly what staff and services are included in the price: resident technicians, box office, bar staff, cleaners, ushers and so on. Be sure you know how far in advance payment is due, as this can have a critical impact on your cash flow.

If you are hiring a non-theatre venue, costs will probably be lower and you will have more room for negotiation. However, remember that you may incur considerable extra expense making the building safe for public performance, and you will have to hire far more technical equipment.

Administrative, sales, support and publicity staff will need office space somewhere. This is potentially very expensive, and many fledgling producers prefer to work out of a spare bedroom to save money. The construction department will need access to a workshop and possibly a paint frame, and the costume

Advertising your show is essential. You will need posters and flyers of different sizes to market the show in different places. More expense.

department to sewing and fitting rooms. Sets, costume and props will also need to be stored securely prior to the move into the theatre.

You may also have to rent premises for auditions and rehearsals. Again, prices vary widely. A church hall or school gym may be hired for a few pounds an hour: custom-built dance studios can cost more than ten times as much. Shop around.

Administration/Sales

Office and administration costs can be a black hole swallowing up hundreds or even thousands of pounds. Postage, photocopying, stationery and computer costs all add up, and it is often difficult to quantify exactly how much is being spent. Record all expenditure in a petty cash account book, and in particular monitor phone usage carefully: you need to know how much that bill is likely to be when it arrives in three months' time.

If you are hiring a theatre it will probably have its own box office operation; if not, you will have to set up your own. Manning a box office all day is tedious and potentially expensive, so you may choose to open only at certain times and/or ask customers to leave sales enquiries on an answerphone – though returning every call will bump up phone costs. You will also have to pay for the printing of the tickets themselves.

Publicity/PR

If people don't know that your show is on, they won't buy a ticket. Advertising is essential.

You will need a publicity budget to cover the design, printing and distribution of posters and flyers, and any advertising in the press and media. In addition you may need to pay for other promotional activity, production photographs, foyer decorations and hospitality on the press night.

Consider how large and varied your advertising campaign will have to be in order to

Production Costs	
Set/props:	Model: construction and materials Materials: wood, metal, plastic, cloth, gauze Paint Workshop hire Paintframe hire Labour
Costume:	Purchase costs: clothes, hats, shoes, accessories Materials: fabric, decorations, haberdashery Hires: uniforms, period costume, animal skins Labour
Lighting:	Equipment purchase Hire charges: lanterns, dimmers, lighting board, cables Other hardware: smoke/dry-ice machines Pyrotechnics Gels
Sound:	Equipment purchase Hire charges: PA system, microphones, amplifiers, mixing desk, loudspeakers, mini-disc players, music stands Recording costs Sound effects
Miscellaneous:	Consumable props – food, drink, breakables Refreshments Other
Transport:	For all the above

Use the limitations of the production budget as a spur to your creativity. A low-budget studio production of Pilgrim's Progress *at GSA Conservatoire. The actors wore modern dress and a single truck was used to create multiple locations. Director, John Gardyne; lighting designer, Mark Dymock.*

reach your target market effectively – half-a-dozen home-made posters may be enough to fill the auditorium for a school production. At the other end of the scale, the advertising and promotional budget for West End and Broadway shows can run to millions of pounds or dollars.

Miscellaneous

There are numerous other areas of expenditure that do not fit into the major categories; these include personal travel costs, taxis, CDs, DVDs, books, research costs, late-night pizzas, tickets to other shows, drinks at meetings ... In some cases the producer may find it impossible to distinguish between everyday personal expenditure and bona fide business costs. Run a petty cash account and keep all relevant receipts.

PRODUCTION BUDGET

In professional theatres, the production budget is controlled by the production manager, with the heads of staging departments managing and recording their expenditure on a daily basis. On small-scale shows, producers sometimes act as their own production managers and deal directly with the HODs themselves.

It is the production manager's job to find ways of realizing the director and designers' artistic ideas on stage as far as is practical and safe within the financial limitations of the budget. As the production takes shape, he or she acts as the arbiter between the creative team and producer, balancing what the former want against what the latter can afford.

If you are working within an organization, the management may already have set a total figure for production expenditure, and you will have to work out with the production manager how this should be most effectively shared out between the various staging departments. In some cases – a school or fringe production, say – the amount of money available may be extremely small.

Ideally no designer's creativity should be limited by budget considerations; in practice, it is essential that they have some idea of the money and resources that will be available before they begin, so they are working on an appropriate scale. Some astounding shows have been produced on very low budgets, and shortage of cash can provide a spur to amazing resourcefulness and creativity.

Costing the Production Budget

The members of the creative team submit their ideas to the production manager for costing in a variety of forms. The set designer builds a scale model of the set, the costume designer provides a series of drawings and fabric samples, and the lighting and sound designers draw up technical plans and lists of the equipment they require.

The production manager then breaks these down into their individual components, works out what can be supplied out of existing stock (if anything), compares the respective cost effectiveness of buying, making or renting the remainder, and produces an accurate overall estimate. It is a painstaking job, requiring great attention to detail and sometimes a degree of lateral thinking. *Stage Management – A Practical Guide* shows an example of a complete production budget extending over five pages (pp 35–39).

Invariably each designer wants more than the production can afford. A prolonged series of negotiations then begins, with the designers cutting and simplifying their plans while the production manager seeks cheaper sources of materials and equipment. This process will continue right up until opening night.

Libretto and Score Purchase or Hire

Depending on which company publishes your show, you will need to buy or hire enough copies of the libretto, vocal book, score and band parts for your cast and orchestra. The costs for a show with a large chorus can be substantial. A deposit may also be required, which will be deducted from your royalties bill on safe return of the material. Lost and damaged copies will be charged for, and they are not cheap.

Performance Rights

Under the terms of your performance licence you must pay to the licensing agent either a fixed fee per performance or a percentage of the gross box office (usually 7.5–15 per cent), whichever is the greater. This is then passed on

Set your ticket prices in order to maximize earned income. Don't undervalue your show, but don't price yourself out of the market, either.

to the writers as their commission. As this cost is dependent on gross sales, you should update it on the budget sheet whenever box office figures or projections change significantly.

Contingency Fund

However thoroughly you may feel you have covered all the possible sources of expenditure, add 5–10 per cent of the total for contingency.

Always, *always* have a contingency fund, because somewhere along the line you will need it.

INCOME

The total expenses budget will dictate how much income the production must generate in order to break even. Income can come from a variety of sources, both earned and unearned, and you should pursue all potential sources avidly.

Unearned Income

Grants

Depending on your circumstances, you may be eligible to apply for a grant from funding bodies, the arts council, your local authority, lottery funds or charitable trusts.

Public funds are limited and much in demand. Extremely strict criteria are applied to their distribution, and you are likely to have to

RIGHT: First draft budget for a profit-share fringe production of Bernice Bobs Her Hair. The theatre hire charge is not cheap, but many administrative and technical extras are included in the cost. As the production is to be staged 'in the round', the set costs are low. Guaranteed wages for the creative team and actors are nominal. Profits will be increased if ticket sales can be raised above 66 per cent and/or the contingency fund is not used.

DRAFT BUDGET – Bernice Bobs Her Hair

2 weeks rehearsal/ 1 production week/ 5 weeks performance (32 shows)
12 staff (Director/producer, MD, 9 × actors, stage manager – plus designer.)

EXPENDITURE

Wages

12 @ £50 per week x 8 weeks	£4800	
Designer (Fee)	£200	£5000

Premises

Theatre hire 6 weeks @ £850	£5100	
Rehearsal rooms	0	
Auditions	£200	£5300

Administration		£250
Publicity		£350

Production

Set/ props	£100	
Paint (floor)	£30	
Costume (10 costumes @ 30)	£300	
Wig (Bernice)	£100	
Lighting (gels)	£10	
Sound (acoustic)	£0	
Misc	£100	
Transport	£100	£740

Rights/ Hire

12.5% × £17067 (66% sales)	£2133	£2133

Contingency @ 10%	£1400	£1400

TOTAL EXPENDITURE		**£15173**

INCOME

80 seats × 32 performances = 2560 seats

2560 seats @ £10 =		£25600
@ 75% sales		£19200
@ 66% sales		£17067
@ 50% sales		£12800

Profit @ 66% sales

$$£17067$$
$$-£15173$$
$$\textbf{£1894}$$

Break even @ 59.3% sales

provide substantial and convincing proof that your production qualifies for funding under government and/or organizational guidelines. Even if you are producing a show with high-profile large-scale community involvement, be aware that any grant is unlikely to cover more than a modest percentage of your total expenditure budget.

Applications can be time-consuming and complex, and must usually be submitted during the tax year prior to that in which the funds are required. It is extremely unlikely that grants will be made to an individual, or to a project that intends to make a profit for private investors or shareholders.

Before applying for any kind of grant, make sure that the time frame is appropriate, and that you feel you have a reasonable chance of meeting their funding criteria.

Sponsorship, Investment and Donations
Private companies may – repeat, may – be prevailed upon to make a donation to your production, either in return for acknowledgement in advertising and/or some form of hospitality at one or more performances.

Target any potential sponsors carefully; they may be local companies, or have some kind of connection with the venue. Pursue any personal connections you may have with company directors, but be sensitive to their response: 'no' probably really does mean 'no'. Lobbying large companies for sponsorship is highly competitive, and all major publicly funded theatre and opera companies have dedicated departments of skilled individuals trying to raise money in this way.

Companies are far more likely to offer support in kind rather than in hard cash. Always approach a company with a specific idea, rather than a vague request for help: for instance, a van rental company may give you free loan of a vehicle for a day; a scaffolding company may build you a temporary stage; a laundry may offer you free dry cleaning. The possibilities are endless.

(Note that if your organization is a limited company or registered charity, you need to identify and put a notional value on any in-kind support that you have received in your annual and/or final accounts.)

Private individuals may choose to become investors in your show, and it is important to make sure that they are kept abreast of developments, and invited to the opening night. Some altruistic individuals may even be prevailed upon to make a direct contribution to your production, without expecting a return of any sort. God bless 'em!

Earned Income
Ticket Sales
Subtract the total unearned income from the total cost of the production, and the remainder is the amount that you must raise through earned income if you are to break even.

Ticket sales are the life-blood of any production and its main source of income. It is vital to maximize the revenue from ticket sales by devising a pricing structure that makes tickets affordable to the various groups who comprise your target audience. Don't undervalue your show and make tickets too cheap: most people are more interested in getting value for money than paying as little as possible.

In a large theatre you may set different prices for front and rear stalls, circle, balcony and boxes. Consider making Friday and Saturday nights more expensive: most people prefer to go out at weekends and are prepared to pay a premium for a ticket. Encourage students, senior citizens and other low-income groups to attend by offering concessionary deals earlier in the week and at matinées.

Set a revenue target for ticket sales based on the break-even point. Experiment with different price bands to see how that target might be achieved if 66 per cent of the total tickets were

Ticket Price Calculations

Target income £28,500

Location/No. of seats	Wed @	Potential	Thur @	Potential	Fri @	Potential	Sat mat @	Potential	Sat @	Potential	TOTAL
Front stalls 300	£12.00	£3,600.00	£12.00	£3,600.00	£15.00	£4,500.00	£10.00	£3,000.00	£15.00	£45,000.00	
Rear stalls 100	£8.00	£800.00	£8.00	£800.00	£12.00	£800.00	£5.00	£500.00	£12.00	£800.00	
Front balcony 120	£12.00	£1,440.00	£12.00	£1,440.00	£15.00	£1,800.00	£10.00	£1,200.00	£15.00	£1,800.00	
Rear balcony 80	£8.00	£640.00	£8.00	£640.00	£12.00	£960.00	£5.00	£400.00	£12.00	£960.00	
100% box office		£6,480.00		£6,480.00		£8,060.00		£5,100.00		£8,060.00	£34,180.00

Sales projection						
100% £34,180.00	Target	£28,500.00	Excess/	£5,680.00		
85% £29,053.00		£28,500.00	Deficit	£553.00		
75% £25,635.00		£28,500.00		−£2,865.00		
66% £22,787.00		£28,500.00		−£5,713.00		
50% £17,090.00		£28,500.00		−£11,410.00		

Calculating ticket prices for a five-performance run in a 600-seat theatre. The target income is not achieved at 66 per cent potential box office sales. The producer may consider making the Saturday night more expensive, or find ways of increasing unearned income and lowering the target. The target is currently reached at 83.4 per cent sales, which may be achievable on a short run.

sold. Never calculate potential box office income from 100 per cent ticket sales: it is virtually impossible to achieve above 95 per cent except on short runs of extremely popular shows, usually featuring big stars in limited engagements. Most producers also calculate potential income on 50 per cent and 75 per cent ticket sales to give them a picture of the possible variations in income.

Of course, if tickets start selling well, you should revise your revenue estimate accordingly.

Note that in some circumstances, ticket sales may incur value added tax or local purchase tax. Double-check your legal position, and do not get caught out.

Other Earned Income

Consider how you could raise additional revenue – from selling programmes, merchandise, posters and refreshments. Check out the local licensing laws to see if you will be allowed to serve alcoholic beverages at the venue.

Look beyond the theatre, and the production, too. Be imaginative – run a car boot sale, have a benefit concert, run a raffle, organize a sponsored walk: it's all money in the kitty.

BALANCING THE BUDGET

In an ideal world no musical would go into production until there was enough guaranteed income to cover all the costs. In reality this never happens, and there is always – *always* – a degree of financial risk.

At some point a decision has to made: is the production going to happen or not? If you are working within an organization, submit your draft budget to the management committee, board of directors or financial controller, and see if they give you the go-ahead. If you are working independently, you may decide to take the risk yourself, based on instinct, belief and optimism.

Once you start spending money on the production, keep a tight control on your cash flow. Even if the budget looks healthy, remember that you will not receive the bulk of your income from ticket sales for months ahead. An organization may inform you that you have been awarded a grant, but the actual cheque may not arrive in the post for weeks.

When dealing with theatres and rental companies, try and negotiate payment in instalments, and always wait thirty days before paying invoices. But never welch on a deal with an individual, especially if they are working for you at below the going rate; there is no quicker way to lose their goodwill and co-operation. Pay them on the day you agreed, in cash or by cheque.

Throughout the pre-production period you will spend a large proportion of your time juggling the figures in the budget, negotiating, fixing, re-organizing – trying every way possible to turn the final balance from a negative to a positive figure. You will only stop revising it when the last performance is over, all the bills paid, and the final accounts drawn up.

Meanwhile, it is time for the director and the creative team to get working on the show.

5 SET AND COSTUME DESIGN

What the audience sees on the stage has the most immediate impact, and can also have the most lasting effect: a stunning set can elicit a spontaneous round of applause, the memory of a wonderful costume may linger in the mind for decades.

The designers of the sets and costumes define a visual style for the show and create a physical world within which the characters can exist and their story can be told. This requires a combination of imagination, artistic skill and clear-eyed practicality: designers not only have to dream up wonderful ideas, they also have to work out how these can be realized in practical terms.

Some professional designers specialize in either set or costume; others like to do both. If time is short it may be a good idea to split up the workload: designing a musical is a big job.

RECENT DEVELOPMENTS IN SET DESIGN

Up until the sixties, musical theatre scenery typically consisted of a number of backcloths

Experienced designers build up large collections of reference material over the years.

Sketch for a composite set for West Side Story *by Alison Cartledge. The action can flow freely through the space on several levels, and there is plenty of room for choreography.*

painted to indicate the various locations required in the script. These were suspended above the stage from a series of bars (known as 'pipes' in the USA), and could be hoisted out of sight when not required.

Scene changes were effected by 'frontcloth' scenes. A painted cloth would be flown in downstage, or a 'traveller' drawn horizontally across the stage like a curtain, and a short scene played in front of it, while a major scene change took place behind. Once the scene was over, the frontcloth or traveller would be removed to reveal the next set, which used the full depth of the stage.

In 1960 Sean Kenny broke the mould with his revolutionary design for *Oliver!* The set was defiantly non-realistic, and featured a revolving construction of bridges, staircases and platforms, which constantly moved to create new locations with cinematic fluidity.

Kenny's work was highly influential. Designers began to realize that audiences did not necessarily need painted images to help them imagine a scene, and that there were less cumbersome ways of moving the action from one place to another. Audiences quickly learned to 'read' stage sets in a new way, and the use of painted backcloths gradually dwindled away.

Librettists began to write scenes that moved fluidly between locations, or which happened in two or more places at once. The opening scene of *Into the Woods* takes place in three different houses simultaneously, and then moves off to a dense forest in just a few bars of music. *City of Angels* continuously leaps back and forth between a naturalistic Hollywood studio and the highly stylized, alternative reality of film noir. The action of *Sweeney Todd* is particularly fluid, rushing us all over London from the docks to Fleet Street, from the Judge's House to Mrs Lovett's Pie Shop, from Sweeney's barber's shop to the grisly cellar below, with barely a moment to draw breath.

Over the past twenty years, developments in stage hydraulics and computer technology have allowed the sets of West End and Broadway shows to become increasingly spectacular – and to swallow up a larger proportion of the production budget as a result. Each new production promises ever-more dazzling stage effects: a massive mansion lifts up from the ground in *Sunset Boulevard*, a helicopter takes off in *Miss Saigon*, a car flies above the audience in *Chitty Chitty Bang Bang*.

However, it is important to remember that being a good designer is not about spending large amounts of money on flashy effects: it is about solving problems imaginatively within the resources available.

Set Design: Preparation

When you are designing a set, start off by reading through the script carefully several times. Get a general overview of the story and its locations. Make a list of the scenes that are required, note whether they are interior or exterior, and highlight any lines that comment on the setting: 'This is the grandest mansion I've ever seen!', or 'You live here? In this dump?', or 'I feel the walls of this damn cell closing in on me'.

Expand your knowledge. Research the show's historical period and its geographical setting. Look at pictures and photographs of the wide-open spaces of Oklahoma, or New York in the twenties, or Berlin in the thirties, or small-town America in the sixties. Watch films, videos and DVDs, browse through books on architecture and fashion. Pin photos and drawings above your desk and let them feed your imagination; start a sketchbook of ideas and research materials. Play a recording of the

Designer Roger Ness's research sketchbook for Oliver.

soundtrack as you work, to get a sense of the show's tone and musical style. Let it into your subconscious mind. Make sketches of rough ideas, and draw or paint particular episodes from the story. Some professional designers 'storyboard' the show – that is, they sketch out the action as a series of pictures, like a strip cartoon – to discover how the actors and action will flow across the stage.

Once you have a grasp of the geographical and historical context, and understand the basic requirements of the story, have a meeting with the director. Take along your sketchbook and share your thoughts. The director may well have a general design concept in mind that you should discuss, but don't be afraid to talk about your own ideas.

Visiting the Venue

Unless it is absolutely impossible, go and visit the venue as early as possible to get a sense of its atmosphere and scale. Just as every show has specific demands, so every venue will have unique physical requirements.

Most theatres have technical drawings, groundplans and elevations that give details of

Standard Equipment in Theatres

Theatres frequently have all, or some, of the following equipment, which may be useful to the designer:

Cyclorama or 'Cyc': A plain cloth at the back of the stage that extends around to the sides to give a feeling of sky and space. Alternatively, there may be a white or pale blue cloth hung on the furthest upstage bar, sometimes called a 'skycloth'.

Black: An opaque black cloth that fills the entire space of the stage.

Gauze: An open-weave cloth that becomes transparent when lit from behind. A gauze may be painted to achieve a specific effect.

House tabs: Heavy drapes – usually red, blue or green velvet – that separate the stage from the auditorium.

Masking: Either 'hard' (painted black flats, or black serge stretched on a wooden frame) or 'soft' (black material). Masking is used to define the edges of the set and to conceal the backstage area from the audience.

If the theatre possesses any of these, check that they are willing to let you use them in your production before integrating them into your design. Making the wrong assumption could prove expensive.

the dimensions and physical peculiarities of the building. If, for any reason, these are not available – or you are working in a non-theatre venue – you will have to measure out the dimensions of the acting and backstage areas for yourself.

In proscenium arch theatres take particular note of the type of flying system and the number of bars. There should be a plan, so make sure you get a copy of it. The more bars there are, the more options you have; though remember that some of them will almost certainly be needed by the lighting designer to hang lanterns.

TRYING OUT IDEAS

The next stage is to move from working in two dimensions to working in three. Using the technical drawings of the theatre, build a model of the theatre space in card or foamboard, and paint it black. Models are usually made to the scale of 1:25, but occasionally – when dealing with a vast open-air venue, for instance – they may be 1:50.

Then start to play. Use card, balsa wood, bits of plasticine, clay, toy soldiers, matchboxes – anything you like – to give an idea of how the stage space can be broken up to give the sense of a variety of locations and moods.

Constantly re-read the libretto and listen to the music. Keep researching, too: who knows what golden nugget you will find next?

DEFINING THE PARAMETERS OF THE SPACE

At this stage you are still working in broad strokes. Concentrate on defining the scale and shape of the acting area for each scene – do not worry about detail, colour or texture. There are a few basic guidelines that you should keep in mind:

* Know exactly where the entrances and exits will be.
* It should always be clear if the scene is an interior or an exterior: always define the difference in a coherent and consistent way.
* Check that there is enough room for any stage action and, in particular, choreography; 'The Rain in Spain', for instance, may

not need much room, but 'I'm Getting Married in the Morning' will. If in doubt, make scale cardboard cut-outs of figures, one for every member of the chorus, and put them into the model box to see if they will fit.

* Many shows are backstage musicals: *Gypsy*, *42nd Street*, *Kiss Me Kate*, *Cabaret*, *Dames at Sea*... You need to make a clear definition between the 'real' world of backstage and the 'fantasy' world of the show-within-the-show.

* Musicals are a heightened reality, in which perspectives can be wilder, windows bigger, roofs steeper, beds larger.

* If there is no orchestra pit, be absolutely, one hundred per cent, unequivocally sure that you know where the band are going to be. This is the first question that the MD will ask you.

* Be sure you have dealt with every scene in the show, however short.

* Keep working with the director: you are collaborators and should support each other.

* Watch out for getting stuck on your first idea. Even if you think you have solved the problems straightaway, give yourself the time and the freedom to consider alternatives. As with all artistic endeavour, the bolder the experiments, the better.

Clarifying the Design Concept

Every libretto has unique and specific requirements, and every theatre is different. Sets may be large or small, simple or complex, realistic or stylized, depending on the designer's artistic response to the libretto.

Of course, the budget has a huge influence too. You may have enough money for several full sets that can be brought in from the flies or built on 'trucks' (mobile castored platforms) and wheeled on from the wings; but if funds are limited you may have to create one basic permanent set and add scenic elements to it as

Trying out ideas in the model box.

appropriate. And if money is really tight, or backstage space non-existent, you may only be able to provide a few rostra to break up the stage space into a series of different areas and levels.

Get a sense of scale. How large do the individual elements of the set need to be to fill the space effectively and harmoniously? If the space looks too stark and empty, a ground row – a flat running horizontally along the back – can be used to conceal the upstage edge of the stage. When shaped and painted to represent a city skyline or a distant range of mountains, it also provides a sense of perspective and environment.

Consider what materials you want to use. Many types of construction material – timber, chipboard, steel decking, staging – are supplied in a series of standard sizes. If you design the set with these in mind it will be much cheaper and easier to build, and the production manager is more likely to be able to give you what you want. Similarly, if you have access to a stock of scenery, find out what flats, rostra, 'treads' (flights of steps), doorframes and windows already exist, and see if you can re-use them, rather than building new ones.

Start to pull your ideas together. Keep playing in the model box, but make informed decisions. Be as ambitious as you like, but keep the physical limitations of the theatre in mind – for instance, there is no point envisaging elaborate use of a revolving stage if the theatre does not have one.

Transitions

You need to pay particular attention to the transitions between scenes, and work out how these will be effected. During the performance of a naturalistic play with three or four different scenes – by Shaw or Chekhov, say – audiences are, within reason, prepared for the action to halt for a few minutes while the curtain comes in and the scenery is changed. A musical, on the other hand, has a tempo that you must not interrupt, and the action needs to keep flowing across the stage. Most scores include 'scene change' music, but it may only be of a certain length. Of course, the music can be extended if necessary, but an audience will soon get irritated by a tune endlessly repeating while a lengthy scene change takes place.

In modern productions, set changes frequently occur in full view of the audience, and they can make a thrilling contribution to the way the story unfolds on stage. The creation of the Paris barricade is one of the highlights of *Les Misérables*. Talk to the lighting designer and consider what you may be able to achieve through the selective lighting of small areas of the stage, or by using a gauze.

Periaktoi are rotating triangular trucks with a painted flat on each side, and these can provide a cheap and adaptable solution to backcloths if multiple locations are required. They will speed up scene changes, too. The original Broadway production of *Dreamgirls* used three continuously moving and rotating towers to propel the action from place to place with cinematic speed and fluidity.

'White Card' Model

At this point the designer needs to make a 'white card' model to show the size, scale, nature and number of the main elements of the set, including all flats, trucks, flown pieces, and any special furniture or structures. Don't forget to include the flats needed for masking the backstage areas from the audience's view.

Each element should be built to scale in card and placed in the model box, though as the name implies they need not be finished or coloured. The director and designer then present this model to the production manager at the 'white card meeting'. The producer will normally come to this to see how you are planning to spend their money. Ideally the costume, lighting and sound designers should attend too: it is invariably the case that the more fully the members of the creative team understand what the others are trying to achieve, the more focused and effective their own contribution will be.

A professional production manager should be able to do an approximate costing of a white card model on sight, calculating roughly what quantities of wood, steel, paint and other building materials will be required. The overall cost will also depend on where the set is going to be constructed, who is going to build it, and whether any special equipment, such as welding or fibreglass-moulding tools, will be needed. The production manager may wish to hold on to the model for a few days while he consults the construction department and phones round for quotes from suppliers.

A good production manager will always be open to a set designer's ideas, and strive to realize them as fully as possible. Quite frequently the estimated cost of the set is beyond the resources of the budget, and they will have to identify where economies can be made. Will it be possible to use cheaper materials? Is there another supplier somewhere who will give you a better deal? Is there a more cost-effective building method that will give the same result? In the end, elements of the set may need to be simplified, altered or cut altogether, but this should only happen after all possible alternatives have been explored.

Decoration, Colour and Style

Once the basic structural elements of the design have been agreed, you need to start working in detail on its decoration, colour and style.

Considerable research may be required. You may have decided on the general layout of Professor Higgins' office, but now you need to consider décor, wallpaper, furniture, ornaments, bookshelves, paintings, cushions and so on. If you are working on a tight budget, consider making your set – especially the interiors – very simple and uncluttered. One or two carefully chosen and well-positioned artefacts or pieces of furniture can say far more about the essential nature of a room and the people who inhabit it than a stage full of random pieces of furniture.

You also need to consider the colour scheme. Decide on a 'palette' a limited number and range of complementary colours – for each scene to create a specific mood or style. Contrasts in colour between scenes inform and enrich the story that is being told. You might use bright silvers and blues for the buzzing streets of New York, and dull browns and yellows for Sarah Brown's mission hall. The prison cell in *Kiss of the Spiderwoman* may be grey, but the stage floods with colour whenever Aurora appears.

Note that scenery painted in a single colour can look extremely dull and shoddy once lit. Experiment with spattering additional colours on the base colour to give extra texture and richness, especially to flat vertical surfaces and the floor. Give a sample of the paint finish to the costume and lighting designers: it will be of great assistance to them in choosing their own fabrics and colour schemes.

Gradually you will start to define the show's visual aesthetic in more detail. How realistic is the set to be, how stylized or abstract? How historically or architecturally accurate are you making it? How are you using perspective?

Keep working closely with the director and the other designers. Make sure you agree with the costume designer on the weight, type and

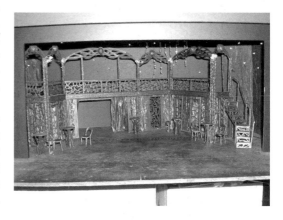

Roger Ness's model box for Cabaret. *The band will sit on the upper balcony.*

The completed set on stage at the Yvonne Arnaud Theatre, Guildford. Director, Peter Barlow; choreographer, Gerry Tebbutt; lighting designer, Richard Jones.
Photo: Mark Dean

69

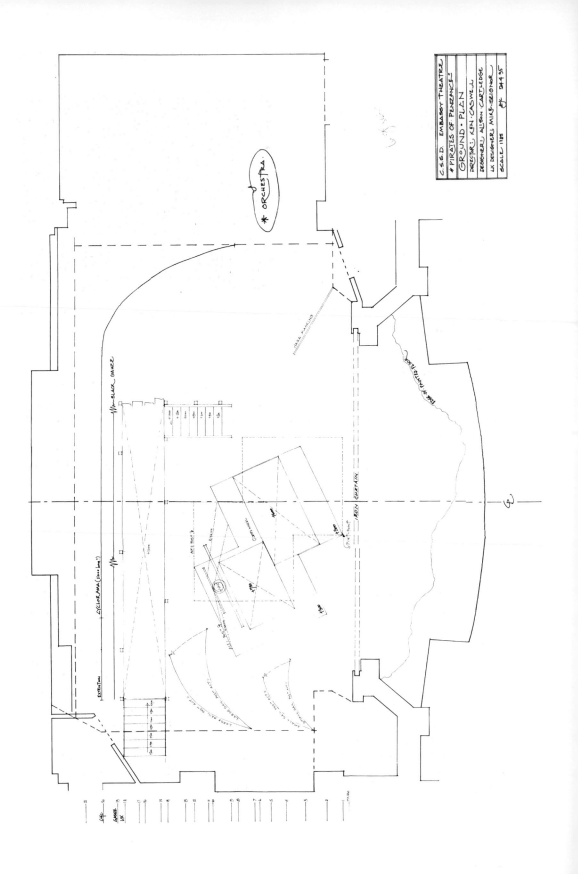

colour of any fabrics used in the set. Let the lighting designer know if there are to be any practical lanterns built into the set, or any illuminated signs.

Making a Model

As decisions are finalized, start building a fully detailed and coloured model of the set. This can be a lengthy and painstaking task, so make sure you leave yourself enough time to complete it properly. The production manager will schedule another production meeting where the model is again presented, discussed and costed. Again, some elements may have to be cut or modified depending on the budget. Have a list of priorities: know where you are prepared to make compromises, and what you can lose most easily without damaging the overall design concept.

When the model is finally approved you need to produce a groundplan and a set of technical drawings, which the construction department can then use as a blueprint for building the set in the workshop.

If scenic artists are painting the set, make sure they are provided with accurate colour samples and finished artwork to copy. Large backcloths and gauzes need to be suspended in a device called a 'paintframe' when they are painted. Most larger theatres have paintframes, and they can normally be hired by the day if required. Schedule the painting well in advance, as paintframes are often booked up months in advance, too.

It is not uncommon for designers to supervise the building and painting of their own

A scenic painter scaling up art work from the designer's model.

sets, particularly on modest-scale and fringe productions. It has been known for designers to build and paint their sets single-handedly when resources are slim.

A last word of caution: make sure that you are entirely satisfied with the model before ordering the wood and starting to build the set. It is much easier to make alterations to the model box than to the completed set.

COSTUME DESIGN

A huge amount of time, effort and ingenuity – and a substantial proportion of the budget – goes in to designing and making the set. However, in the final analysis it is just that: a *setting*. Musicals are about people, and how those people look and what they wear in that setting are both absolutely fundamental to the audience's understanding of the story that is being told. If *My Fair Lady* were to be performed on a bare stage with no set, to an audience who spoke no English, the changes in Eliza's costume and appearance alone would be enough to enable them to grasp the core of the story.

LEFT: Ground plan for The Pirates of Penzance *at the Embassy Theatre, Central School of Speech and Drama. Director, Ken Caswell; designer, Alison Cartledge. The numbered lines on the left-hand side show the location and use of fly bars.*

71

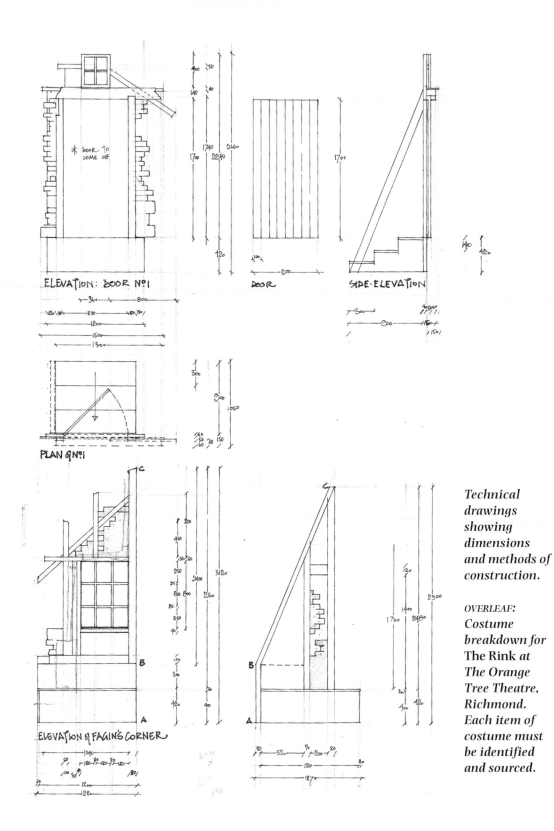

ELEVATION: DOOR N°1

* DOOR TO COME OFF

DOOR

SIDE·ELEVATION

PLAN OF N°1

ELEVATION OF FAGIN'S CORNER

Technical drawings showing dimensions and methods of construction.

OVERLEAF:
Costume breakdown for **The Rink** *at* **The Orange Tree Theatre, Richmond. Each item of costume must be identified and sourced.**

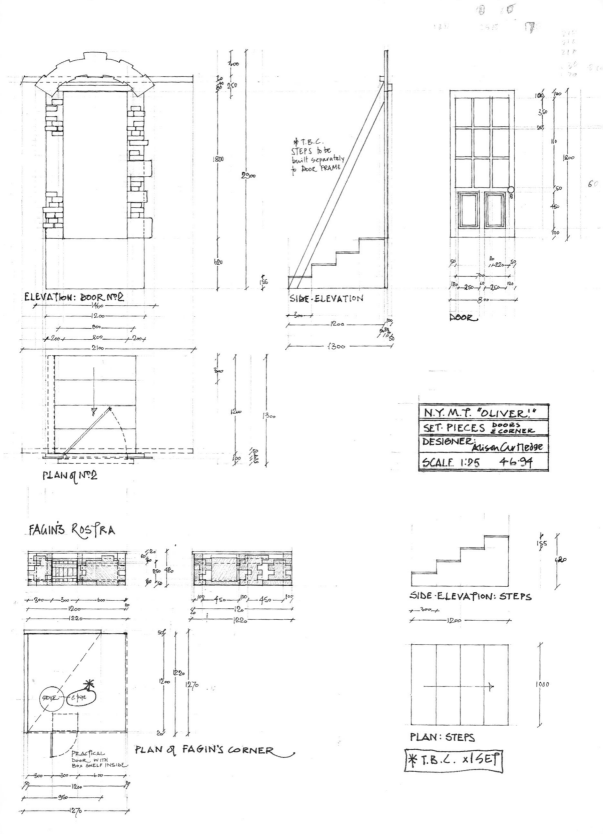

ELEVATION: DOOR Nº 2

SIDE·ELEVATION

DOOR

* T.B.C.
STEPS to be
built separately
to DOOR FRAME

PLAN of Nº 2

| N.Y. M.T. "OLIVER!" |
| SET·PIECES DOORS & CORNER |
| DESIGNER: Alison Curtledge |
| SCALE 1:25   46·94 |

FAGIN'S ROSTRA

PLAN of FAGIN'S CORNER

PRACTICAL
DOOR WITH
BOX SHELF INSIDE

STOVE   & PIPE

SIDE·ELEVATION: STEPS

PLAN: STEPS

* T.B.C. x1 SET

CHARACTER	(PARTS)	Nº of cost...	COSTUME	EXTRA BITS	SHOES/BOOTS
ANNA.		make male Buy 1	Coat Suit Skirt Shirt Shoes Jewelery Earings/Necklace	Tights Polo Knicks Scarf	Shoes / Knee High Boots.
ANGEL.		1	Jean. Coat. Shirt Jewelery Earings W'coat.	Rucksac Duffle Bag	Shoes / Boots
LITTLE GIRL.			Skating OUTfit. Dress		Roller Skates.
		2	Dress. Socks Socks Cardigan.		Shoes.
LINO. (sévan)		✓	Overalls Hat		Boots Skating 1 2
	LENNY 1953 60		Shirt / Tie (either after party) Trousers Jacket		Shoes. 3
	'43		(Teen Lenny) Trousers Shirt Vest Jumper		(↑)
	FAUSTO 43/46/65	o	Suit Shirt Tie Hat / Glasses	1943 Work Jacket. coat & Hat Lei. (63) +scarf	(Shoes ↑?)
	PUNK 78	✓ o ✓ 5	Trousers / Pants Shirt Vest Vest Bandana Bomber Jkt.		Boot (4)
BEN. (Gary)		✓	Overall. Hat.		Boot Roller Skate.
	DINO'S FATHER 52/53/56.		Trouser Vest Shirt Jumper/cardigan	Work Jacket.	Shoes.
	MRS SILVERMAN 78	o	Padding Dress Coat Hat / Gloves / Bag Wig		Shoes.
	SIS. PHILO.	make 4	Nuns outfit.	Lei	Shoes.
TONY (Graham)		✓	Overall. Hat.		Boots Skates.
	TOM '53	Shoes↑ AEH	US Army Uniform. tkt		Boot. / lace ups
	PUNK.	7 ASN o o	Trouser / Pants Vest Bandana.		Boots
	SUITOR 56/60	( )	Shirt Suit Tie		Shoes (lace Ups)
	PETER REILEY	5	Trousers Hawaiian Shirt.		(4).

CHARACTER	(PART)	N° cost.	COSTUMES	EXTRA BITS	SHOES/BOOTS
BUDDY (Gary)		✓	Overalls / Hat		Boot / Skate.
	MIRAM 53	ASN ø	US Army Uniform.		Boots / (lace ups)
	MRS JACKSON		Padding / Dress / Coat / Wig / Glasses ...		Shoes.
	SUITOR 56/60	( )	Suit / Shirt / Tie		Shoes. / (lace ups)
	CHARLIE. 43	✓	Trouser (Red Sox) / T Shirt / BB Hat.		BB Boots ?
	JUNIOR '65 MILLER.		Hawaiian Shirt.	? Disguise.	(↑↑??)
		8 +			
GUY (Martin)		✓	Overalls / Hat.		Boots / Skate.
	YOUNG MAN		Skating Outfit		
	DINO. 43/46/50/53		Vest / Shirt (plaid) / Trousers		Shoes.
		ASN	US Army Uniform		Boots / Blk lace-ups
		ø	Dk Suit / Shirt (Vest) / Tie		Blk (Shoes)
	OLD DINO	denim 70	Chefs outfit	Working skr / cardigan Disguise	
	F. ROCCO 56/60	Make	Priest Cassock		(As 4)
	DEBBIE DUBERMAN '65	Make Make 7	Padding / Wig / Dress skirt / Gloves etc / Top	(Lei)	Shoes.
LUCKY (Niel)		✓	Overalls / Hat		Boots / Skates.
	SUGAR '53	Make Make	Padding / Dress / Wig / Gloves etc		Shoes.
	PUNK 78	ASN ø ø	Trouser. / Pants / Vest / Bandana		Boots
	ARNIE. 43	ø	Trousers / Shirt T Shirt / Vest Jumper BB Jacket		Shoes
	SUITOR 56/60		Suit / Shirt / Tie		Shoes
	BOBBY 65		Hat	Hawaiian Shirt	
	DANNY 70	ø ø	Jeans / Cheesecloth Shirt / Waistcoat / Head Band		

Do not underestimate the power of a good costume. Even though hundreds of thousands of pounds were expended on the sets of mega-musicals in the eighties and nineties, the abiding image associated with many of them has become a figure in costume – or even a single costume element. Think of the ragged girl in *Les Misérables*, the lycra-clad dancers in *Cats*, or the half-face mask of *Phantom of the Opera*.

Do not underestimate the value of a good costume designer, either.

Preparation

If you are designing the costumes for a musical, start off by reading and re-reading the libretto carefully. Certain basic facts can be ascertained immediately: what historical period is the show set in? What country? What season of the year? Some musicals are set in a very specific place and time: a South Pacific island during World War II, the banks of the Mississippi in 1890, New York City a month after the Wall Street crash. Others whisk the audience off to strange dream worlds of fantasy.

Write out a list of all the characters who are named or who play a significant part in the action. Remember that every character – even the tiniest walk-on role – will require a costume of some sort. As you work through the libretto, make notes about each character and the factors that might affect the clothes they wear: age, social status, occupation, nationality, income, relationship to their peer group and so on.

How Many Costumes?

You need to work out early on the total number of costumes you are likely to need, as this will affect what proportion of the budget will be allocated to you, and how you go about spending it. Identify the absolute priorities first. Does anybody undergo a significant transformation in the course of the story? In *Honk!* Ugly changes from duckling to swan; in *Into the Woods* the witch changes from ancient hag to beautiful young woman; Eliza changes from flower girl to society beauty. Many shows are 'rags to riches' stories, and even if you are working on a miniscule budget, these costume changes will be absolutely essential to tell the story.

Ask the director how large the chorus is likely to be, and how they will be used in the show. Do they remain the same characters throughout – townsfolk, soldiers, flappers, servants and so on – or do they play many different roles? Ask the choreographer how many actors they plan to use for each number. If money is tight you may need to negotiate: it is one thing to choreograph twenty Brazilian sailors into the conga scene in *Wonderful Town*, and quite another to costume them all.

Other factors also need to be taken into account: for instance, how much time passes in the show? Will characters need different clothes for winter and summer? Or do decades pass and fashions change? How many places do the characters go to? Do they dress differently at work and at home? Will they need indoor and outdoor outfits? Do they attend any formal or public events, such as weddings, funerals, parties, balls? Alfred Dolittle cannot get married in his dustman's outfit, nor Calamity Jane in her buckskins. Remember that clothes will be more important to some characters than to others: thus Sky Masterson will be more fashion conscious than Nathan Detroit; and the King of Siam will have a larger wardrobe than Tevye.

Keep working through the script until you have produced a basic costume plot that meets all the requirements of the production. As ever, budget restraints mean that you may not be able to have as many costumes as you would ideally like, and you may have to discuss cutbacks with the director and choreographer.

First costume sketches, using a silhouette as a starting point.

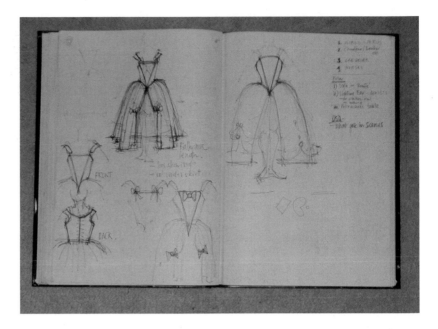

Research

Start researching. Look at photos, paintings, magazines and newspapers from the period and country you are dealing with. Films show period clothes in motion, and may provide vital information on accessories, bags, canes, hats, hairstyles and so on. If the show is set within living memory, talk to people who were alive at the time; you may find out all kinds of unexpected details that never made it into a book.

Get some clothes from the period or country and find out how they are made: how are they strengthened, shaped and supported? What fabrics, materials and colours are used? Build up a sketchbook of drawings, photos, sketches, useful quotations, samples of material and anything else that you think may be useful. Don't limit your research to one source, and keep an open mind.

Designing the Show

Each designer works differently, but the great majority start off by sketching out a few rough ideas as soon as possible, often in the sketchbook that contains their research materials.

Establishing the general shape, or 'silhouette', of a costume is essential. Consider the different way a thirties' suit, a World War II uniform, a fifties' leather jacket or a sixties' 'flower-power' smock hangs on an actor's body, and how each will transform him into a different character. Use the silhouette as a starting point for your sketches. Of course it is an enormous help if you know who will be playing each role before you begin, since the actors' body shapes, height, build, hair, colouring and appearance can have a huge influence on the way you plan to dress them.

As you work, always bear in mind that ordinary living, breathing human beings will be wearing your creations, not catwalk models. A professional dancer with a highly trained body and a perfect physique may have no problem about wearing an extremely skimpy or revealing costume; but a middle-aged amateur performer may well feel differently.

Also remember that your costumes have to be functional: actors have to be able to perform while wearing them. You may think the leading lady will look fabulous in a tight skirt and sky-high stilettos, but if she cannot dance a step in them, forget it. Be considerate of the actors' needs, too: for instance, avoid dressing someone in a woolly jumper and heavy overcoat during a scene with a particularly long and exhausting dance number. Liaise with the director and choreographer so you know if and when actors are going to be performing any particularly spectacular or strenuous physical action, and keep this in mind as you design.

As ever, it is important not to get bogged down in your first idea. Spread your net wide: look around clothes shops and haberdashers; flick through hire companies' catalogues, or visit their storerooms. Continue to sketch and experiment.

Start to think about which fabrics you want to use, and which fabrics you are likely to be able to afford. What would be appropriate to the period, the climate, the social status of the characters? As you go around fabric shops and market stalls, collect 'swatches' – small samples of the material – and make a note of the price per metre. This will make costing the final designs quicker and more accurate.

Keep in close contact with the set designer. Ensure that you are both aware of the materials and colours that the other is planning to use, and that you share a common vision of the visual style that you wish to achieve.

Expanding the Imagination

Television is a naturalistic medium. For costume designers working on a period film or television drama, historical accuracy is often the top priority. A huge amount of effort goes into finding out *exactly* what a well-to-do lawyer in Paris in 1813 would have worn, and then making a costume that reproduces it in every last detail.

It cannot be repeated too often that, unlike TV and film, musicals are non-naturalistic. They use a heightened form of dramatic expression and require a heightened visual style to match. Of course as the costume designer you must be aware of the style of the period, but there is no need to reproduce it with slavish accuracy: lapels can be wider, pinstripes broader, hats bigger, colours brighter, gowns longer, uniforms more highly decorated. Real eighteenth-century pirates probably wore filthy old rags, but the very unrealistic, all-singing, all-dancing pirates of Penzance need to wear something colourful and bright.

Enjoy this freedom, and use it to extend the boundaries of your imagination. Be bold in

Swatches of fabrics for **The King and I.**

Costume drawings for **The Pirates of Penzance** *at the Embassy Theatre, Central School of Speech and Drama. Director, Ken Caswell; designer, Alison Cartledge.*

your ideas; try pushing them further. Of course, there is always a danger that the style may overbalance and become 'camp' or downright silly. Use your taste and judgement to stay on the right side of the line.

Costume Drawings

You will need to make a series of coloured drawings that shows each character in each of his/her costumes. Draw both a front and back view if necessary, and identify the scene or scenes in which the costume will be worn. Add in a description of each component, and add explanatory diagrams and/or notes on any unusual decorative features. Attach swatches of the fabrics you are planning to use if you

have them. If a specific hairdo or wig is required, or an unusual make-up, these should be shown, too.

A set of costume drawings needs to be complete and comprehensive. Don't forget any characters, even if they only appear for a few moments. Identical chorus costumes need only be drawn once, but you may choose to draw a few to show how they will look together in a group on stage.

You should pay particular attention to drawings of costumes that will have to be made from scratch. The more accurate, detailed and helpful they are, the easier it will be for the dressmaker or tailor to produce exactly what you want. If a costume needs to be made in a specific way – if it needs velcro seams for a quick change, for instance – make sure this is specified.

Your drawings should aim to give as clear an indication as possible of how the character will look on stage. You don't have to do brilliant portraits of the actors – in any case, it is unlikely that every role will have been cast when you are preparing your drawings – but if you do know who is playing the part, at least give them the right hair and skin colouring.

During the rehearsal period you will build up a personal relationship with each member of the cast (unlike the set designer who may see very little of them). Many people have extremely fixed ideas about what clothes look good on them, and you may need to use gentle persuasion to get them to wear your creations. Make your drawings as attractive, bright and exciting as you can, as they will help to 'sell' the costumes to the actors at the first rehearsal, and make them keen to wear them.

Costing the Design

The costume drawings go through a similar costing procedure to the model box. In most professional productions this costing is done by the costume supervisor working alongside the designer, but for smaller shows the designer may do it on his own.

The costume supervisor needs to assess the most cost-effective way of sourcing the costumes. Some will have to be made, some adapted from existing stock, some bought, and some hired.

Making costs can include fabric, transport, fastenings, zips, braiding, padding, decoration and labour. Large producing theatres have their own teams of cutters and makers, while freelance supervisors have teams of makers – often people working from home – to whom the work is subcontracted on a casual basis.

Many professional theatres raise extra revenue by renting out costumes from their wardrobe department. In the UK both the Royal National Theatre and the Royal Shakespeare Company offer this service: the quality is fantastic, but the price is high. In addition there are numerous specialist theatre hire companies that you may consider using.

To Hire or Buy?

It is obviously more satisfying for the designer if the costumes are made specially for the production. A brand new costume made of carefully chosen fabric, cut perfectly to fit a certain actor, will always look better than a five-year-old one that has been dug out of stock and altered.

However, inevitably there are practical and financial considerations to be taken into account. There are some costumes where you will almost certainly find it easier to hire than to make, such as military uniforms, tuxedos, top hat and tails, police uniforms, animal skins and certain historical costumes (Mister Bumble's beadle's gown, for instance).

Hired costumes will be cheaper for a short run, but if they are needed for several weeks there will come a point where it is less expensive to make or buy them outright, than to continue to pay a weekly hire charge. Circumstances will, of course, vary from production to production, and the various options need to be weighed up and costed.

Where to Save Money

When the designs have been costed, the overall price will invariably exceed the budget, and the designer and director then have to embark on the all-too-familiar process of finding ways to save money.

Like set designers, costume designers need to know where they are most prepared to make sacrifices, and where they are not. Some costumes have to be just fantastic, and money, care and attention need to be lavished on them. Hire dresses for everyone else at the ball

Costume drawings for The King and I *at The Freemasons' Temple, produced by Mark Watty for the Covent Garden Festival. Director, John Gardyne; designer, Alison Cartledge.*

if you have to, but whatever you do, don't skimp on Eliza's ballgown.

Look for cheaper suppliers of fabrics and materials: markets are nearly always cheaper than shops. Go to unglamorous industrial estates and buy direct from wholesalers and importers. The last few metres of a roll of fabric may be sold off at a cut price. Check out charity and thrift shops and see what you can find.

If you are doing an up-to-the-minute show set in the present day such as *Rent* or *Songs for a New World*, see if the cast own any suitable clothes which they are prepared to wear themselves, or lend to the production. Many men have their own dinner jackets or business suits: see what you can borrow. Shoes are always troublesome: again, if the cast will wear their own, you will make a significant saving.

Is it possible to cut down on the number of costumes? Can the King of Siam make do with three outfits rather than four? Maybe Dolly can make do with just one outfit right up to her triumphant entry for the title song? Can you just add a jacket or coat to an existing costume, rather than creating a whole new 'winter' outfit? If you have access to a wardrobe store, see if there are costumes from previous shows that can be adapted and re-used.

Any musical worth its salt works towards a musical and dramatic climax, and many demand an equivalent visual climax. If you have to cut or economize on costumes, do this in Act One, as early on in the show as possible. Save your money for the big moments, and especially the finale. That is what the audience will remember when they leave the theatre buzzing with excitement – they will have forgotten all about those dreary chorus costumes you had to use in the first few scenes.

The tradition of the 'walkdown' in pantomimes – where the cast take their final bows in extravagant, glittering costumes – is an extreme example of this principle. It has been

A Chorus Line

In the finale of *A Chorus Line*, the dancers we have come to know and empathize with during their audition – and whom we have only ever seen in their rehearsal clothes – appear on the stage in gold lamé top-hat-and-tails outfits, high-kicking their way through the song 'One'.

It is the high point of the show, a huge moment of celebration: look, they've got the job. But as more dancers appear on stage in identical costumes – and then yet more – it becomes increasingly difficult to tell who is who. Their individuality disappears, and they turn into little more than walking scenery, whose only function is to frame the performance of the star.

It is an astonishing moment of musical theatre, brilliantly encapsulating both the triumph and tragedy of the chorus dancer's life in a single, deeply ambiguous image. It is the whole point of the show.

Don't try staging *A Chorus Line* unless you can costume that finale.

known for productions to spend nearly 40 per cent of the wardrobe budget on the walkdown, even though it only lasts for a few minutes.

Finalizing the Design
Trade-offs are made, compromises reached, cuts agreed. Eventually the costume design is agreed.

Organizing and scheduling the making and delivery of the costumes is the responsibility of the costume supervisor, though in amateur and fringe productions the designer will often do this himself. The production manager provides a cash float, and the supervisor and/or designer goes out shopping. Try and get a discount for paying in cash, keep a careful record

COSTUME MEASUREMENTS

NAME
CHARACTER

DRESS SIZE
HEIGHT
SHOE

CHEST/BUST
BRA SIZE
UNDER BUST
WAIST
HIPS

INSIDE LEG
OUTSIDE LEG
ACROSS FRONT (armpit-armpit)
ACROSS BACK
M: CB-SHOULDER-ELBOW-WRIST
UNDER ARM
OUTSIDE ARM (bent)
SHOULDER MMT
CF (PIT-WAIST)
CB (NAP-WAIST)
NAP-GROUND (cloak)
NECK
WRIST
HEAD

ARMHOLE-WAIST
CB NAP-CF WAIST
SIDE FRONT(shoulder seam-over bust-waist)
BUST-BUST
TOP OF ARM (bent)
FOREARM (bent)
THIGH
ABOVE KNEE
BELOW KNEE (breeches)
CB-CF (crotch)
GIRTH (neck-crotch-up back)

Actor's measurement form.

of everything you spend, and always get a receipt.

Hired costumes need to be checked and ordered as far in advance as possible, but are usually only delivered on the day of the technical rehearsals.

Measurement Charts

The wardrobe department cannot start work properly until they know the measurements of the actors, and it is the wardrobe supervisor's job to prepare a measurement chart for each member of the cast. How many measurements are required will of course depend on the style and complexity of the costumes, but it is as well to get as much information as you can as early as possible.

As soon as actors are cast, you should contact them and get their details. It is best if you can measure them yourself, as people will sometimes give misleading information about their dress size or waist measurement. If this is impossible, send them a copy of the chart and ask them to fill it in themselves – stressing the need for accuracy.

Completed measurement forms with actors' photographs attached.

6 CASTING

asting is a critical task. A good, strong, committed cast can overcome shortcomings in the venue, set and costumes and make the production a success. A weak cast can have the most expensive resources, the biggest budget and the most fabulous theatre, and the show will still be a disappointment.

A few musicals have tiny casts: *I do! I do!* is written for two actors; *Starting Here, Starting Now* and *What About Luv?* for three; and *Closer then Ever* and *Songs for a New World* for four. The vast majority, however, demand a cast of twenty or more, depending on the role of the chorus.

SCENE/CHARACTER BREAKDOWN

When starting to cast a show, many directors find it useful to draw up a grid showing which characters appear in each scene. This gives a general idea of the size of the cast, the relative importance of the roles, and a sense of the overall shape and structure. Include all the speaking roles, no matter how small, and any non-speaking roles that play a significant part in the stage action. For the time being crowd scenes should just be identified as including 'male chorus' and/ or 'female chorus'.

Vocal Range

Make lists of all the named characters, one for men, one for women. Start with the leading roles, and work down in rough order of size and importance. Put the vocal range of the singing roles next to the name of the character – soprano, alto, tenor, baritone or bass. This may be indicated in the score: if not, go through it with the MD.

THE CAST BREAKDOWN

The cast list in the libretto will probably supply a certain amount of information about the characters. For example:

MARY: Mezzo-soprano, 50s, Irish. Mother to Connor.
CONNOR: High baritone, 25, Irish. Mary's son.

Plays vs. Musicals: Vocal Range

When casting straight plays, vocal range is not really an issue: within reason, any actor of approximately the right age may – theoretically at least – be eligible to play any part.

In musicals it is crucial. If the actor cannot sing within the required range – no matter how suitable he or she may be in every other respect – there is no point considering them for the role.

A casting grid for **Guys and Dolls,** *showing which characters appear in each scene.*

'GUYS and DOLLS' – SCENE/CHARACTER BREAKDOWN

	ACT ONE										ACT TWO						
	1	2	3	4	5	6	7	8	9	10	1	2	3	4	5	6	7
NICELY/NICELY	✔				✔		✔			✔	✔	✔	✔	✔	✔		✔
BENNY SOUTHSTREET	✔				✔		✔			✔			✔	✔	✔		✔
RUSTY CHARLIE	✔																
SARAH BROWN	✔	✔			✔	✔		✔	✔	✔		✔			✔	✔	✔
ARVIDE ABERNATHY	✔	✔			✔	✔	✔		✔			✔			✔		✔
MARTHA	✔				✔	✔				✔					✔		✔
CALVIN	✔				✔	✔				✔					✔		✔
AGATHA	✔				✔	✔				✔					✔		✔
HARRY THE HORSE	✔						✔			✔			✔	✔	✔		✔
LIEUTENANT BRANNIGAN	✔						✔			✔					✔		✔
NATHAN DETROIT	✔		✔	✔			✔			✔			✔	✔	✔		✔
ANGIE THE OX	✔						✔			✔			✔		✔		✔
ADELAIDE	✔			✔			✔			✔	✔			✔		✔	✔
SKY MASTERSTON	✔	✔			✔	✔		✔	✔	✔	✔	✔	✔		✔		✔
MIMI (HOT BOX GIRL)			✔														
GENERAL CARTWRIGHT						✔									✔		
LIVER LIPS LOUIS							✔			✔			✔		✔		✔
SOCIETY MAX							✔						✔		✔		✔
BIG JULE							✔			✔			✔	✔	✔		✔
WAITER (CUBA)								✔									
WAITER (HOT BOX)											✔						
CUBA DANCE TRIO								✔									
MC (HOT BOX)				✔							✔						
FEMALE CHORUS	✔				✔			✔			✔						
MALE CHORUS	✔				✔			✔	✔	✔	✔		✔	✔	✔		✔
JOEY BILTMORE	(✔) – VOICE ON PHONE ONLY																

85

The director should add other significant aspects of the roles to this bald outline: the main qualities the characters display, notes about their background, any special accomplishments they have, and any unusual action in which they are involved. Include any specific quotes from the text if that helps to build up a general picture of each character. For example:

MARY: Mezzo-soprano, 50s, Irish. Mother to Connor. Loving mother, very moral, careworn but resilient. 'Jeez but she was a beauty when she was a girl.' Has to clog dance in Act 1 finale.
CONNOR: High baritone, 25, Irish (but has lived in New York for ten years). Lovable rogue, irresistible to women. Lots of jazz dancing inc. two solos. Jumps out of bedroom window naked in Act 2.

Keep your descriptions brief and to the point. Don't feel you have to psychoanalyse the characters like this: 'Lovable rogue, possibly due to absence of paternal role model in early youth. Still obsessed with tragic death of his younger sister aged 6 ...' and so on. You may, of course, wish to go into that in rehearsal with the actor once he has been cast.

As you work down the list your notes will get shorter. 'Ice-cream seller (could be male or female).' For reference you may wish to identify in which scene the character appears.

How Many People?

From your character grid you can identify how many named roles you need to cast. Smaller roles that appear in only one or two scenes may be played by members of the chorus, and may be doubled up.

Be careful not to overdo this, however. In *Guys and Dolls* General Matilda B. Cartwright may only appear in two scenes, but she is a very important character: you risk lessening

Auditions need to be carefully organized. Let people know where to go.

her dramatic impact if the actress who plays her keeps popping up in the chorus. Similarly, it will be very confusing for the audience if the actor who plays the waiter at El Café Cubano in Havana (Act 1 Scene 8) also plays a different waiter at the Hot Box Club in New York (Act 2 Scene 1).

The Chorus

In the professional world the size of the chorus is dictated by how many actors the management are prepared to pay. In amateur shows it may depend on the size of the stage, how many people are available, or on the costume budget.

The director, MD and choreographer need to confer on how many chorus members they require. The director needs to be sure that all the small parts can be filled, and that there are enough actors to fill the stage effectively in crowd scenes. The MD will have the musical balance in mind. Resident choruses in opera companies contain equal numbers of the four main vocal types; the ensemble numbers will sound weak if there are nine baritones and only one bass. Similarly the choreographer may have special requirements: the Hot Box girls in *Guys and Dolls* do not necessarily have to be the world's greatest dancers, but you need a trio who can really dance up a storm for the Havana scene.

When you are all agreed, add the ensemble players to your cast breakdown, then type it up and check it. It is very reassuring to have it in your hands, since now you know what you are looking for. Make sure the costume designer gets a copy, too.

Professional Casting

In the professional world the stars of musicals are cast early; indeed, the show may be written for them. They are often the biggest single draw and selling point of the show. Sometimes they have a financial stake in it, too.

Professional producers may employ a casting agent to assist the director in casting the supporting roles and ensemble. Casting agents – the good ones, anyway – have an encyclopaedic knowledge of actors, their abilities and their availability for work. Using the cast breakdown for guidance, the casting agent will draw up a list of potential actors for each role, who will then be auditioned by the director, the MD and the choreographer.

Of course, it is quite possible that the director will have particular actors in mind anyway, in which case they are contacted through their personal agents. Alternatively, the director may fax or email the cast breakdown directly to actors' agencies, and ask for suggestions.

Open Auditions

Producers may also hold open auditions, where anyone who likes can turn up. These are invariably crowded and tense, and can be brutal. Michael Bennett mythologized the Broadway open audition in *A Chorus Line*, one of the greatest musicals of all time. (Come to think of it, an open audition for a production of *A Chorus Line* must be a pretty surreal event.)

Spread the Word

Lots of people want to be in shows, and the more people that know about your production, the larger pool of potential actors you will have to choose from. Let people know you are casting. If you are producing the show for an existing drama club or society, put it in the newsletter; stick up notices and posters; hand out flyers.

Photocopy your cast breakdown and distribute it so people are aware of what roles are available. Talk up the show: make it sound as exciting as you can. Take out an advertisement in the local press if that seems appropriate; or try and get on to your local radio.

If you are producing a heavy dance show such as *West Side Story* or *Grease* you might organize a dance workshop to stir up people's interest. If the show is obscure – or even if it isn't it can be a good idea to organize an informal sing-through of some of the music with the MD.

Do everything you can think of to make people want to be in it.

ORGANIZING AUDITIONS

Exactly how you structure your audition process will vary according to the nature of the show and your particular circumstances. Thus, dance auditions will be essential for

---

Beware of Pre-Casting

It is highly inadvisable to promise a juicy leading role to an actor before you have held auditions – especially if that actor is your friend, lover, husband or wife. Someone may turn up who is twice as good and three times as suitable for the part, putting you in a compromised and difficult position. Marriages have been wrecked for less.

42nd Street, probably unnecessary for *Sweeney Todd*.

It takes time to put a good cast together, so don't expect to get all your auditions completed in one day, especially if you are dealing with large numbers. Decide on two or three dates and times when the director, MD and choreographer are available. In amateur productions it is best if you have a mixture of weekday evenings and weekend afternoons. Hire a dance studio, rehearsal room or hall with a good piano, and make it very clear on all your publicity exactly where and when the auditions are taking place.

If people cannot attend for some reason, give them alternative dates if you can. Accommodate them as far as possible, though try not to organize several individual auditions on separate days. Avoid auditioning in private houses unless there is absolutely no alternative: everyone will function better in neutral territory, and the whole process will feel more professional.

Ensure there is somewhere clean and quiet for your auditionees to wait.

DANCE AUDITIONS

Dance auditions should be supervised by the choreographer, with the director in attendance. They can be time-consuming, so plan to see your auditionees in groups of twenty to thirty, depending on how much room you have. If at all possible run the audition in a dance studio with a properly sprung floor and mirrors. Get your auditionees to bring appropriate clothing and footwear, and make sure that there is somewhere relatively private to change.

Dancers wearing identical black leotards with their hair tied back can look very similar, especially women. Encourage your auditionees to wear a coloured headband, top or tights. When reviewing a group of dancers a director may not remember names or faces, but may recall 'The girl in the red top was good', or that they 'liked the boy in the blue T-shirt.'

Be organized. Have someone who is not involved in the selection process at the door to greet the auditionees. Some may bring professional-style CVs, resumés and photographs; if they don't, be sure to make a careful record of their names and contact details. If you are expecting a lot of people who are largely unknown to you, give them a badge or a sticky label with a number on it for ease of identification. This may seem brutal and de-personalizing, but if you are dealing with dozens of people it is the only way you will ever be able to keep track of who's who.

Many amateur performers are extremely self-conscious about expressing themselves through their body, and the choreographer must work hard to create a non-threatening atmosphere in which everyone feels confident to have a go. It is time-consuming and frustrating to keep messing around with cassettes and CDs at this stage: use a rehearsal pianist, or ask the MD to play for you.

Teaching a Routine

Start with a few stretching moves to loosen people up, then work through a few basic steps and moves that suit the style of the music. Use a number from the show, or at least something in a similar style; there is no point in working on an elaborate tap dance if you are casting *Cabaret*.

Professional dancers in auditions pride themselves on their ability to learn a routine quickly and accurately. When dealing with non-professionals, however, don't try and teach too much: eight bars of music should be enough, sixteen at the most. In any case, don't let the audition run for more than forty minutes or so.

The choreographer should keep leading the group, demonstrating and calling out the steps. Let people get confident in the basic moves before introducing points of style and technique. Once they have a basic grasp, run the routine through in smaller groups, first with the choreographer leading, then with the actors on their own.

Watch how people are doing; it is usually very clear who has a natural sense of rhythm and timing, and who does not. The choreographer and director should make individual notes on the candidates they think have potential, and then confer. Usually there are one or two 'definites', one or two 'maybes' and quite a few 'definitely nots'. Do not, however, immediately write off the latter, certainly not until after the singing audition. Girl number 37 may have two left feet, but she might sing like an angel.

It may be appropriate to ask some of the more promising dancers to come back and run through another routine later, especially if the choreography involves several different dance styles.

As with all auditions, always be polite. Don't waste people's time, and don't give them a false sense of optimism. If there really is no place for

Good casting is about building a team who will work well together and look right. The male cast of The Rink *at The Orange Tree Theatre, Richmond, directed by the author.*

them in the show, thank them for coming, but tell them your decision there and then.

If you are undecided about people, or if you may be recalling them at a later date, double check their contact details. Above all, if you tell someone you will get back to them, make sure you do, even if it is only to say 'No thank you'. Courtesy is free.

SINGING AUDITIONS

These may take place immediately after the dance auditions, or completely separately; they are usually run by the MD and the director together. As with dance auditions, be organized: give people a specific time to attend, allowing ten minutes for a singing audition, fifteen if you are combining it with the acting auditions. If you are seeing a lot of people all afternoon, schedule in a tea break: you will need it.

Type up a list of the names of the people you are seeing, and leave plenty of space for your notes. As with the dance auditions, it is best if you have someone else to receive and organize auditionees as they arrive, check their details and bring them into the room to introduce them to the auditioners.

In the professional world, singers are asked to prepare two contrasting songs and bring the sheet music with them to the audition. The songs need not be from the show (indeed it is sometimes better if they're not – if everyone is singing the same number it can get very dull for the auditioners), but it should be in an appropriate style; usually a song from one of the composer's other shows is a good bet.

If you are dealing with young or inexperienced actors you may choose to audition them less formally. Some MDs like to start by teaching a song from the show to everyone in a group, then getting them to sing it solo one by one. If time is extremely short – if you are auditioning a large number of children, for instance – it may be sufficient to hear them sing a few bars of a standard song such as 'Somewhere over the Rainbow', or even 'Happy Birthday to You'.

Whichever approach you choose, the music should be played live on a piano. You will need a highly competent pianist who can play anything that is put in front of him or her at sight. Singing auditions are nerve-racking enough as it is, without the pianist fumbling away and making mistakes. Some MDs like to play themselves, others find that this distracts them from listening carefully to the voices of the auditionees.

Assessing the Voice

Listen to the tone of the singing voice. Is it light or strong, bluesy or folksy? Can you hear the individual words? How about the phrasing? Can you understand the meaning of the lyrics? Do they make you laugh, or cry – or do they send a tingle down the back of your neck? The MD may also wish to check the singer's vocal range if they are considering them as a possible candidate for a solo role.

Sometimes actors just click with each other from the start. 'Chemistry' is difficult to define, but impossible to miss. Billy Bigelow and Julie Jordan in GSA Conservatoire's production of Carousel, *director Val Macardle. Photo: Mark Dean*

Again, always be polite. Don't make derogatory comments, however bad you may think someone is – but don't be afraid to stop a singer in mid-song if they are going on for too long: usually one verse and a chorus is enough to give the MD the information required. If you sit through every verse of 'I am a very model of a modern major general' you will be there all night.

Once the auditionee has left the room, have a brief discussion about their musical potential straightaway. Don't wait till the end of the session: in two hours' time you will have forgotten all about the person you saw first.

Don't be afraid to ask people to come back at a later date, especially if you want to hear them sing a duet with another actor.

ACTING AUDITIONS

Acting auditions take many different forms. When casting a play, the director may just chat informally to the actors, then ask them to read part of the script. Alternatively, the actors may be asked to take part in day-long company workshops, especially if the work is to be devised.

Some directors find it best to meet actors individually when considering them for an acting role; others like to ask two or three to come at the same time. Either way, they should be invited to read some of the dialogue aloud.

Don't ask them to do too much – a page or so should be sufficient. Take time to talk about the scene, then read it a second, or even a third time. Remember that the actor may have prepared an interpretation of the role that is radically different from the director's, and it is worth seeing if they are willing and/or able to respond to the director's comments. This is also a good moment to check on accents.

If an actor expresses a particular interest in one role, always ask them at the audition if they are prepared to take on another, or to be in the chorus. Four actors may fancy themselves as Nathan Detroit, but remember you are also looking for Benny Southstreet, Rusty Charlie and Harry the Horse.

Recalls

Don't hesitate to recall actors to read scenes with others. If you have two potential Sarah Browns and a potential Sky Masterson, get each of them to read their scenes with him and see what happens. Sometimes actors respond to each other immediately and the sparks fly – the elusive 'chemistry'. This is unpredictable, but when it happens it is unmistakable.

Always try out combinations of lovers, parents and children, and characters who work as a double act such as the gangsters in *Kiss Me Kate*. Apart from anything else, this will also give you a chance to see how actors look together on stage. Do you really believe they're brothers? Do you mind the leading man being a bit short? Isn't she just a little bit old for him?

Casting Children

Casting children can be a minefield. It may be that the parents are keener for their son or daughter to be in a show than the children are themselves. Beware the stage mother who is going to be attending every rehearsal making helpful comments like Rose in *Gypsy*.

When casting children remember that, unless you are only doing three or four performances, you may have to cast more than one child in each role.

Remember also that children who can sustain a leading role such as Oliver, the Artful Dodger or Annie are rare. You may have to search far and wide for them.

GUYS AND DOLLS – WOMEN

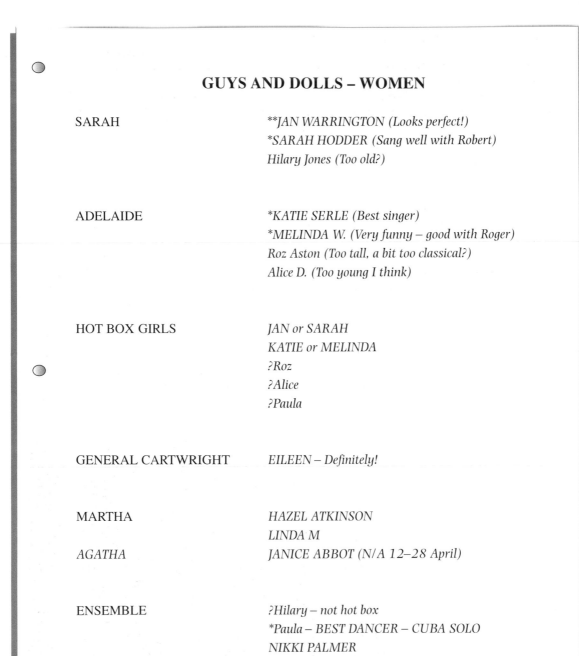

SARAH	**JAN WARRINGTON *(Looks perfect!)* *SARAH HODDER (Sang well with Robert)* *Hilary Jones (Too old?)*
ADELAIDE	*KATIE SERLE (Best singer)* *MELINDA W. (Very funny – good with Roger)* *Roz Aston (Too tall, a bit too classical?)* *Alice D. (Too young I think)*
HOT BOX GIRLS	*JAN or SARAH* *KATIE or MELINDA* *?Roz* *?Alice* *?Paula*
GENERAL CARTWRIGHT	*EILEEN – Definitely!*
MARTHA *AGATHA*	*HAZEL ATKINSON* *LINDA M* *JANICE ABBOT (N/A 12–28 April)*
ENSEMBLE	*?Hilary – not hot box* *Paula – BEST DANCER – CUBA SOLO* *NIKKI PALMER* *?Do we need one more?*

DECIDING ON THE CAST

As auditions progress, the director, MD, choreographer and producer will draw up their lists of first, second and third choices for each role. Some actors fit certain parts like a glove; other roles seem impossible to fill. Keep looking, and always remember that the right person is out there somewhere.

It can be a tricky process, and you need to weigh up the qualities that each actor would bring to the role. The choreographer may favour an actress who moves like a dream, but sings a little off-key; the MD may prefer the slightly awkward one who sings like Liza Minelli; the producer may want the dazzling beauty whose face will go on the poster and sell tickets. Everybody will have an opinion, but the final decision rests with the director, supported – one hopes – by the producer.

Where to Compromise

Inevitably some compromises will have to be made, and it is usually best to compromise

---

Double Casting

Occasionally a role is double cast, meaning that two actors share it, each appearing at every alternate performance. Child roles are almost always double (or even treble) cast because there are laws limiting the number of public performances a child can give in any one period.

Double casting is frequently used in drama schools, where giving everyone a fair crack of the whip is a major priority. Furthermore, it may seem an attractive compromise if no agreement can be reached. Be aware, however, that double casting can add considerably to rehearsal time, and inevitably it has an impact on the wardrobe budget.

---

least on vocal ability. Wigs, 'lifts' in shoes and well-cut costumes can help to shave off the years and transform people physically. Choreography can be modified or simplified to

LEFT: *Weighing up the options between actresses for* Guys and Dolls.

Henrik in A Little Night Music *has to play – or appear to play – the cello. An actor who can play an instrument is always a bonus. GSA Conservatoire production, directed and designed by David Flaten; lighting designer, Mark Dymock. Photo: Mark Dean*

GUYS AND DOLLS

CAST LIST

SARAH BROWN	JAN WARRINGTON
SKY MASTERSON	ROBERT DAVIDSON
ADELAIDE	MELINDA WIENEKE
NATHAN DETROIT	ROGER COOOPER
NICELY-NICELY JOHNSON	IAN FINLAY
BENNY SOUTHSTREET	TIM HARRISON
RUSTY CHARLIE	SIMON BAXTER
ARVIDE ABERNETHY	ARTHUR SMEATON
MARTHA	HAZEL ATKINSON
AGATHA	LINDA MAHER
CALVIN	TBC
HARRY THE HORSE	PETER RICHARDS
LIEUTENANT BRANNIGAN	JON LAIRD
ANGIE THE OX	ANDY TAYLOR
GENERAL CARTWRIGHT	EILEEN McCRAE
LIVER LIPS LOUIS	ALAN STRINGFELLOW
SOCIETY MAX	DAVID FLOYD
BIG JULE	ROB TEBBUTT
HOT BOX GIRLS	SARAH HODDER
	KATIE SEARLE
	ROZ ASTON
	ALICE DAVIDSON
FEMALE ENSEMBLE	PAULA REDWAY*
	HILARY JONES
	NICKI PALMER
MALE ENSEMBLE	JONAS PFEIFFER*
	ALDO PELOSI*
	CHRIS GASCOINE
	IAN ROBINSON
	*- HAVANA DANCE SOLOISTS

WAITERS, MC, DRUNKS, TOURISTS, VOICE OF JOEY BILTMORE etc TO BE CAST FROM ENSEMBLE

FIRST REHEARSAL: TUESDAY 14 MARCH, 7-30pm ROOM 606, CARLTON COMMUNITY COLLEGE, OFF ST LEONARDS ROAD, LONDON W13 8PN.
(SEE MAP)

PERFORMANCES 7:30 pm MON 12 – SAT 24 MAY – CRESCENT THEATRE
(No performance Sunday 18th)

MANY THANKS TO EVERYONE WHO AUDITIONED.

RACHEL JONES – DIRECTOR

suit a performer of lesser ability; music cannot. Thus a Lady Thiang who is slightly too old but can sing 'Something Wonderful' like a dream is preferable to one who looks better, but sounds worse.

Consider the real demands of each role. Tevye has been married for twenty-five years, so he should be in his mid-forties or fifty; but more importantly, he has to carry the whole of *Fiddler on the Roof*. It is therefore better to choose someone too young who can carry the show, rather than someone the right age who can't.

Understudies

If your run is a long one you may consider appointing understudies for the main roles. Understudying can be a thankless task, and it is best to discuss the possibility with the actor involved, with tact and discretion.

Professional understudies are often guaranteed one or two performances a week, usually at midweek matinées, and you might consider letting your understudy perform the part at least once during the run.

Announcing the Cast

Casting is an emotional business, and inevitably many people will be disappointed. Twenty actresses may want to play Miss Adelaide, but only one will get the part. It is best to wait until the cast list is complete before you announce it, but do not delay for too long: try and publish it within a few days of your recalls.

Type up the cast list and check it; if there are still some smaller parts to be filled, put a note to the effect that these are TBC ('To be cast'). Note that the odd 'TBC' for a supporting role is perfectly normal, but too many can make the show look under-resourced – and never leave a leading role as 'TBC', as it will lead to awkward questions from actors who are surprised to find themselves in the chorus.

If appropriate, pin up the cast list on a noticeboard, or fax or email it to your auditionees. Some directors like to beat a hasty retreat at this point, to let the dust settle. If you have to contact people by phone, it is best if this is done by someone who was not involved in the decision-making process. Avoid at all costs getting involved in discussing your casting decisions with the actors; this may quickly lead to destabilizing gossip and bad feeling amongst the cast.

The cast list is final. If an actor objects violently to his or her casting, it is probably better that they leave the show before rehearsals begin.

LEFT: *The final cast list for* Guys and Dolls. *'Calvin' has yet to be found, but the rest of the parts are cast.*

7 REHEARSALS: GETTING STARTED

In the professional theatre, financial considerations dictate that the rehearsal period should be as short and intensive as possible. Older British actors sometimes speak fondly of 'weekly rep' that flourished until the sixties, when plays were rehearsed from scratch in one week and performed the next. Even today, pantomimes are lucky to get two weeks' rehearsal. Repertory theatres might rehearse a straight play for three weeks, but would probably allow four for a musical; five would be a luxury.

At the other end of the scale, a West End show might rehearse for two months, and for longer if there is rewriting to be done. Many large-scale Broadway shows start life on out-of-town try-out tours, which give the writers and creative team weeks, if not months, to re-work and re-rehearse the material before they open in New York.

Amateur performers are unlikely to be available every day, so their rehearsals, by necessity, must take place over a longer period. Just as there is never enough money, so there is never

When working with young or inexperienced actors it is often useful to use theatre games and exercises to build trust and confidence at the first few rehearsals. Photo: Tina Bicât

enough time: however long you rehearse for, be prepared for a rush of activity in the last week.

'SESSIONS'

Professional actors and musicians usually work in three-hour periods, known as 'sessions', with a fifteen-minute coffee or cigarette break about half-way through. After three hours everybody begins to flag. A professional rehearsal week comprises two sessions a day for five or six days a week; so four weeks of rehearsal would work out at about forty to forty-five sessions in total.

If an amateur cast rehearsed three times a week, it would take between thirteen and fifteen weeks – three to four months – to achieve the same amount of rehearsal, which is an awfully long time to ask people to commit to voluntarily. Moreover, it is dispiriting to start rehearsing a show whose opening night seems impossibly distant, to the extent that some of your cast may lose interest and drift off, which is bad for everyone's morale. Also, remember that people's circumstances and availability may change, especially in school holidays and during the summer.

Aim to rehearse for about eight weeks, ten at the most. Remember that not all the cast will be called to all the rehearsals, so the overall time commitment is not as daunting as initially it might sound. Plan on at least four rehearsals a week; evening rehearsals should not exceed three hours. Sunday afternoons are useful for whole company calls, and you may be able to work on for an extra couple of hours into the early evening.

DRAFTING A SCHEDULE

The director should liaise with the MD and choreographer and agree how the rehearsal time will be divided up between them. When you do this be aware that – as with all aspects of the production – everyone will have very good reasons why they need a larger proportion of the production's time and resources than anybody else. Use tact and diplomacy – and a sense of fairness.

When working on professional productions, directors usually have a rough rehearsal plan in their head, based on their experience and the size of the show.

In a professional production the schedule does not have to be planned in much more detail than this. All the actors are – theoretically at least – available whenever they are required, and as professionals it is possible to make a fairly accurate estimate of how long it will take them to learn their material.

In an amateur show, things will go more slowly. Allow two or three sessions early on for learning music, and more if it is complicated. Depending on the cast's level of expertise and experience, the choreographer may want a full company rehearsal early on to introduce basic steps and style guidelines. Allow a whole session for staging company dance numbers, and two if they are long and involve a large number of people.

A page of dialogue runs on average for two minutes on stage, and you should allow fifteen to twenty minutes' rehearsal for each page. Of course, you will be able to rehearse some scenes more quickly than others – thus work on a scene between two characters will always move faster than work on one with thirty.

Use the scene breakdown to work out how you will organize the work during the rehearsal period. Mark in any 'N/A's that have been previously agreed with the cast, and as far as possible plan rehearsals around these so that actors' non-availability causes minimum disruption. Don't feel that you have to rehearse scenes and numbers in the order that they appear in the show: it is more important to

Draft rehearsal plan – professional

WEEK 1:	Read through Learn all company and solo music Start Act 1 company choreography	
WEEK 2	Rehearse Act 1 scenes and solos Complete Act 1 choreography Begin Act 2 choreography Saturday am: Stagger through Act 1 (No scripts)	
WEEK 3	Rehearse Act 2 scenes and solos Complete Act 2 choreography Saturday am: Stagger through Act 2 (No scripts)	
WEEK 4	Revise and polish Act 1 scenes/choreography Revise and polish Act 2 scenes/choreography Brush-up music rehearsal Run whole show	
WEEK 5	Technical week	

Typical outline rehearsal schedule for a professional production.

make good use of the time available than to observe strict chronology.

Once everything has been covered, set a definitive date for a 'stagger-through' of each act, or of the whole show. From this point on, no more scripts or sheet music should be used.

Once you have been through the whole show, scenes and numbers will need to be recapped, revised – and possibly re-rehearsed again from scratch. Give everybody some leeway by designating some of the later rehearsals as 'TBA' ('to be arranged').

Towards the end of the rehearsal period plan to run each act in its entirety, and schedule at least one complete run of the whole show. The schedule for moving into the theatre – and for the final technical and dress rehearsals – involves considerable liaison with the design and technical departments, and is dealt with in Chapter 12.

Remember that this is a draft schedule and is therefore liable to alteration. Circumstances change: an actor may get sick and miss a week's rehearsal, the MD may be called away for a few days, a train strike may cause upheaval one weekend, a complicated number may take more time to choreograph than you thought it would. You will need to be flexible.

However, it is very important – and comforting – to have a plan, and also to stick to it as far as possible: don't fall into the trap of spending a month endlessly polishing the opening number, and then finding you only have three weeks left to rehearse the rest of the show.

RIGHT: Typical outline rehearsal schedule for an amateur production.

Draft rehearsal schedule – amateur

WEEK 1

Mon 7.30	COMPANY – read through
Tue 7.30	COMPANY – music
Thu 7.30	COMPANY – music
Sun 2.30	COMPANY – dance workshop/music

WEEK 2

Mon 7.30	COMPANY – choreography
Tue 7.30	COMPANY – music
Thu 7.30	COMPANY – choreography
Sun 2.30	COMPANY – recap/start rehearsing scenes with principals

WEEK 3

Mon 7.30	COMPANY – choreography/music
Tue 7.30	PRINCIPALS AS REQUIRED – scenes/music
Thu 7.30	PRINCIPALS AS REQUIRED – scenes/music
Sun 2.30	COMPANY – recap all work so far/rehearse scenes

WEEK 4

Mon 7.30	COMPANY – choreography/music/scenes
Tue 7.30	PRINCIPALS AS REQUIRED/COMPANY – TBC
Thu 7.30	PRINCIPALS AS REQUIRED/COMPANY – TBC
Sun 2.30	Stagger through Act 1 NO SCRIPTS

WEEK 5

Mon 7.30	COMPANY – choreography/music/scenes – Act 2
Tue 7.30	PRINCIPALS – rehearse Act 2
Thu 7.30	TBC
Sun 2.30	COMPANY – choreography/music/scenes – Act 2

WEEK 6

Mon 7.30	TBC
Tue 7.30	Stagger through Act 2 NO SCRIPTS
Thu 7.30	TBC
Sun 2.30	COMPANY TBC

WEEK 7

Mon 7.30	TBC
Tue 7.30	TBC
Thu 7.30	TBC
Sun 2.30	COMPANY Run show

WEEK 8

Mon 7.30	COMPANY – Act 1
Tue 7.30	COMPANY – Act 2
Thu 7.30	COMPANY – Run show
Sun 2.30	COMPANY – Run show

WEEK 9 – TECHNICAL WEEK SEE SEPARATE SHEET

Splitting Rehearsals

Save time by splitting rehearsals where you can, so that the director works with some members of the cast while the MD and/or choreographer work with others. Do not, however, make a splitting system too complicated; you don't want actors wandering about looking lost, and wondering which rehearsal they are meant to be in.

Be aware also that a split rehearsal means needing extra rehearsal space, and possibly even an extra pianist and piano.

PLANNING REHEARSALS FOR CHILDREN

Many musicals feature child characters – maybe one or two (*The Rink*, *The Ballad of Little Jo*), maybe dozens (*Oliver*, *Bugsy Malone*, *The King and I*). In the professional theatre there is extensive legislation regarding the employment of child actors, which managements ignore at their peril.

If your show involves children, you may have to make separate arrangements for them, particularly in the early stages of rehearsal. Young children cannot rehearse for three hours; they will not normally be available late in the evening when you may be doing the bulk of the work with the adult members of the cast; and they will also need to be chaperoned. For parents, the logistics of transporting their children to and from rehearsals can also present difficulties.

Arrange a definite rehearsal time for the children two or three times a week, and don't change it. Early evening is a good time, straight after school. Plan to rehearse their music and choreography separately from the adults until they have learnt it properly. Keep their rehearsals short and focused.

If the children have a lot of material to learn, it may be a good idea to consider starting work with them before the main rehearsal period begins.

THE STAGE MANAGEMENT TEAM

A series of rehearsals that takes place over several weeks or months and involves dozens of people obviously requires a great deal of practical organization: this is where the stage management team comes in.

Stage management is a complex, multifaceted job that is difficult to define precisely. The team is responsible for facilitating and organizing all aspects of the rehearsal, from booking the rehearsal room studio to buying the coffee. They are the main liaison point between the members of the creative team and the technical departments; they help organize the move from the rehearsal room to the theatre; and they are responsible for the day-to-day running of the show once it has opened.

Every show goes through fraught and difficult moments during the long journey to the first night. The whole production process is very demanding, and can be extremely emotional at times. During low moments it is often stage management who hold the company together, providing a much-needed shoulder to cry on for actors and creative team alike. The best stage managers possess a rare combination of sensitivity, understanding, practicality and diplomacy – and above all a sense of humour.

The team typically comprises a stage manager (SM), a deputy stage manager (DSM) and one or more assistant stage managers (ASMs). Make sure you recruit the right people for these jobs: they could save your life!

The Team Roles

The SM heads up the team, and is responsible

Rehearsing The Ballad of Little Jo *in a church. Custom-built rehearsal rooms are expensive, and may be beyond your budget.*

for organizing and sourcing anything and everything that is required to make the show happen that is not covered by one of the other staging departments. The SM spends a great deal of time running around chasing props, organizing transportation, fixing meetings, managing the petty cash budget, and attending to general administration.

The DSM attends all the rehearsals and is often closest to the creative team and cast. In the UK, the DSM is responsible for recording everything that goes on in rehearsals, and for distributing all the relevant information to the other production or creative departments. During the performance the DSM runs the show, cueing the actors and all lighting, sound, flying and scene changes from a prompt desk in the wings or control box at the rear of the theatre.

In professional theatres in the USA the organization tends to be slightly different, with the director, prompter and SM sharing out many of the DSM's jobs between them.

The ASM is the most junior member of the team, and assists the SM in prop-making, running errands, shopping, general administration, and anything else that needs to be done. On the night the ASM will usually be in the wings, helping to organize props, actors and the stage crew. If your show is complex and has a big cast, you should aim to have two ASMs, one for each side of the stage during performance.

Further details of the specific jobs undertaken by members of the stage management team during rehearsals can be found in Chapter 10.

THE REHEARSAL ROOM

One of the SM's first responsibilities is to go out and find a suitable room for rehearsals – and that is easier said than done! It needs to be big enough to accommodate a full-size mark-out of the stage area and set. You will also need access to a piano that is tuned, in good working order, and that can be unlocked. If there isn't one, you will have to source a clavinova or electric piano, and arrange transportation and/or storage for it. Ideally choreography

101

rehearsals require a dance studio with full-length mirrors along one wall and a properly sprung floor.

If you are planning to split rehearsals, make sure there is a second room you can use; and a second piano in a side room is invaluable for additional solo music calls. Ideally there should also be an area that can act as a 'green room' where the actors can sit, relax and run through lines with each other without disturbing the main rehearsal.

Tea- and coffee-making facilities are a must. You will also need enough chairs for the cast, director and DSM, and at least a couple of tables.

Finding a Rehearsal Room

Ideal rehearsal rooms are difficult to find and can be extremely expensive to hire. Make sure you know what your budget is before booking up eight weeks in a brand new, state-of-the-art, fully equipped dance studio in the trendiest part of town. Of course, if you are mounting your show in your school or college, there will probably be plenty of spare rooms available that you may be able to use free of charge.

If your organization does not have its own building and you are hiring a theatre, there may be a rehearsal room there that you can book. If not – or if it is too expensive – church halls, community centres, municipal facilities, sports clubs, scout huts, college lecture rooms and school gyms may provide affordable alternatives.

Ideally, try and find a venue that is available for all your rehearsals: better one shabby rehearsal room that you can use all the time than four glamorous ones scattered all over town. The more different venues you rehearse in, the more work and expense will be involved in transporting props and equipment; plus the greater possibility of actors going to the wrong place and wasting valuable rehearsal time.

You should also consider public transport links, car-parking facilities, and issues of personal security. Remember that your cast will sometimes be leaving the venue late at night, so check that the access is well-lit and feels safe.

It may well be that the perfect, affordable, light, clean, airy, accessible rehearsal room simply does not exist, so be prepared to make some compromises. If you have misgivings, ask the director to visit the venue with you before booking it; at the very least make sure you have described it and pointed out any shortcomings that you have noticed.

When you book up the room, make sure you know what the arrangements are for picking up and returning the key, and exactly what is, and is not, included in the agreement. If there is a caretaker or janitor, make friends with him: you will need his co-operation.

STAGE MANAGEMENT PREPARATION

If there isn't already a definitive list of the entire company – the creative team, the cast and the staging departments – then the SM should collate one.

Professional stage managers would normally ensure that the cast had received a score, libretto and a rehearsal schedule before rehearsals begin. If this is impossible – for example, if the libretti and vocal books are due to arrive the day before rehearsals begin – they may be distributed at the first rehearsal. At the very least, ensure that all cast and company members have clear and unequivocal information regarding the date, time and location of the first rehearsal. Include as much information about public transport, parking and accessibility as possible; and if appropriate, draw a map and post or email it to everybody.

RIGHT: *Part of the props acquisition chart for* **The Most Happy Fella.**

A/SC/PG	PROP	CHARACTER	BUY	MAKE	BORROW/HIRE	REH PROP	IN REH	N G	DETAILS
	Menu x5	table-used by Cleo		✓					DESIGN FROM NIGEL.
	Tablecloths: 3 square-mint green	waitresses	✓		BENTLEY BROWN ✓				
	3 round-cream	waitresses	✓		'' ✓				
	Tea cup				'' ✓	✓			
	Something from the floor								
	Cup	Cleo			BENTLEY BROWN ✓	✓	✓		
	Canadian Dime	Cleo			✓				
	Pin – tie pin	Rosabella/set		✓	✓				
	Fluff (possibly)	in Cleo's coat pocket		✓	✓				
	Sandwich board and camera kit	photographer			✓	✓			MR. MURPHY - HIRE MAKE - BOARD.
1.2	Mailbag	Postman		✓	✓				
	Packet of letters	Postman - in mailbag		✓	✓				
	Whistle	Postman			✓ STOCK		✓	✓	
	Photograph	Tony - in a letter		✓					
	Wooden crate	set		✓			✓	✓	
	Bundle of letters	Tony - inside pocket		✓					

Props List and Acquisition Chart

Large theatre and opera companies have dedicated props departments to source and build props and furniture. In smaller-scale productions, this job is usually shared by the stage manager and the ASM.

Before the first rehearsal, the stage manager should go through the libretto carefully and make a list of all the props that are mentioned in the stage directions and dialogue, such as newspapers, books, suitcases, coins, wallets, maps and so on. Draw up a props acquisition chart showing the scene in which they appear, which character uses them, how many are required, and whether or not they are 'practical' (that is, do they have to work). The chart is also used to record whether the prop is to be bought, made or borrowed, and where it is being sourced from.

Some shows demand props that are so stylized and complex that they are effectively part of the set – the plant in *Little Shop of Horrors* for instance, or the oversized bed in *Once Upon a Mattress*. In such cases the set designer should supply the workshop with the necessary technical drawings so they can be built by the construction department.

Smaller, specialized props will be made and painted either by the props department or by an ASM. Always check their size, colour and shape with the designer before starting to make them, and remember that they need to be resilient enough to last to the final performance. There is nothing worse than having to re-make a prop that you have slaved over for hours because it isn't right, or has fallen to bits at the dress rehearsal.

Each individual prop or piece of furniture makes its own contribution to the overall visual effect of the production, so the set designer must give the stage manager clear guidance on the period, size, colour and shape of items that are required.

When hunting for props always, as ever, try and save money. There will inevitably be some props – a period wheelchair, a 1930s telephone, an elaborate samovar – that will have to be hired from a specialist firm or professional theatre. Otherwise see what you can beg or borrow: professional stage managers become experts at this. Fortunately you will be surprised at the things people are prepared to lend a production, as long as they know they will be returned safely. When you borrow an item, reassure the owner that it will be looked after carefully, and arrange a definite date and time both for its pick-up and its return.

Real items of food and drink are known as 'consumables', and have to be freshly prepared for each performance. Similarly, if a prop is broken or destroyed as part of the stage action – Dino breaking a glass in *The Rink*, for instance – a new one will be required for each performance. Make this clear on the acquisition chart, too.

Pin up the chart in the stage management office, if you have one, so you can easily see what has been sourced and what you still have to find.

Preparing the Prompt Copy

The DSM should buy a ring binder and make up a copy of the libretto and score with interleaved blank pages. Over the course of rehearsals all the information on blocking and technical cueing will be recorded in this, and it will be the definitive script for running every performance. The DSM's script is known as the 'prompt copy' or simply 'the book'.

THE FIRST REHEARSAL

The first rehearsal is unlike any other, and reaching this stage represents the culmination of months of work for the producer. The director is like the host of a party, hoping that all the guests will turn up and get on with each other. The actors feel as if they are reliving their first day of school: who is going to be there, will they make friends, will it be scary?

Organizing the Room

The stage managers should arrive early and get the room organized. Unload any practice furniture or props, and store them out of the way. Then make sure that there are enough chairs for everybody, and a table for the model box.

If you are rehearsing in one room or studio all the time, use the designer's ground plan to mark out the limits of the stage and the set in adhesive tape on the floor, using a different colour for each major scene.

First impressions last a long time, so it is important to consider the details: for instance, are the toilets clean? Is there plenty of toilet

First day of **Pippin** *at GSA Conservatoire. The director, Tim Flavin (extreme right), addresses the cast.*

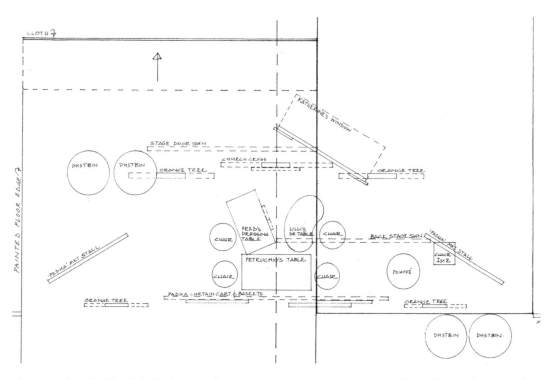

Ground plan for **Kiss Me Kate,** *which the stage management team will use for marking up the rehearsal room floor.*

paper? Make sure there are tea- and coffee-making facilities available; one electric kettle will not be enough to make drinks for forty people, so find a tea urn or bring a spare kettle. Splash out and buy a few packets of biscuits out of the petty cash.

You need to make people feel secure. The cast may be about to give up hours of their free time for weeks to come for no payment, and they may already be having doubts about their ability to do what is going to be asked of them – may even be considering giving up the whole idea. As people start to arrive, do everything you can to make them feel welcome in a relaxed, pleasant environment.

Checking Information

The first rehearsal is one of the very few occasions when the entire creative team and the cast are together in one room, so it is a very useful time to assimilate information. The stage manager should go round with a cast list and double-check that everybody's name and contact details are recorded correctly.

The costume designer and/or wardrobe supervisor should go round with measuring tapes and get the cast's measurements. They should do the measuring themselves, and not leave it to cast members to tell them their size: they may give inaccurate or over-optimistic information. Be tactful and discreet.

An actor playing a huge lead role may already have been given their script and score by the director, but inevitably many of the cast will not have these yet. Number the scripts, scores, and/or vocal books, and as you distribute them make a note of who has which copy. Make sure that everyone understands that only light pencil should be used when writing in them.

In some cases it may be worth asking the cast to pay a small deposit on their scores, refundable on return. Collecting in books after the last performance can be a chore, and peo-ple are more likely to make the effort to return them if they have a financial incentive.

When everyone has arrived, the director should call the company to order. This is it!

Making a Start

Some directors like to launch straight into warm-ups and theatre games to break the ice, or play name games to help the members of the company meet each other. This can help raise the energy level in the room, increase trust amongst the cast, and allow people to lose some of their inhibitions – and it also establishes the director's authority and working methods. Other directors like to start more formally, introducing themselves, the creative and stage management teams, and talking through the various aspects of the work ahead.

Remember that people need information and reassurance at this stage; they want to know what they are letting themselves in for. Make sure that everyone has a rehearsal schedule, and reiterate any details of dates, times and places that may be potentially unclear or may cause confusion. Make doubly sure that people are aware of matinée performances, as these can easily get overlooked.

The stage manager should run through the practical and safety features of the building – fire exits, any potential hazards, parking restrictions, the location of the toilets and so on.

If the actors are being paid, the producer or company manager should explain when and how payment will be made. Don't mention figures or get into any form of negotiation: all payment should have been agreed and negotiated before this point.

The director needs to run through the rehearsal ground rules: there is no need to be humourlessly authoritarian as you do this, but make sure the message gets across. Stress that these rules are for everybody's comfort, safety and convenience.

Once the formal details are out of the way, move on to talking about the play. Directors have sleepless nights worrying about what they should say at this moment. However, don't feel you have to make some earth-shattering pronouncement about the meaning of the universe: concentrate on sharing your enthusiasm and belief in the show. Say how the production has come about, why you are keen to direct it, and what you hope the cast and audience will get out of it.

If you have a particular interpretation of the show, or have moved it into a radically different setting from the original, explain why you have done this.

The Model Box

After talking generally about the show, the

First day of **Pippin.** *Designer Roger Ness prepares to show the model box.*

Rehearsal Ground Rules

Rehearsals will run more smoothly and efficiently if a few basic ground rules are observed:

- Arrive on time.
- Come ready to work.
- Wear appropriate clothing and footwear, especially during choreography rehearsals.
- Always bring a pencil.
- No smoking, eating or drinking except bottled water.
- No drugs or alcohol before or during rehearsal.
- Take care of personal hygiene, especially when working in close proximity with others.
- Respect other people's work and needs, and co-operate at all times.
- And a new rule that has arisen in the last few years: turn off all mobile phones.

director should introduce the set designer and show the model box. Models – finished, painted, even lit – are impressive, and a good model will significantly boost cast and company morale.

The director and the designer should decide in advance who is going to do the talking. Go through each scene change in order, using the model to show how pieces of the set will fly, truck or revolve. As you reach the end of the show the director should thank the set designer for their work: don't be surprised if there is a round of applause.

The Costume Drawings

Once you have dealt with the set, introduce the costume designer. This can be a sensitive area. Everybody has certain ideas about their body shape, their physical appearance and what suits them, and people often have very fixed notions about what they will or will not wear, and may need reassurance. Any particularly skimpy or revealing costumes should not come as a shock. If you're dressing your Kit Kat Girls in not much more than leather lingerie and fishnet tights you should at least have mentioned it during the auditions.

The costume designer has a tough job. It is hard enough to create and realize a style and design concept for the whole show: convincing living, breathing actors to wear your costumes can be harder. Be prepared to listen to people's concerns, but have the courage of your convictions, and be ready to stick to your decisions. Tact and diplomacy may be required.

The Read-Through

The next stage is to read and sing through the whole show. In a play this is simple: open

First day of **Pippin.** *Musical director Peter Roberts leads the sing-through.*

the script at Act 1, Scene 1, and off you go. In the world of professional opera, soloists are expected to arrive at the first rehearsal knowing their music: open at page one of the score, and off you go.

In a musical the situation is usually different. Some actors will have learnt all their songs and can't wait to start belting them out, while others may be so paralysed with self-conscious terror that they cannot open their mouth.

If there is a lot of chorus singing, organize your cast into vocal groups – sopranos, altos, tenors and basses: there is security in numbers. It helps to break the ice if the MD volunteers to sing the show, inviting people to join in as and when they can. Everybody will sing along to 'Wilkommen', though you might have fewer takers for the complicated harmonies of 'Telephone Dance'. Underscoring should be played quietly under dialogue: it boosts the actors' confidence to know that their scenes will be supported by music, especially at emotional moments.

This may well be the first time that members of the cast have heard any of the music played live. And don't underestimate the effect your MD's musicianship can have on the cast: like a good model and good costume drawings, it helps to create a sense of excitement and anticipation in the room.

Keep things moving. There is no need to play all the way through lengthy dance breaks – at this stage they can cause panic. Have a coffee break when you get to the end of Act One; let the cast chat informally with each other and with the creative team. Someone will always approach the costume designer in a corner and say, 'I didn't like to say anything earlier, but that dress in Act Two...'. Let people look at, and admire the model. It represents many

hours of work for the designer, and should be shown with pride.

At the end of the play, thank the cast. Never underestimate the emotional strain of the read-/sing-through for everyone; and it's ten times worse for the writers if they are in the room. Everybody needs a break, so have lunch, or simply call the rehearsal to an end.

If it's the end of the day the stage manager should make sure that everybody knows when they are next required to rehearse: this is known as the actors' 'call'. Also clarify if they need to bring any special equipment or clothing next time.

Afterwards

Directors often say: 'The first day is just something you have to get through so you can start rehearsing properly on the second day.'

If you are carrying on rehearsing after the read-through, do not attempt too much. It may be more useful to have discussions with the other members of the creative team than to start work on a musical number: seeing the real flesh-and-blood actors together for the first time often brings up a whole lot of new issues.

The stage manager should make sure that the room is left clean and tidy: don't alienate the caretaker on the first day. If the model box is being sent off to a builder's workshop, make sure that it is neatly packed away. Similarly, make sure the costume drawings are looked after; they are valuable.

You may have mixed feelings after the first rehearsal: exhilarated by the sing-through, daunted by the amount of work ahead. Don't worry: this is perfectly normal.

The first rehearsal is a huge landmark in every production. Now the real work can begin.

8 SELLING THE SHOW

There is absolutely no point in staging a musical unless people come to see it: it is the audience that makes the actors' performances come alive. There is nothing more exciting than playing to a full house, nothing worse than playing to a dozen people scattered around an otherwise deserted auditorium. Plus, of course, you need their money. So it is vital that you let people know that your show is on, and – more importantly – that you make them want to buy a ticket.

Of course, you could just hand write a few notices and pin them up. Thirty years ago London fringe theatres did not need to do much more than this to sell out their shows. Today, however, you are competing with dozens of TV channels, the Internet, multiplex cinemas and video games – not to mention all the other live shows that are being performed.

Marketing your show properly is vital: take it very seriously indeed.

CREATING A BUZZ

The advertising for big West End and Broadway shows starts early: posters and press ads may start to appear a year, or even eighteen months, before the opening night. These are sometimes referred to as 'teaser ads', designed to grab people's interest and build up their sense of expectation – and, of course, to generate advance ticket sales.

Even if you are producing a show in a school or college with a more or less guaranteed audience, it is important to keep telling people that the show is on. Create a buzz: the cast will walk tall knowing they are in a show that people are talking about.

THE PUBLICITY OFFICER

Appoint a press and publicity officer for your show, preferably someone with experience of working in, or dealing with, the press and the media. Experience in graphic design, commercial art and/or photography is also valuable.

The publicity officer's task is to create a growing wave of excitement and interest in the show that will culminate in the first official performance. As this is the performance to which newspaper reviewers are invited, it is usually known as 'press night'.

The publicity officer's underlying objective is to get as many tickets sold as possible, and to maximize the show's potential revenue both before and after the opening night. However small your publicity budget, it should be spent with this end in mind.

'BRANDING'

'Branding' is a commonly used marketing technique that involves giving a product a single recognizable identity, and then using it across a wide range of sales and promotional activities. The Macdonald's 'M' sign is recognizable the world over – even a child who cannot read knows that the sign means Macdonald's.

The Dominion Theatre, London. The musical We Will Rock You *announces its presence with a bold design.*

Hollywood studios brand movies with visual images, logos and musical themes, none more successfully than the James Bond movies. They may also use short 'strap lines' under the title, which, if successful, become inextricably linked with the movie; for example, '*Alien*: In space no one can hear you scream', '*Reservoir Dogs*: Let's go to work'.

One or two musicals have been successfully branded around the world on a single image and a few words: '*Cats* – Now and Forever'; and a simple line drawing of a ragged child has become the internationally recognizable brand symbol of *Les Misérables*.

It is unlikely that you will be selling your show on this kind of scale (and if you are, you probably don't need this book!) but it may be useful to apply these principles to your own sales campaign. Take one image and/or phrase, use it consistently in all printed publicity, and your marketing campaign will be more coherent, focused and effective.

CREATING A VISUAL IMAGE

At the very least you will need some posters and flyers to advertise your production. The poster is the public's first impression of the show, so it needs to be immediate, eye-catching and intriguing. Above all, it needs to convey the message 'Hey, this show is worth seeing – buy a ticket and you won't regret it!'

You do not need a gigantic budget to produce a stylish and effective poster, especially now that digital cameras and visual modification and desktop publishing software packages

111

Poster/flyer design for The Frogs, *silver printed on rich blue. A striking, epic image for a striking, epic production.*

are widely available. If the publicity officer does not have practical experience in graphic design, find somebody who does and ask them to help. Then get together with the producer and the director, and brainstorm ideas to produce a visual image.

What is the tone of the show? Is it funny or dramatic, entertaining or tragic, intimate or epic? Does it have some special element that gives it a unique quality?

Are people likely to have heard of it? Will they know the story? If so, exploit that knowledge as you try out visual images: a pair of hands holding a bowl for *Oliver*, a bloody razor for *Sweeney Todd*, lovers on a moonlit beach for *South Pacific*.

Try to convey a flavour of the show's period and/or style: twenties' flappers for *The Boyfriend*, thirties' ships and sailors for *Dames at Sea*, forties' Raymond Chandler-style private eyes for *City of Angels*, the psychedelic sixties for *Hair*.

Play around with different ideas; sketch them out – what do you think will be most effective, a photograph (possibly treated in some way), a line drawing, a cartoon, or a

Poster/flyer design for **Bernice Bobs Her Hair.** *An intriguing period snapshot, printed brown on white to give a sepia effect, sets the tone for a show set in 1920.*

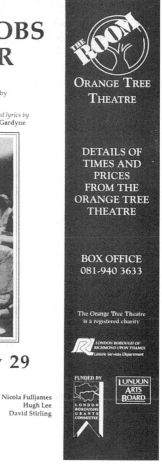

BERNICE BOBS HER HAIR

A NEW MUSICAL
based on "Bernice Bobs Her Hair" by
F. Scott Fitzgerald

Music by
Matthew Miller

Book and lyrics by
John Gardyne

April 28 – May 29

with

Constance Barrie	Jacqueline Charlesworth	Nicola Fulljames
Patrick Jamieson	Abigail Lee	Hugh Lee
Carol Mounter	Emma Parish	David Stirling

Directed by **John Gardyne**
Musical Director **Matthew Miller**
Designed by **Jesse Schwenck**

THE ROOM

ORANGE TREE THEATRE

DETAILS OF TIMES AND PRICES FROM THE ORANGE TREE THEATRE

BOX OFFICE
081-940 3633

The Orange Tree Theatre is a registered charity

LONDON BOROUGH OF RICHMOND UPON THAMES
Leisure Services Department

FUNDED BY

LONDON BOROUGHS GRANTS COMMITTEE

LONDON ARTS BOARD

'David Merrick Red'

The legendary Broadway producer David Merrick had little time for complex poster art. He once said that his ideal poster was four words: CAROL CHANNING HELLO DOLLY: in big capital letters; in red.

He used exactly the same colour red on the posters for all his shows, and this shade has become known in the USA as 'David Merrick red'.

painting? Do you want the image to fill the whole page, or be framed within a border?

Don't forget that your image may be reproduced in different sizes for different purposes. A complicated, detailed, full-colour image may look fabulous in a large sketchbook, but will you be able to reproduce it for a small black-and-white newspaper ad?

Also, remember that full-colour printing is expensive. Keep costs down by limiting the number of colours you use, and/or printing on coloured paper. As ever, use the limitations of the budget as a spur to your creativity, not as a hindrance.

Designing the Poster

Once you have an idea for a visual image, decide what information you need to put on the poster. The title, venue and dates are obviously crucial, as are the box office number and details on any other methods of buying tickets.

Check your publisher's agreement – it will almost certainly dictate that the names of the writers must be credited in type size proportionate to the title (usually 50 per cent). There may also be acknowledgements regarding the original production that have to be included. You are legally obliged to include this information. Also, don't forget to include the logo of any funding bodies or organizations that may have given you money.

If the writing team is better known for another show, consider mentioning that on the poster: *70 Girls 70* may not mean much to the general public, but if you add 'by the writers of *Cabaret* and *Chicago*' you will attract more attention. A few years ago, a professional theatre was not above advertising a production of T. S. Eliot's intense verse drama *Murder in the Cathedral* as being 'by the author of *Cats*'.

The etiquette of who gets credited on the publicity is endlessly negotiable in the professional world. It is an awkward and troublesome area, and you need to tread carefully; for instance, if some of the creative team are credited and not others, this can cause considerable friction.

Amateur casts are not normally credited on posters, though you should credit the name of your organization or club if appropriate. On the other hand, professional actors expect to be credited if possible – especially if they are providing their services for little or no payment, and are hoping to get professional casting directors or agents along to see them in the show.

Adding the Text

Designing the layout of the text on a poster used to be a complex, time-consuming job that involved either fiddling about with letter transfers for hours, or using expensive professional typesetting equipment. Modern publishing and design PC software has cut down costs and work times significantly.

Play around with different fonts and pitch sizes to achieve the most striking effect. Resist the temptation to have numerous different typefaces on one sheet of paper, as this looks untidy and can be difficult to read.

Do not feel you have to wait until casting is completed to get your publicity material produced. It is more important to get marketing the show than to risk offending an actor. Plus, of course, you may be able to add names at a later date if required.

Designing the Flyer

Flyers allow you to get information about your show into peoples' hands and pockets, propped up on their bookshelves, and stuck to their fridge doors. Most flyers are printed on A5 or DL-sized paper or card. Big West End shows are sometimes advertised on folded A4 sheets with lavish full-colour photography, but these are very expensive. Remember, the purpose of your flyer is to sell tickets, not to gobble up the budget.

Use the same image as the poster. If you have to crop the image to make it fit, make sure it looks harmonious and balanced, and that no vital information has been missed out. You can print more information on the back, such as ticket prices, cast details, details of any special price reductions or offers, directions on how to get to the venue and so on.

A few lines about the setting or milieu of the plot may help to whet the audience's appetite; use these as teasers to set the scene – for example:

'Berlin, 1938. The Kit Kat Club. Everything's for sale. What would you do?'

Do not use up valuable space giving a dull précis of the plot, as:

'Cliff Bradshaw, recently arrived in Berlin, struggles to write his novel. A chance encounter on a train leads him to the Kit Kat Club where he meets Sally Bowles. Sally splits up with her boyfriend and moves in with him ... blah blah blah ...'.

This is very boring; and anyway, the audience will find out all about this when they come to a performance.

If the show features hit tunes, you may wish to list these somewhere on the flyer. The general rule is, if you think it will sell tickets, then do it.

Once you have everything laid out as you wish, ask the producer to check it. Then get three more people to check it; then check it again.

Calculating Quantities

Unfortunately, there is no magic formula whereby you may calculate that to sell x tickets you need y posters and z flyers. The simple fact is, that the more tickets you want to sell, the more leaflets and posters you will need. If you are hiring a theatre, the resident publicity department should be able to advise you on the quantities that you will need, based on their experience and local knowledge.

If in doubt, order more flyers and fewer posters than you think you will need; certainly you should get at least ten times more flyers than posters.

PRINTING MARKETING MATERIAL

If your show is aimed at a very specific, relatively small potential audience – pupils and teachers within a single school, for instance – it may be possible to produce all the printed marketing material you need on the printer of a home computer. If, on the other hand, you require several hundred posters and thousands of flyers, you will need to get them produced professionally.

Phone round local print companies and get some price quotes. Give them the details of how many copies you need, how many colours there are, and whether you want it printed on coloured paper or card. Glossy paper is more expensive, but will make your show look slicker and more professional; it is usually worth paying the extra.

Inevitably there will be economies of scale. It will always be significantly cheaper to order one large print run than several small ones, so make sure your first estimate is as realistic as possible. Find out the costs for additional print runs just in case, and how quickly the company can complete and deliver the job. Similarly it will always be cheaper to get your printing done on standard-sized paper, and in standard ink colours.

Don't feel you have to order posters in lots of different sizes. You may find it difficult to find places to exhibit posters larger than A3; on the other hand, A4 posters are surprisingly ineffectual and can easily get covered up on notice boards. Flyers should be A5 or DL in size.

Find out who offers the best deal, and fix a delivery date. Before taking the final artwork to the printer, check once more that all the information and spellings are correct. It is sickening – not to mention potentially expensive – to spot a mistake once the printing has been completed.

USING A DISTRIBUTION NETWORK

Contact the arts department of your local or district council: they may well run a distribution network of information on local events to libraries, information centres, civic amenities,

Make your flyer as eye-catching as possible – it will be competing with many others.

sports centres and so on. Find out well in advance how many posters and leaflets they require, and when their deadlines are for receiving material. Then make sure that you meet them.

In larger cities it may be worth employing a professional distribution company to leaflet pubs, cafés, theatres, arts amenities, shops and so on. If you are hiring a theatre, liaise with their publicity department to ensure that your material is properly displayed in the foyer.

Remember that your flyers and posters are not doing any good if they are sitting in a box in the office: get them out there, spreading the word. However, do not hand out all your print publicity at once: keep some of it back to supply any new distribution opportunities that may crop up, or to make a final sales push in the couple of weeks before opening night.

T-Shirts

Get a price for printing the show's image and title on T-shirts. Amateur actors love to have souvenirs of the shows that they are in, and are usually prepared to pay for them if they are reasonably priced. Professionals, on the other hand, may prove a tougher nut to crack. In either case, remember that the better the design, the greater will be the demand for them.

Encourage the cast to wear their T-shirts outside rehearsal so they become mobile advertising hoardings for the production.

USING THE MEDIA

Write a press release about the show, and send it to the arts/events editor of your local and regional newspapers, radio stations and – if you have one – television channel. Most theatres have a press and media contact list; if they do not, ask for help at the local library. It is worth ringing up and checking that the names on any contact lists are current before sending in material; journalists move around all the time, and reviewers can be sensitive.

Make the press release as newsworthy and interesting as possible. If you have professional actors in your cast mention any high profile TV, film or stage plays that they may recently have been in, and any famous actors with whom they have worked. Marketing professionals talk about identifying a product's 'unique selling point', or USP: does *your* show have a USP? If so, push it for all it's worth.

A press release for The Ballad of Little Jo *at* The Bridewell Theatre, *stressing the pedigree of the show, the leading actor, the director and the MD.*

Bridewelltheatre

Bride Lane, London EC4Y 8EQ ■ tel: +44 (0)20 7353 0259 ■ fax: +44 (0)20 7583 5289
email: admin@bridewelltheatre.co.uk ■ web: www.bridewelltheatre.co.uk

The Ballad of Little Jo

June - July 2003

Thursday 26th June - Saturday 26th July 2003
7.30pm (3.30pm Sunday matinees, no performances on Mondays)

Bridewell Theatre, Bride Lane (off Fleet St.), London EC4Y 8EQ

Tickets: £16.50/£12.50 (previews 26th - 29th June £7.50)
Box Office: 020 7936 3456 (Tuesday - Saturday 12-6.30pm)
Press nights - Tuesday 1st July

A stunning new, award-winning musical by American writers, **Mike Reid** (composer) and **Sarah Schlesinger** (lyrics), based on the film *The Ballad of Little Jo* by **Maggie Greenwald,** will receive its **European premiere** at the **Bridewell Theatre, London,** in June/July 2003.

Starring **Anna Francolini** in the title role, *The Ballad of Little Jo* is an archetypal American frontier legend which draws on Irish/American folk-forms. Full of poignant melodies and true toe-tappers, it packs a powerful emotional punch.

The Ballad of Little Jo is based on the true story of Josephine Monaghan who lived as a man in Silver City, Idaho, in the late 1800s. Her true identity was only discovered on her death. Abandoning her home after having an illegitimate child, Josephine travels to the West coast and works in a silver mine, disguised as a man until her true identity is revealed ... A traditional 'yarn' is woven with questions of prejudice and injustice and the way small communities behave under pressure.

The Ballad of Little Jo is directed by the Bridewell Theatre's Artistic Director, **Carol Metcalfe,** whose credits include the world premiere of Sondheim's *Saturday Night, Damn Yankees* and *On a Clear Day You Can See Forever.* Musical Direction is by **Michael England,** whose West End credits include *The Phantom of the Opera* and *Les Miserables.*

First staged in the Steppenwolf Theatre, Chicago in 2000, The New Yorker Magazine described it as:

> ... the real thing ... the best piece of musical storytelling I've seen in a decade ... a compelling drama.

For further information contact:
John Jones @ Calan Communications
T: 020 7357 7604/E-Mail: jej@dircon.co.uk

Artistic Director: Carol Metcalfe   Executive Director: Tim Sawers

Your press release will be competing with many others that will arrive that day, so anything that really grabs the attention is much more likely to be covered. Aim to get an article into the paper about the show: it is good publicity, and it is free. Be aware, however, that press ads are expensive, and display ads can be very expensive. If you decide to take out a newspaper ad, be very selective and monitor sales afterwards to see if it has had any effect.

Local radio exposure is invaluable. If the director or an actor is asked in for an interview, make sure that they have a rough idea of the questions they are likely to be asked in advance. Remind them that, above all, they are there to sell the show, and that they should mention the performance dates and box office number at least twice during the interview.

If you are very lucky and/or have a particularly interesting show, you may get on television. Even a couple of minutes' exposure on a local channel would cost you a small fortune if you had to pay for the airtime, so be properly prepared and make the very best use of it you can.

Diary Listings

Nearly all local and national newspapers and magazines print diary listings of local arts events and performances; there is also a growing number of dedicated listings magazines, many of which are free. Make sure your show appears in all of them. Again, the theatre's publicity department may be able to help you contact the relevant people; they may even send in the information on your behalf, though don't rely on this.

Newspaper and magazine listings will not normally include your show until the week before it opens. If you are not working with a theatre's publicity department, check out whom you need to contact, and find out what their deadline is for submissions and exactly what information they require. Beware: these may be a lot earlier than you think.

The Internet

Increasingly, of course, all this information is being made available to a global audience over the Internet. Many theatres now provide details of booking and information at their web sites, and there are already thousands of

Publicity shot for **Bernice Bobs Her Hair.** *Ironically, this scene does not occur in the show: Bernice's fateful haircut takes place offstage. Photo: Paul Thompson*

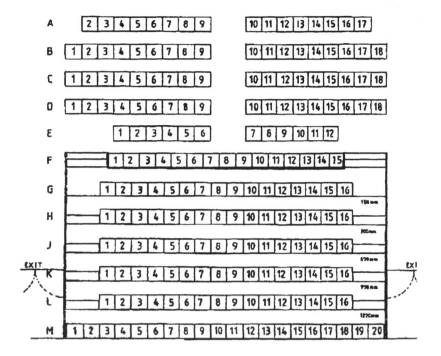

Seating plan for a small theatre. If your box office is not computerized you will need a separate seating plan to record the sales for each performance.

local and specialist information services on-line. Research the sites that may be of use to you in contacting your target market, and get in touch with them. Scan the poster and send it as an attachment. If you have web design and programming skills, or know somebody who does, you might even consider creating your own web site. It's the most effective method of distributing information ever invented, and it's virtually free.

PUBLICITY PHOTOGRAPHS

As the press night approaches, papers and magazines may ask for a publicity photograph, almost invariably of the leading actors. Some newspapers will send along their own photographer, but you should make sure that you have some photos of your own in case they do not.

The publicity officer should organize the photo shoot with the costume designer and the actors. Depending on the nature of your show, get them into the classiest or the most outrageous costumes that they wear in the performance. If the set is not ready, photograph them against a neutral background, not against a half-painted piece of scenery.

Find someone who knows what they are doing to take a roll of black-and-white photographs. Choose two or three images, print them out on good quality paper, and on the back write the names of the actors, the dates and location of the show, and the publicity officer's contact details.

REVIEWERS

Find out who is responsible for theatre reviews in your local newspapers, magazines, radio and TV stations, and invite them to the press night. Critics get booked up early, so contact them well in advance. If someone cannot attend the press night, offer them seats for another performance: it is better that they come late than not at all.

Ring up a few days before to check that they are still coming. Most critics are friendly and charming; a few are not. In either case, always be polite and positive when talking to them: it is never worth alienating the critics.

ADVANCE SALES

To repeat: the whole purpose of all this activity is to generate interest in the show and to sell tickets. The more advance sales, the better your cash flow, and the less pressure there will be on the producer and production manager as they struggle to balance their budgets.

Good advance sales lift everyone's spirits, and help to boost the cast and crew's belief in the show. They also operate as a self-fulfilling prophecy – if word gets round that you are selling out, people are more likely to book up early.

If you are hiring a theatre, it will probably have a computerized box office with a resident sales staff who can make credit and debit card sales on the phone or over the Internet. If you are not, appoint your own box office manager and set up your own. Either way, it is vital that you make sure the box office is operating efficiently before you start advertising.

SETTING UP A BOX OFFICE

When running the box office yourself, make sure that the details of how to book by post, telephone and/or email are printed clearly on all your print and press material.

You will need to order printed tickets from a specialist printer, or get someone to produce them on a PC. Make sure the date and time of the performance are clearly marked on each ticket. You can save money by writing on row and seat numbers yourself: do this before you

---

Payment by Personal Cheque

If you can only accept payment by cheque, accept telephone bookings provisionally, and hold them for three or four days pending arrival of payment. If customers want their tickets sent to them in the post, add the price of a stamp to their booking; otherwise, give them the option of picking them up at the theatre on the night of the performance.

At the time of writing this process already seems hopelessly old-fashioned and amateurish; in a few years it will seem positively prehistoric. No doubt by then inexpensive, secure and instantaneous electronic payment systems and paper-free booking methods will have become widely available to everyone.

---

start selling seats, so there is less chance of making a mistake and double-booking.

You will also need a copy of the plan of the auditorium for each performance. Register all sales on your plan, marking each seat as you send out the tickets. Keep a record of who has bought each ticket or block of tickets – a contact number will be very useful in the event of double-bookings, lost tickets or last-minute cancellations.

Make sure that your box office staff are fully aware of any special offers that may apply for group bookings, or concessionary rates for children, pensioners and so on. It's all good PR.

Ask your customers how they found out about the show, and keep a note of the responses: they will help you see where your publicity campaign is working most effectively.

If you cannot find someone to man the phone all day, leave a clear message on the answerphone, and follow up all sales leads daily.

And get selling those tickets!

9 REHEARSALS: DOING THE WORK

The director is the ultimate arbiter and controller of all artistic aspects of the production, with responsibility for making sure that the contributions of all the other members of the creative team and cast gel together into a harmonious whole. No matter how brilliant individual elements may be, if they do not work together, the show will never reach its full potential on stage.

A film director controls the auditory and visual information that the cinema audience receives through such devices as cutting, editing, camera angles, close-ups, and the use of music and sound effects in order to tell a story in the most effective possible way. Similarly, the director of a musical must marshal and control the action on stage in order to guide the audience through the plot; provide them with insights into the characters' lives, loves, dilemmas and dreams; and finally give them an emotionally satisfying and meaningful conclusion.

Singing, movement and a strong group dynamic come together in this dramatic scene from Pilgrim's Progress. GSA *Conservatoire production; director, John Gardyne; movement director, Ayse Tashkiran; lighting, Mark Dymock.* Photo: Mark Dean

It cannot be emphasized too strongly that the director's main responsibility is to the *audience.* If the audience cannot understand what is happening from moment to moment, they will not be able to empathize with characters on stage, and the emotional life of the production will be stillborn. Or to put it another way: make 'em laugh, make 'em cry.

WORKING AS A TEAM

In the early stages of the rehearsal process, the show needs to be broken down into its component parts – music, dance, dialogue, action – and each rehearsed separately, song by song, routine by routine, scene by scene. The latter stages of rehearsals involve bringing the parts together and moulding them into a seamless whole.

Whether you are directing a musical for the first or the fiftieth time, it is extremely important that you have a fruitful working relationship with the members of your creative team, and that you recognize their talents. Talk to them openly about your ideas, listen to their points of view, and respect their expertise. In the end, though, the buck stops with you: stick to your guns if you are convinced that you are right, but be prepared to take some flak, too.

Call Sheets

When rehearsing you should only call the actors who are required. Rehearsing is a time-consuming, and at times delicate business, and you need to create a sense of trust and focus in the room. A lot of bored actors sitting round the side, staring at their watches and tapping their feet in irritation, will not help.

Get the DSM to produce a call sheet, indicating which scene is being rehearsed, and who is required. (Further details of stage management's duties during rehearsals are dealt with in Chapter 10.) If an actor is only required for part of the rehearsal, so be it: better one hour's

intensive work than three hours' sitting around with nothing to do.

It is theatrical etiquette to refer to the actors as 'Mr Smith' and 'Miss Jones' on the call sheet, and your actors may appreciate this being observed. Only in the most formal of rehearsals would a director not refer to the actors by their first names, however.

STARTING MUSIC REHEARSALS

The quality of the singing is obviously a key element in the success of any show. Singing is also wonderful exercise for the vocal chords, and the more you do, the better you get at it.

Once the first rehearsal is out of the way, the MD should start teaching the music as soon as possible. There is nothing better than singing a big chorus number to create a good company spirit. This is also a good way to begin the cast's learning process, as everybody is working together as a group, and nobody will feel too exposed and vulnerable.

The MD should always start off music rehearsals with a warm-up that will stretch and stimulate the vocal chords, the lips and the tongue, and help to prevent overstraining and damage to the voice. All MDs have their own favourite warm-ups, but most involve a combination of physical, vocal and mental exercises.

First of all ask the cast to stand, and to stretch out and shake their arms, necks, shoulders and upper bodies, especially if they have been sitting around all day or it is cold. Start with humming some sounds on the lips. Play a few scales or arpeggios, and get the cast to sing up and down the scales on a series of open vowel sounds. Move up the keys one semitone at a time, telling the cast to stop when they feel the notes are getting too high or too low. Over

RIGHT: *Rehearsal call sheet for* No No Nanette.

NO NO NANETTE

REHEARSAL CALL

Date: 12 October 1999

Venue: St Jude's Church Hall

2:00pm	MS BECHGAARD	"I want to be happy"
	MS CHAPMAN	Choreography
	MS LOVELESS	
	MS SLADE	
	MR ALEXANDER	
	MR DENNISON	
	MR LIVINGSTONE	
3:30pm	MS NAPTHINE	"Too Many Rings…"
	MR ALEXANDER	Choreography and music
	MR LIVINGSTONE	
	MR RAMSDIN	
	MR THOMAS	
5:30pm	BREAK	
6:30pm	MS ALEXANDER	Scene pages 43 – 48
	MS LE RICHE	
	MS STEVENS	
	MR DENNISON	
7:30pm	MS. ST CLAIR	To join. Pages 48 – 53
	MS CHAPMAN	
	MR LENNON	
9:00pm	CALL ENDS	

WARDROBE CALLS – AT 23 SMITH STREET

2:00pm	MR THOMAS
2:30pm	MS ST CLAIR

Thank you

Carola Kuester DSM

DISTRIBUTION: DIRECTOR/ PRODUCTION MANAGER/ STAGE MANAGER/
NOTICE BOARD/ PRODUCER

the weeks to come their vocal range and power will gradually increase.

Work on breath control. Ask the cast to breathe in for four counts, and then out for eight, maintaining a steady tone and a constant flow of air over the vocal chords as they do so. Gradually increase the length of the outbreaths: the better your singers' breath control, the better their musical phrasing will be.

Articulation exercises help get the lips and tongue moving. Try speaking or singing tongue-twisters. You may wish to put simple physical actions to well-known songs such as 'Heads, Shoulders, Knees and Toes' or 'My Bonnie Lies Over the Ocean' to wake up the brain and stimulate physical and vocal co-ordination. If your cast have been at work all day, they need this stimulus to energize them and help them concentrate on the rehearsal ahead.

Chorus Parts

When teaching chorus numbers, the MD should organize the cast around the piano in their vocal groups (soprano, alto, tenor and bass). At this stage everybody will invariably bury their heads deep in their scores and stare at the floor. Give everyone a boost by kicking off with the best-known or most upbeat number in the show.

MDs sometimes refer to the process of teaching the music in early rehearsals as 'note-bashing'. When dealing with an inexperienced cast this can be a tedious and frustrating process; however, there is no avoiding it, it simply has to be done. Identify which vocal group is singing the main tune, and start with them. Play through eight bars or so, and get them to sing along. Then move on to the next group. Play through their line, get them to sing it, and then try putting the two vocal lines together. After a few attempts move on to the third group, and repeat the process. And so on.

Keep the rehearsal energized, and make sure that no group is sitting around not singing for too long. Note-bashing may seem very daunting to inexperienced singers, and some people will insist that they 'Can't get it'.

Encourage the cast to listen to each other. Be positive and upbeat. Keep recapping, and gradually you will start to see progress.

There is a limit to what your cast will be able to take in at one rehearsal, so add some variety. Learn sections from two or three songs, rather than bashing on for hours on the same one. Tell the cast to bring in personal mini-disk or tape players, and record their vocal line so they can practise in the car or at home. Some MDs have been known to prepare practice tapes in advance, and hand them out at the first rehearsal: very impressive. Gradually the music from the show will start to infect the cast's DNA, and they will have the numbers running round in their heads in the middle of the night. Keep at it: the more secure they are in their music, the better.

At the end of each music rehearsal ask the cast to stand up and sing out with as much gusto as they can; not only will this give them a sense of achievement, it lets the MD hear how the harmonies are balancing against each other. If one vocal part sounds weak, consider moving some people across from one that is stronger. If the tenor line is very high and your men are struggling to get the notes, try adding a few altos to it.

Encourage the chorus to do their homework. At the next rehearsal, recap everything that you have learned so far before moving on.

Solo Numbers

The process for working with soloists begins in the same way: note-bash the music, concentrating in the early stages on accurate learning rather than interpretation. The singers should agree on a provisional tempo for each song with the MD, but this may change once they start developing their roles and assimilating their vocal delivery with their acting.

(a) Extract from a company section of Bernice Bobs Her Hair, *with six-part vocal harmony. Music, Matthew Miller; book and lyrics, John Gardyne.*

(b) Solo number from Bernice Bobs Her Hair. *The piano accompaniment is sparse, but the actor can pitch his first note from the sustained B flat on the third beat of the opening bars. Music, Matthew Miller; book and lyrics, John Gardyne.*

If the show is American or requires an accent, it is as well to start singing in it from the beginning. However, don't overstress accents to such an extent that they detract from the musicality of the melody. Watch out for imitations. Some roles – Henry Higgins, Audrey (and Audrey II for that matter) in *Little Shop of Horrors*, the Emcee in *Cabaret* – have become inextricably linked with a particular actor's vocal delivery. In these cases, encourage the actors to learn the song accurately in their own voice, and let the phrasing and delivery evolve once they have started developing characterization with the director.

Some comic songs – 'Adelaide's Lament' is a classic example – rely on a particular vocal delivery to work in performance. Again, resist the temptation of imposing a stylized or 'comedy' voice too soon.

Always rehearse duets, trios and quartets with all the relevant singers together. They will learn their music more quickly and more accurately, and will start to listen to each other, and this will in turn affect their relationship and enhance the sensitivity of their acting.

Learning and fine-tuning the music can be a long process, but it brings with it a wonderful sense of achievement and *esprit de corps*. However, be prepared for songs to sound different when the choreographer starts moving the actors about – a song that sounded great when everybody was standing round the piano, suddenly disappears into thin air once the dancing starts.

DANCE AND THE CHOREOGRAPHER

The role of choreographer in rehearsal is entirely dependent on the requirements of your show. Obviously the choreographer of a dance-heavy show such as *Cats* or *A Chorus Line* will have a proportionally bigger influence on a production than the choreographer of

Transposition

Normally, actors are cast in a musical on the understanding that their vocal range fits the demands of the role. If, however, you have had to cast from a limited pool of people, this may not always be possible.

Transposition – playing the song in a lower or higher key to make it easier for an actor to sing – is, however, a rocky road, and you should only go down it if you think there is no alternative. Do not offer this as an option at the outset, or half your cast will want their parts transposed before they open their mouths. Remember that the musical accompaniment will also have to be transposed if your pianist is not confident about doing this at sight, and so too may the band parts.

Sweeney Todd or *A Little Night Music*, which only require a few odd snatches of social dance. Some directors have very specific ideas about how numbers should be choreographed, others want to do little more than give a few outlines on style, and are content to leave it all to the choreographer from then on.

Rehearsals can get sweaty and intimate: the cast members need to lose their inhibitions and build up a sense of mutual trust.

Types of Dance Number

Musicals contain many types of dance number, which contribute to the style and method of telling the story. There are social dances such as the waltz at the Embassy in *My Fair Lady*, or the General's reception in *Calamity Jane*; in these the characters are partaking in an organized dance occasion appropriate to their social milieu. The characters know they are at a dance and behave accordingly: Colonel Pickering may not dance, but Eliza – effortlessly, triumphantly – does.

There are numbers that are self-consciously presented as entertainment performed to an implied or actual on-stage audience, such as the Hot Box songs in *Guys and Dolls*, the night-club songs in *Pal Joey*, and in all of *Chicago*. In such numbers the emphasis may be on the style, physique and dance skill of the performers, rather than on expressing subtleties of plot or characterization.

Then there are company numbers such as 'I'm getting married in the morning' or 'It's a fine life' or 'The Lambeth Walk', where the characters' mood means that they just can't help dancing, and before they know it, they are. At these heightened moments, dance becomes their natural form of expression.

Some musicals have large sections of pure dance, breaking into narrative forms beyond naturalism. Laurey's unspoken fears about Jud and Curly are expressed non-verbally in the *Oklahoma!* dream ballet. It would be inappropriate for farm boy Curly to dance ballet steps, but his 'dream' *alter ego* certainly can. The crap-shooters of *Guys and Dolls* dance their own stylized ballet in the sewers below New York as the big game finally gets started. The Prologue section of *West Side Story* outlines the 'story so far' in dazzling dance shorthand that is entirely appropriate to the streetwise cool of the Jets and the Sharks: after all, they are far too hip and energized to talk about it.

Preparation

However much dance there is in your particular show, the choreographer and director need to have agreed a general style and approach to the dance sections before rehearsing with the cast. Sometimes there will be extensive descriptions of the stage action during a dance number in the libretto; on others there may just be the bald instruction 'They dance', and the choreographer must respond to the mood and dynamics of the score. Before rehearsals begin, the choreographer and director need to identify where the dance numbers occur, discuss what each dance number contributes to the dramatic line of the show, define what specific action (if any) needs to take place during it, and decide how the dance style should relate to characterization.

Musical Staging

Apart from the obvious dance sections, there may also be songs or scenes that are primarily acted, but are so deeply informed by music that they demand some form of solo or group movement; this is known as 'musical staging'. For example, in 'Christopher Street', the opening number of *Wonderful Town*, a tour guide takes a group of tourists round Greenwich Village, pointing out the landmarks and introducing the main characters in a series of short vignettes. The choreographer and director would obviously have to work carefully together to ensure that the interplay of characters in the scenes relates to the musical accompaniment, while supporting both the narrative and the larger sense of space, mood and place that the number is creating.

A dancer warming up at the barre.

Some slow tunes, especially contemplative love songs, don't need a great deal of formal choreography. Transformed by love, a character may be lighter, better, more elegant in their movement, and unconsciously dance a few steps with the effortless grace of Gene Kelly. Or they may not – it all depends on the character, the actor and the milieu of the show.

Some directors love to do their own musical staging, as they feel it is an extension of character and plot; others hand over responsibility to the choreographer at the first note of music. This can sometimes lead to a jarring shift in style in performance: the ingénue who performs her scenes like Shirley Temple suddenly starts dancing like Chita Rivera. Alternatively, after two hours of elegant thirties' dance, the big love duet is suddenly static and prosaic.

The best musical staging usually involves a degree of collaboration, as it allows the director to maintain continuity of character and narrative, while allowing the choreographer to maintain and refer to the physical language of the show, and make reference to certain gestures or combinations that appear elsewhere in the choreography.

Working on musical staging can be thrilling for everyone involved, but it is complex, and involves a level of confidence, and musical and movement ability among the cast that may not exist at early rehearsals. For this reason in early rehearsals it is usually a good idea to concentrate on simpler, self-contained, defined dance numbers.

The director should give the choreographer time and space to do their work. If it is a dance rehearsal, then the choreographer is in charge, and the director should resist the temptation to jump up every two minutes to make some minor point. Remember that dance is conjured up out of thin air, and a choreographer in the process of creation is in a delicate frame of mind.

Feed your ideas and thoughts to the choreographer by all means, but never criticize or undermine their work in front of the cast.

STARTING DANCE REHEARSALS

Professional dancers pride themselves on the speed and accuracy with which they can pick up dance routines. For many actors, though, both amateur and professional, learning dance is difficult and takes time. If you are working with a cast without much dance experience – or even if they are experienced – start as early as possible, certainly in the first week of rehearsal.

Let your cast know in advance which rehearsals will be dance rehearsals, so they can bring appropriate clothing and footwear.

Thirty people sweating away in a hot room can get smelly, so encourage people to pay special attention to their personal hygiene. Tell them to bring bottles of water and a towel; men may need a dancer's belt or athletic support, especially if they are doing lifts; and if appropriate, women should wear practice skirts.

Warming Up

Dance can be dangerous, and dancers are therefore particularly vulnerable to injury, so choreography rehearsals should always start with a physical warm-up, led by the choreographer or dance captain. Make sure that whoever does the warm-up knows exactly what they are doing: this is no job for the well-meaning but untrained amateur. Professional dancers always arrive early and do their own stretching exercises before rehearsals start, and you should encourage your cast to emulate this practice as rehearsals progress.

Beware the tendency for warm-ups to eat into valuable rehearsal time. Unless you are doing a particularly strenuous and ambitious number, fifteen minutes should be ample.

Learning a Dance Routine

If you are choreographing a show that demands a specific style – tap, for instance – you may choose to use the first rehearsal as a class to run through basic steps, techniques, technical terms and working practices. As this will almost certainly be the first time you have seen the full cast together, it will also allow you the opportunity to assess their potential.

It is good to start off with a big number that involves as many people as possible; let the cast get used to the sweaty intimacy of dance rehearsals. Initially the choreographer should simply teach the steps to a series of counted beats. Build up numbers slowly, teaching four or eight beats at a time, showing which movement goes with each count. Demonstrate feet patterns first, naming the steps as you go, and

explaining how the dancers should balance and distribute their weight. Add arm, hand and head movements, and re-run the pattern. Don't be afraid of touching people: you may need to move them into the correct position to get the feeling of a correct placement or move.

It is an enormous help if you rehearse – if only for some of the time – in a proper dance studio with mirrors. Dancers who can see what they look like can make adjustments much more easily than those who cannot.

Like the MD, the choreographer needs to keep recapping material, and simultaneously keep the rehearsals moving forward, so that everyone feels that progress is being made. Don't try and finish off a long or complex routine in one rehearsal: there is a limit to the amount of information your cast can assimilate. Have a break, then move on to something else. There is also no point rehearsing and rehearsing an upbeat number until everyone is dropping from exhaustion; come back to it another day.

If you need people to work in pairs, set up partners early on. Always use your strongest dancers for solos or featured duets, trios and quartets. If there are weaker dancers in group numbers, consider pairing them with stronger partners who will help them improve. Encourage people to write down what they have done, and to practise on their own at home. There are formal methods of notating dance, but most untrained dancers prefer to work out their own method for recording steps, and to write them down in their own hieroglyphics. As long as it makes sense to them, and the steps are recorded accurately, that is fine.

At the end of each rehearsal run everything that has been learnt so far with music, preferably played live on the piano. You will be amazed at the cast's sense of achievement in performing even a small section of a routine.

Initially the learning process may seem unbearably slow. Worse, when you return at

Rehearsing a scene from Pippin *at GSA Conservatoire.*

Checking positions in the mirror.

the next rehearsal to the sequence you have just worked on for hours, people may seem unable to remember a single step. Don't panic: it takes time for untrained bodies to get used to memorizing physical movement in this way. Recap what you did, and then add a bit more to the routine. As the weeks go by the cast will 'learn how to learn', and the routines will start to be retained in their muscle memory.

Achieving a Sense of Style

Unless you are working with skilled professionals, a sense of 'style' may be hard to achieve. Inexperienced actors are often extremely self-conscious about their bodies, and may be horrified at the thought of presenting themselves in an upfront, charged, stylish or sexy manner.

Define a couple of simple style points, and encourage the cast to use them: the particular drop of a shoulder, or turn of a leg. Attitude is important, too; for example, when Velma and the cast of *Chicago* kick into 'All that Jazz', it is more important that they ooze detached cool than do a lot of flashy dance steps. Self-belief can go a long way in selling a number to an audience.

Spacing

As your cast grows in confidence in their steps, take a look at the bigger picture. Everyone may be doing the same moves, but if there are five couples stage left and two stage right, the overall picture will be unbalanced. Your cast need to develop a sense of spatial awareness, as they need to know where they are in relation to the other dancers on the stage, and may need to maintain equal distances between themselves and others. Use the mirror if you have one.

Accidents can, and do happen at dance rehearsals. Beware of slippery floors, and mop up any spilled liquids immediately. Find out if there is a trained first-aider in the company, just in case. Also be aware that if you are performing on a raked stage, it will feel very different from the horizontal floor of a rehearsal room.

Keeping a Balance

The task of learning both the music and the dance steps may seem so daunting that the director may be tempted to hand over rehearsals for the first few weeks entirely to the MD and choreographer. However, don't fall into this trap.

It is important to keep a good balance between music, dance and acting in rehearsals. You should not think of them as totally separate disciplines – they are completely interdependent. Dancing will heighten the actors' sense of rhythm and musicality, and this will help their singing. Learning lyrics and musical phrasing will inform characterization and physicality, so their acting will improve. This in turn will boost their performance skills and confidence, which will feed back into their dancing.

DIALOGUE SCENES

Once the music and choreography rehearsals are under way, the director needs to start work with the cast on the dialogue scenes. Even if your show is extremely heavy on dance, get started early; a professional director would probably begin towards the end of the first week. If you are rehearsing an amateur cast for eight weeks, certainly get started in week two. Apart from anything else, it is important that the actors retain the sense of the show's story, and realize that the song-and-dance numbers they are learning are not self-contained, but part of a larger whole.

Some professional directors like to spend several rehearsals sitting round a table poring over the text with the actors, especially when dealing with a complex and elusive modern play. The majority, however, prefer to get the actors up on their feet as soon as possible, especially if rehearsal time is at a premium.

There are no hard and fast rules about how to direct a scene. Some directors like to work out everything in minute detail in advance and give the actors very specific instructions on every movement and gesture; for example:

'Oh, Henry!' Move towards him three paces, stop, look him in the eye. 'I love you.' Hold his gaze for a count of three. 'But I know it's

Pippin *in performance at the Electric Theatre, Guildford. Director/choreographer, Tim Flavin; designer, Roger Ness; lighting, Mark Dymock.* Photo: Mark Dean

hopeless.' Break away, slightly stagger, and slump down on the sofa.

Other directors launch into improvizational games, de-constructing the text and re-imagining the narrative in different ways.

Extraordinary and brilliant work has been created using both approaches. However, over-direction can produce arid, rather lifeless performances, and certainly professional actors like to move as and when they feel the impulse, rather than when told to do so. On the other hand, inexperienced actors, and especially children and adolescents, may benefit from very clear instructions.

Directors can only learn by experience how much blocking they should prepare in advance for each scene, and how much they should let evolve during rehearsal. The larger the number of people on stage and the more complicated the action, the more preparation will be needed.

The following is an outline of some rehearsal practices that the author has found

131

useful and effective when directing both plays and musicals. It is intended only as an outline of one possible approach.

Understanding the Scene

At the start of the rehearsal, get the actors to sit or stand in a circle, and read through the scene. If there are any meanings that are unclear, sort them out. If there is an obscure reference, make sure you have checked it out and understand it. Your credibility with your cast may depend on little moments like this.

Well-written scenes are little three-act dramas, with a beginning, a middle and an end. Often the arrival of a new character, or the revelation of a vital and hitherto unknown piece of information, completely alters the mood and emotional quality of a scene. Discover where these turning points are. Encourage the cast to talk about the scene in their own words. Keep it straightforward: where does the scene take place, what concerns and expectations do the characters have when it starts, what happens during it, how have things changed by the end? Concentrate specifically on the scene: do not talk about what happens later in the play. After all, the actors may know what will happen in Act Two, but the characters do not.

Blocking

The placing and organization of the actors on stage is known as 'blocking'. Once the meaning of the scene is clear, set up any furniture that is in the scene, and get the actors on their feet into position for the opening, whether this is standing, sitting, at the table, lying on the bed, at the door, wherever.

Encourage them to work through the scene, moving as feels appropriate. Inexperienced actors tend to move about a lot, getting up, sitting down and marching round the room on every line. Let them try – experiment: if the scene is too 'busy' it will be difficult to follow. Usually, blocking gets simpler as rehearsals progress and the actors grow in confidence.

Concentrate on what is going on in the scene, and what it means to the characters. Don't invent extraneous comedy business or engineer self-consciously funny moments. Trust the integrity of the script.

Most actors love writing notes in their script, either blocking ('move to sofa') or character points ('he killed my brother!!!'); it gives them a sense of ownership of the character and of the show. Remember to tell them always to use a pencil: their notes may need to be rubbed out later.

The director should keep an eye on the clock. If you start running out of time, speed up. Don't get bogged down in detail, keep things moving, and make sure you reach the end of the scene.

Leave enough time at the end of the rehearsal to run the entire scene through once – though remember, you are not making a film, so it doesn't have to be a perfect 'take'. Inevitably there will be things that you don't like, but you have made a start, and that is the main thing.

Director/choreographer Gerry Tebbutt rehearsing with the Orphans in Annie. *GSA Conservatoire production.*

Rehearsing Chorus Scenes

Do not overlook acting rehearsals for the chorus. There is a danger that all their rehearsal time gets taken up with music and choreography, so although they may look sensational during their numbers, they then spend the rest of the performance standing around at the back of the stage wondering what to do while the lead actors play a scene in front of them.

Of course, sometimes the chorus's function is to provide a visual setting for the leading player: that is the job the dancers in *A Chorus Line* are auditioning for, and they then effectively become walking props and scenery. Busby Berkeley's astonishing staging of musical numbers in films such as *42nd Street* and *Gold-diggers of 1933* takes this approach to its ultimate conclusion.

However, in the vast majority of cases the chorus have a clear identity. Whether they are cowboys propping up the bar at Henry Miller's saloon, guards at the King of Siam's palace, or the street traders of Covent Garden Market, they need to relate to the main action in a convincing and meaningful way.

The same basic principles apply when rehearsing with the principals, but the director will probably have less specific information to work with, and may have to exercise a greater degree of creativity.

Ask yourself: who are these people, what are they doing here, what kind of lives do they have? It often helps to give the chorus specific characters to increase their sense of identity. A busy street scene will come to life on stage if it is full of recognizable individuals. Set up social and family groups – parents with children, a delinquent trio of adolescent girls, two road-sweepers, a streetwalker, a couple of cops, a businessman and his wife, a beggar. Wardrobe permitting, you may encourage the chorus to make up their own characters; this can provide a fruitful basis for developing their acting skills.

The director needs to come to a chorus session well prepared. Working with a large number of people is tricky, and unless you are highly focused and well organized, rehearsals can slide into anarchy.

If you have to move large numbers of people about the stage, divide them into manageable groups and work out in advance where their starting points and what their routes around the stage will be. You may appoint a 'team captain' for each group, who should take responsibility for leading and cueing the others. Keep a list of who is in each group. In a large cast show someone will almost always be absent from rehearsal, so the 'team leader' should take responsibility for passing on instructions on their return.

Be practical, and remember the physical constraints of the stage. Ensure that there is enough time and space for people to get on and off the stage safely. Thirty people will not be able to exit simultaneously through one small doorway on stage left. If you have an assistant director, delegate some of the work to them. Be prepared for the rehearsal to be very noisy. Some directors in desperation have been

---

Rehearsing Fights

Start rehearsing fights as early as you can. They are potentially dangerous and need to be choreographed more carefully than anything else in the show. Fights should only be set by an experienced fight director, initially in slow motion and gradually speeded up.

Once the fight is set, get the actors involved to run it through several times at each rehearsal. The more they rehearse it, the better and more convincing it will be. The same goes for any special skills that have to be acquired, be it tumbling for *Barnum* or roller skating for *The Rink*.

If there are animals in the show give them plenty of time to get used to their human co-stars.

Animals

A few shows require animals: *Annie* needs a dog, so does *Anything Goes. Gypsy* asks for a cat, dogs, a monkey and a lamb!

Professional producers would normally contract the services of a professional 'wrangler' to supply and train animals, but this can be very expensive. If you can't afford this, choose your animal very carefully. Make sure it has plenty of time to get familiar with the actors with whom it will primarily come into contact, then bring it to plenty of rehearsals so it gets used to being around a large number of people and the volume of the music. And keep your fingers crossed.

---

known to take along a referee's whistle so they do not have to keep shouting their heads off asking for quiet.

If there is a big dance number in the scene you should consult with the choreographer so that you both know who will be where when the dance begins. You should normally let the dance emerge out of the action, rather than blocking the scene to accommodate the dance. The exception to the rule is when a song is self-consciously performed by an actor in a theatre or club setting to an on-stage audience.

Big chorus rehearsals can be exhausting and overwhelming. Keep them short and snappy, and intersperse them with small cast scenes to retain your sanity.

REHEARSING CHILDREN

As mentioned in Chapter 7, if your show features children you may need to rehearse with them separately at first. A group of very young children together needs special care: *The March of the Siamese Children* can be a daunting prospect for a four-year-old!

If you have an assistant director, make it their responsibility to teach the children their material and run through it with them. Keep children's rehearsals short and sweet. A large group of adults can be extremely intimidating, so let the children get confident about performing their sections before you mix them up with the rest of the cast.

Encourage the adults to be supportive of the children's efforts. They probably will be anyway: it is always exciting when a new bit of the show arrives in the rehearsal room.

PUTTING THE ELEMENTS TOGETHER

Once the individual elements of song, dance and dialogue have been covered, start running scenes through and combining them. If you are new to directing, start with smaller scenes that involve only a few actors. Run a dialogue scene, and let the actors get a sense of how the emotional content of the scene develops into a song and/or a dance number. Involve the MD and the choreographer, and try and make the transitions as seamless and apparently effortless as possible.

Always establish how the first actor to sing will get his or her starting note: from a musical introduction, from underscoring played in the scene, or from a 'bell note' – a single note timed to a particular word or pause in the dialogue.

An actor should never look at the MD when a music cue is about to be given. If the scene is played convincingly, the audience will feel that, just at that moment, the music is welling up from the character's inner soul: they must not give the game away by drawing attention to the pianist on the side of the stage.

Most numbers work to a musical climax, and actors should be bold. They should relish the scale and intensity of the emotion that the song expresses: it is in such moments that the musical breaks out of the constraints of naturalism. They should celebrate it, hold the moment, believe in it – and provide the audience with the opportunity to applaud.

Applause also gives the audience a few seconds to readjust from listening to song, to listening to spoken dialogue. In filmed musicals, these transitions can sometimes feel jarring, precisely because there is no opportunity for applause.

Learning Lines

Learning lines is the most unglamorous aspect of the actor's job; for many it is an almost unbearable slog. Nevertheless, it has to be done.

Set a definite date on the rehearsal schedule for *no books*, and always encourage your actors to learn their lines 100 per cent accurately. It is easier and quicker to learn lines correctly in the first place than to learn them inaccurately,

Annie in performance – the Orphans. GSA Conservatoire production at the Yvonne Arnaud Theatre. Director/choreographer, Gerry Tebbutt; designer, Roger Ness; lighting, Richard Jones. Photo: Mark Dean

then have to unlearn the wrong lines and re-learn the right ones.

Some actors will learn more quickly than others, and may want to rehearse without a script very early on. That is fine, as long as they are accurate. Actors who ask for a prompt every other line and wildly paraphrase the text are wasting everybody's time and being disrespectful towards their colleagues. The usual explanation for this is: 'But this is the only way I can learn them.' In such cases be diplomatic, but be firm.

The Stagger-Through

This is the first attempt at running a whole act (or the whole show) in sequence, without using scripts or scores. Make sure that the cast know well in advance when this is going to be: it is a major milestone in the rehearsal process.

The DSM will be prompting on the night, and needs to learn where the actors pause or slow down their delivery. At the outset make it clear that, from now on, the DSM, and only the DSM, will prompt. Wish everybody good luck, and off you go.

135

The DSM setting up props for a run-through.

The stagger-through can be a fraught experience for everyone: there may be gaps; the choreographer may have run out of time and not completed the staging of a number; songs that people have been learning for weeks fall to pieces; actors forget their entrances; scenes that zipped along wonderfully last week now seem leaden and witless. The show seems interminable. This is all perfectly normal: why else would it be known as a 'stagger-through'?

Keep things moving forwards. If a scene falls apart (and it will), don't try and fix it there and then. Don't stop to recap mistakes in music and choreography. If an actor is repeatedly calling for prompts and holding up the show, tell him to use his script (this would be the ultimate humiliation for a professional actor). The point of the stagger-through is that, one way or another, you get through to the end. Afterwards the cast may feel dispirited.

However, keep positive and upbeat, and be polite. Thank everybody for their efforts, and emphasize how useful the exercise has been.

Get together with the MD and choreographer, and discuss any particular areas of concern. Make a note of any glaring gaps and any sections that you really do not think are working well (as opposed to sections that worked well last week but came apart at the stagger-through). Prioritize the work that has to be done, starting with scenes or numbers that have had little or no rehearsal. Agree a date for another run of the whole act or show, and make sure everyone is focused on that as the next landmark. However much you may feel like it, don't sink to the floor and burst into tears – not until you are in the privacy of your own home, anyway.

THE SECOND PHASE OF REHEARSALS

After the stagger-through, the MD, choreographer and director will each have a list of sections that need work: vocal harmonies that need to be tightened up, dance sections that need to be finished off, a dialogue scene that needs to be re-blocked. Divide up rehearsal time between you, and nail these individual problems as quickly as possible.

Once you have done that, you need to start developing a sense of pace and continuity through individual scenes, through each act, and ultimately through the whole show. Rehearsals should no longer be classified as 'dance', 'music' and 'acting', but 'Act 1, scene 3' and 'Act 2, scenes 1 to 3', working on the synthesis of the various performance elements in each.

It is now that all that note-bashing and those endless dance rehearsals in the first few weeks start to pay off. The actors have so much to worry about that muscle memory and unconscious knowledge start to kick in. Thus, actors who are concentrating hard on a particularly complicated acting moment may find that an elusive dance routine or musical phrase effortlessly slots into place. Chorus members who are hoofing their way through a company number find that complex vocal lines they have been struggling to find for weeks are suddenly second nature.

The director can now start to see the show beginning to take shape. Run the scenes and watch them carefully: are the actors on stage relating to each other? Is the story clear? Is there a clear point of focus throughout? Enlist the help of the choreographer, who may not have seen some of the acted scenes before, and who can provide a useful objective point of view.

Keep moving forwards, and keep leading. As far as possible let scenes run uninterrupted;

rather, make notes, and give these to the actors afterwards. Always be polite, tactful and clear in giving notes – and do not be afraid to give a note that you suspect will be unpopular.

Watch out in particular for bits of comedy business developed by chorus members that are now likely to 'pull focus' from the main action and distract the audience. Never get into a public argument with individual members of the cast; if necessary, take people to one side and conduct a mature, responsible conversation with them.

Check on accents. Even if they are not 100 per cent accurate, ask yourself if the relevant members of the cast sound as if they all come from the same place. And if you don't have a dedicated accent coach, get someone who has more or less the right native accent to watch a rehearsal and give specific notes.

Scenes from the final run-through of **The Secret Garden** *at Arts Educational School, London. One actor is wearing full costume, the others practice clothes. Director, Ian Watt-Smith; choreographer, Aiden Treays.*

Actors watching a run-through from the sidelines. Note the fan: in the summer the rehearsal room can get very hot.

As rehearsals continue, start creating a sense of performance. Add more props and elements of costume. Play sound effects, if appropriate (*see* Chapter 11, 'Lighting and Sound Design'). Organize another run-through of each act, or the whole show. Invite members of the staging departments and stage management to watch: not only will it give them a greater understanding of the show, it will get the cast used to performing for an audience.

BUILDING TO A PERFORMANCE

If there are still specific problem areas, take the time to break them down to their component elements, and sort them out. Often this is a fairly simple matter: simplify a dance step, reblock a scene, cut a piece of business that seemed wonderful in week three but is now laboured and unconvincing.

It is usually easiest to give notes to the whole company at the end of run-throughs and rehearsal. Make them as succinct and entertaining as possible. Delicate and potentially unpopular notes may need to be given in private. Encourage the cast to write down their notes as you give them; there is nothing more dispiriting than giving the same note over and over again.

Try not to make notes too negative. It's easy for a notes session to become a series of 'don't do this, don't do that'; rather, phrase them as far as possible in active, positive terms: 'Standing up during the argument looks great: keep standing right till the end' is a better note than 'Don't sit down in the middle of the argument, it looks terrible.'

Notes should not always be critical. If you think a scene or a number went particularly well, let the cast know; but there is no need to get involved in an orgy of gushing congratulation.

Successful performances require pace and energy – don't let them flag, or the show will drift away. Some directors say that all the notes ever given add up to two words: 'Faster, louder.'

Before you leave the rehearsal room behind, make sure you run the whole show uninterrupted, in its entirety, at least once. It will be the last time you do so before the dress rehearsal.

BAND REHEARSALS

The band does not usually start to rehearse until late on in the process. Most professional musicians need only one or two rehearsals before they are ready to play the whole score; amateurs may need more time.

On Broadway, band members are recruited and contracted by the 'music co-ordinator', known in the UK as the 'fixer'. In many cases, however, MDs go out and recruit the band themselves.

Remember that you will need competent musicians or the show will sound awful. And even if you need only two or three players,

start recruiting early: it may take weeks to find a good bass player, and finding half-a-dozen violinists may take considerably longer. In the UK, many part-time and semi-professional instrumentalists belong to the Musicians' Union (MU), which has, over the years, established strict working conditions and levels of payment for its members. Musicians' Unions in other countries are traditionally strong and well supported, too.

Be aware that, unless you are recruiting from within a school or college, you may have to honour MU practices and pay rates when dealing with your band members. A professional actress may agree to play Dolly Levi for no money because it is her lifetime's ambition to do so; a professional musician, stuck down in the orchestra pit, is unlikely to feel the same way.

SITZPROBE

One of the last rehearsals before technical rehearsals begin is the *Sitzprobe*, at which the cast sing through the score with the band for the first time. The sound of the band always comes as a shock – though usually a pleasant one. After weeks of rehearsal, the cast will be used to working with a pianist. Suddenly the familiar music of the show is transformed with orchestral colour, and the room is filled with new tones and moods.

The *Sitzprobe* is usually a thrilling rehearsal, and can be relied on to give the whole company a boost as they prepare to move out of the rehearsal room and into the theatre.

10 Rehearsals: Keeping Track

Rehearsal is an organic process. As the production develops and grows in the rehearsal room from day to day, so its practical and technical requirements will keep changing. Props and furniture may be added or cut, sound cues may be altered, extra chorus members blocked into crowd scenes. An actress suddenly finds she needs a pocket in her dress to hide a letter; a singer needs an off-stage microphone; an actor needs to make an ultra-quick costume change; and so on.

Simultaneously, outside the rehearsal room there is a mass of activity going on in the staging departments: work in construction, props, wardrobe, lighting and sound will constantly be affected by the availability and costs of materials, shortage of time, limitations of space – and, of course, ever-changing budgets. These in their turn may produce constraints on what it will be feasible for the actors to do on stage.

A two-way flow of information between rehearsal room and staging departments is therefore vital, and controlling this on a day-to-day basis is one of the most crucial responsibilities of the stage management department.

Rehearsal Reports

At the end of each day's rehearsal the DSM should make up a rehearsal report outlining decisions that will affect, or will need clarification from, the staging departments. These reports need to be unequivocally clear and precise; they should be numbered and dated, and the information organized department by department as per the example shown.

Keep items on the report purely practical and specific. There is no point writing an abstract comment such as: 'The director feels there should be a growing sense of evil in Act 2.' You can avoid confusion by always referring to actors both by their own name and that of the character they are playing; this is particularly important when referring to chorus members who may be playing more than one role. Therefore do not write: 'Jeff needs a stick', but 'Daddy Warbucks (Mr Johnson) needs a silver-topped period walking cane for "N.Y.C." (page 36).'

If there are no notes for some departments, write 'No notes': they can then be 100 per cent confident that nothing has been omitted by accident. Clarity and certainty at this stage will prevent last-minute panic later on. It is worth checking through the rehearsal report with the director (and/or the choreographer if appropriate) before it is typed up and distributed, so they can double check that you have noted their requirements correctly.

Never include a note or suggestion given to you by an actor without first checking it with the director. That can lead to confusion and acrimony.

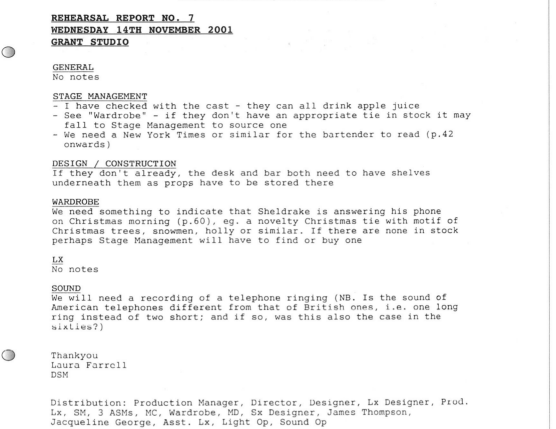

PROMISES, PROMISES

REHEARSAL REPORT NO. 7
WEDNESDAY 14TH NOVEMBER 2001
GRANT STUDIO

GENERAL
No notes

STAGE MANAGEMENT
- I have checked with the cast - they can all drink apple juice
- See "Wardrobe" - if they don't have an appropriate tie in stock it may fall to Stage Management to source one
- We need a New York Times or similar for the bartender to read (p.42 onwards)

DESIGN / CONSTRUCTION
If they don't already, the desk and bar both need to have shelves underneath them as props have to be stored there

WARDROBE
We need something to indicate that Sheldrake is answering his phone on Christmas morning (p.60), eg. a novelty Christmas tie with motif of Christmas trees, snowmen, holly or similar. If there are none in stock perhaps Stage Management will have to find or buy one

LX
No notes

SOUND
We will need a recording of a telephone ringing (NB. Is the sound of American telephones different from that of British ones, i.e. one long ring instead of two short; and if so, was this also the case in the sixties?)

Thankyou
Laura Farrell
DSM

Distribution: Production Manager, Director, Designer, Lx Designer, Prod. Lx, SM, 3 ASMs, MC, Wardrobe, MD, Sx Designer, James Thompson, Jacqueline George, Asst. Lx, Light Op, Sound Op

Rehearsal report from Promises Promises. *Key information from the rehearsal room is distributed daily to each staging department.*

When whole acts are run in their entirety, use a stopwatch to get an approximate running time, and include that on the report. The sound department may also request timings of individual scenes and sequences to enable them to create and edit sound effects efficiently and accurately. (*See* Chapter 11 for more information on the lighting and sound departments.)

Call Sheets

However meticulously the director may have planned the rehearsal schedule, the day-to-day progress of the work – plus unforeseen circumstances such as changes in people's availability, alterations in room bookings, sickness and so on – will inevitably mean that it will be modified as the weeks go by.

The DSM is responsible for producing call sheets for the cast, showing the venue and date of each rehearsal, which actors are required, the times they will be needed, and the scenes that will be rehearsed. Costume and wig fittings should also be detailed, as should the time the rehearsal will end. The DSM should let

DSM recording blocking in the prompt copy.

you know if they will need longer with specific individuals. Also, remember to allow travelling time if actors have to travel from the rehearsal room to another building for fittings.

The costume designer will usually attend at least one fitting to ensure that their intentions are being kept on track.

BLOCKING AND THE PROMPT COPY

As rehearsals progress, the DSM is also responsible for keeping a record of the blocking in the prompt copy. At later rehearsals technical cues and front-of-house calls will be added in, so the prompt copy becomes the definitive record of the production, and is used for 'calling' the show during performance.

There are different ways of laying out prompt copies, and different conventions for

everyone know where the call sheet will be posted, and encourage the cast to take responsibility for checking it regularly.

In the professional theatre, the DSM posts the next day's call sheet on the company notice board and at the stage door. They may also call the actors individually to confirm their calls. If you are working with a large amateur cast and/or you are not based permanently in one building, getting this information to everybody may be more difficult. It is obviously easier to contact three actors than fifty, so the director should not change around full chorus rehearsals unless absolutely necessary.

Always let actors know if a schedule change means that they are no longer required to attend a certain rehearsal. They will appreciate your courtesy and thoughtfulness.

COSTUME FITTINGS

The DSM should liaise with the costume supervisor to schedule fittings for the cast. There will normally be at least two for each actor and, depending on the number and complexity of the costumes, possibly many more. Allow half an hour for each actor; the wardrobe will let

A costume fitting in progress. Photo: Polly McDonnell

recording blocking. The DSM needs to agree on one method with the SM and ASM early on, so they can take over either running rehearsals or calling the show if the DSM is ever absent. The prompt copy is also a useful *aide-mémoire* for the director and actors when they return to a scene after a time lapse and there is confusion over exactly what was set at the previous rehearsal.

In dance numbers and big ensemble scenes the DSM should not attempt to record every detail of the choreography: concentrate on recording where each member of the chorus starts and finishes, and how they are disposed around the stage in the major stage pictures. In an ideal world, every member of the chorus would be present at all chorus rehearsals. However, this is often not the case with large amateur choruses, and there may frequently be absentees, so the DSM needs to be able to tell the director exactly where those missing people should be.

In rehearsal the blocking will keep changing all the time. Never record anything in the prompt copy in ink, and always have a good supply of pencils, a pencil sharpener and a rubber in rehearsals.

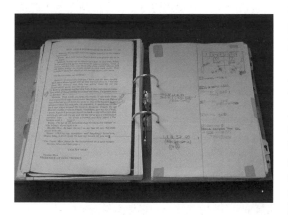

The prompt copy. On the right-hand page, cue points are recorded in the left-hand column, blocking in the right.

Prompting

Once actors start to rehearse without their scripts they will inevitably need the DSM to give them a prompt from time to time, some more frequently than others. In theory, at least, these should get fewer and fewer as the first night approaches. Actors should ask for a prompt by saying 'line'. There is no need to say 'please', but thank the DSM at the end of the scene.

Professional actors are expected not to need prompts during a performance; if someone 'dries' or makes a mistake, it is up to them and their fellow actors to get the scene back on track. Inexperienced performers may not have the expertise or confidence to do this, and you may decide that it is better to provide a prompter than to risk the show grinding to a dead stop in the middle of the scene.

During performances the DSM will be far too busy calling the show to give actors prompts. If you feel it is necessary, recruit a designated prompter and get them to attend as many 'books down' rehearsals and run-throughs as they can so they get used to the actors' pace and delivery, and note any significant pauses that occur in the dialogue.

PROPS STORE/SETTING LISTS

As the stage manager and ASM gradually acquire the props needed, they should be kept all together in a safe place, preferably under lock and key. Anything – literally anything – can be a prop, and it is easy for people to take or move them inadvertently. Practice props should be kept in, or as near as possible to, the rehearsal room: endlessly moving boxes full of props backwards and forwards is time-consuming and can prove expensive. If you are sharing

your rehearsal space with other people, try and find a lockable cupboard or chest that you can use; then make a big sign asking people not to touch them, and display it prominently.

During rehearsals the DSM should make a record of where props need to be at the start of the show, and/or which side of the stage they first appear from. The SM will then be able to use this information to draw up a 'setting list', showing where each prop has to be placed prior to each performance. Clear and accurate setting lists will save a great deal of time at the technical rehearsal.

Building a stool to the designer's specifications in the workshop.

PRODUCTION MEETINGS

The production manager should call regular production meetings throughout the rehearsal period so progress can be monitored and discussed. On a professional production these would be held weekly; if you are rehearsing less intensely over a longer period, one every two weeks or so may be sufficient

An elaborate prop like this may require a great deal of time and effort, but it is worth it.

The director, as many of the creative team as possible, and the heads of all staging departments should attend, and give a brief report on their progress. Production meetings are usually the only times when the various HODs meet each other before the move into the theatre, and it is a good time to clarify matters about which people are confused or unsure. As rehearsals progress, the schedule and plan for production week will be discussed in detail, and will need to be agreed (*see* Chapter 12). Minutes of the meeting are taken and distributed by the stage manager.

Production meetings deal with the practical nuts and bolts issues of getting the show on to the stage, and how the production budget is being managed. Meanwhile the producer, publicity officer and box office manager will be having their own regular meetings to monitor ticket sales, publicity and PR. The producer will also report back occasionally to the managing committee of the organization or company, to inform them of artistic developments and to present an overview of the ongoing financial situation.

Depending on how things are going, the producer may also be having meetings with potential new investors, funding bodies – and the bank manager.

Weapons and any other potentially dangerous props should be controlled by the stage manager. Hand them out at the start of the rehearsal to the actors who are using them, and point out anything particularly hazardous, such as sharp edges and points. Collect them at the end of the rehearsal, and never leave them lying around.

Be aware that there are very strict laws regarding the use and storage of firearms and replica firearms. If in doubt, speak to your local police station.

STAGE LEFT

UP STAGE LEFT

- Waitress pad
- Doctor's Bag
- White Sheet
- Scissors
- Comb
- Mirror
- Rocking Chair

CENTRE STAGE LEFT

- Parasol
- Mesh Shopping Basket
- Shopping Basket
- Photograph of Tony
- Rocking Chair
- Gifts
- Wheelchair

DOWN STAGE LEFT

- Rosabella Suitcase
- Rosabella Shoulder Bag
- 7x Grape Baskets
- Washing Basket
- Sheets for washing basket
- Pail of Water, Flannels
- Broom
- Dustpan
- 3x Sewing
- Patchwork Quilt

STAGE RIGHT

UP STAGE RIGHT

- Coffee Pot
- 4x Trays
- 2x Brooms
- Stepladder
- Travelling Bag
- Stool
- Tin Box (inside box, dollar bills)
- Accountants Book
- Pistol and Holster
- Camera Kit
- Straw

CENTRE STAGE RIGHT

- 3x Crates
- Banquet Table
  - Pink Table Cloth
  - 2x Cheeses
  - 3x Cakes
  - 2x Bowls of fruit
  - 3x Fans
  - 2x Bunches of Flowers
  - Wine Bottles
  - 22x Wine Glasses
  - 4x Trays
  - Wedding Cake
  - Small Bouquet of Flowers
  - Jug of Water and Glass
- Present containing Rosabella's Shawl
- Clipboard and Pencil
- Table
  - Glue Pot
  - Glue Brush
  - Labels
- Dolly (Crate and Fruit Crate tied onto it)
- Lantern
-

DOWN STAGE RIGHT

- Suitcase and Shoes
- Train Ticket

Setting list for The Most Happy Fella, *showing where each prop has to be set for the start of the show.*

11 LIGHTING AND SOUND DESIGN

Technological developments in lighting, amplification, microphone and recording equipment have radically altered the look and sound of musicals over the last fifty years. Shows used to be lit with crude washes of coloured light, occasionally interspersed with a follow spot or two. Only a generation ago, actors had to coat their faces in make-up in order to be seen properly. Today, the best lighting design brings a hitherto undreamed-of variation and complexity to the illumination of stage and actors, which can now approach the subtlety of film.

There have been similar developments in sound. Up until the sixties, the technology of sound amplification was very basic; microphones and amplifiers were large and cumbersome, instruments still mainly acoustic. Performers would sing largely unamplified over the orchestra, and it was up to the conductor to do what he could to ensure some kind of sound balance. Meanwhile, sound effects were created live in the wings by the stage manager. Nowadays, the 'landscape' of a musical's sound, its control and balance, are as much part of its overall aesthetic as the costumes or set.

Responsibility for these vital functions falls respectively to the lighting designer and sound designer. They must not only have the imagination to create new worlds of light and sound that will support and enhance the director's overall vision of the show, but also have the technical knowledge and practical expertise to turn those ideas into reality.

Light brings colour, atmosphere and magic to an empty space. **Guys and Dolls** *at the Jerwood Vanbrugh Theatre, RADA. Director, Geoff Bullen; lighting, Andrew Turner.*
Photo: Neil Fraser

LIGHTING A PLAY

In a production of a naturalistic play such as Chekhov's *Three Sisters*, lighting is normally used purely to enhance the audience's sense of time, place and environment. The director would probably ask the designer to light the stage as naturalistically as possible, creating the moods of a bright summer's day, a grey rainy afternoon in autumn, or a clear and frosty moonlit night in winter. In interior scenes, the light would give the impression of coming from an identifiable source – streaming in through windows by day, from candles, gas or oil lamps by night.

The designer might take great care in creating the effect of a long slow sunset, full of myriad colour changes in the sky and the lengthening shadows of evening. Of course the audience would not know – nor necessarily care – how those effects were being achieved: if they believed that the sunset was 'real', then the lighting designer would have achieved their objective.

The further plays move away from pure naturalism, the more abstract and expressionist lighting may become. For a production of *Macbeth* the lighting designer might create a disorienting mix of harsh white light and deep shadow to express the nightmarish atmosphere of the play. Productions of opera may take this approach further: lighting can become a visual correlative to the sound of the orchestra and singers, with swirling colours and shapes expressing the dynamics of the music.

LIGHTING A MUSICAL

As we have seen, most musicals move backwards and forwards between the naturalism of dialogue scenes, the heightened reality of song, and the pure physical expression of dance. A scene in a musical may start just like a naturalistic play, in a living room, an office or a backyard. However, once characters wish to express sentiments that are just too big for mere words, they have no choice but to sing – Tony can't *speak* the words to 'Maria', nor Annie 'Tomorrow', nor Desirée 'Send in the

Clowns': they must sing them. This outpouring of their feelings momentarily changes the world around them, and that demands a change in the stage picture that we are watching, a change in focus and tone that can most effectively be conveyed through lighting.

If characters then start to dance – tapping up a storm for 'I Could Be Happy', or breaking into the 'Somewhere' dream ballet – they move to yet another new world of pure abstract expression, the focus shifting from the actors' faces to their bodies. Stylistically, almost anything becomes permissible: non-naturalistic shifts in colour and tone, flashing lights, special effects. Eventually the action returns again to the world of naturalism, only for the process to begin once again.

These enormous shifts in style and tone are unique to the musical. When designing the lighting for a show, you may need to create a plot that can accommodate and express them all.

Preparation

The lighting designer should begin by reading the libretto carefully. Make a list of the various locations and time shifts that occur, along with any references to lighting in the dialogue or stage directions, and any special effects that may be required.

Make a note of all the songs, including reprises, and listen to a recording to get a sense of their mood – upbeat, wistful, raunchy, comic and so on. Time them, too: an eight-minute number that starts as a solo and ends with the entire company hoofing across the stage will require multiple lighting cues as it builds to its climax.

Be aware that several different styles of lighting may be needed. This is particularly true of backstage musicals such as *42nd Street* and *Kiss Me Kate* where the 'on stage' scenes may be lit more artificially than the naturalistic 'off stage' scenes.

Working with the Creative Team

You will probably meet the other members of the creative team for the first time at the production meeting at which the full colour model is shown. As the designer and director go through the show scene by scene, make notes of the position of any large structures or major pieces of furniture. Make sure you understand the scale, form, colour, materials and textures of the elements of the set.

Talk to the director and set designer about their ideas on how the lighting should support the design and style of the production. Do they envisage it as primarily naturalistic, atmospheric, impressionistic, or a mixture of all the three? Will figures be picked out in spotlights? How highly coloured should the stage be? Do they want smoke, special effects or projections? How are they planning to cover scene changes? Are the front cloths going to be opaque or gauze? If the latter, do they want one scene to 'bleed' into another?

This is also the time to check out if there are any working or 'practical' lights on the stage: these could be anything from a table lamp, to an illuminated stairway that the cast will dance down in the finale.

Lighting designer Neil Fraser working on a design.

In proscenium arch theatres the fly bars are used to suspend both lighting and scenery. Double-check on the plan as to which bars the designer is intending to use, and which ones will be available for you. The designer may be planning to break down flat surfaces by spattering them with paint. Find out what colours will be used, and get a sample if you can. Pay particular attention to the floor – is it to be black, or painted? How reflective will the surface be?

Have a good look at the costume drawings, and any swatches of material that the costume designer has produced. Are the actors going to be dressed in chic silver and black, in muted pastels, or in bright primary colours? All these will affect your decision on what colour lighting to use.

Don't forget that the other designers are your collaborators, and that you will be working as a team for weeks to come. The model box and costume drawings are the result of a great deal of time and effort, and the showing of them can be a nerve-racking experience for all involved. Be appreciative of their work, even if it is not entirely to your taste. If you spot a technical issue that will create major lighting problems, point it out tactfully, and be as open-minded as possible in considering solutions.

Checking the Venue

Visit the venue as soon as you can to get the feel of its scale and atmosphere. If you are working in a proscenium arch theatre, check the flying system: some bars may be out of order or unsuitable for hanging lanterns, and it is as well to know this early on. Identify where the front-of-house lighting and follow spots are to be positioned.

Most theatres have a resident electrician or technical manager who will be able to provide you with a plan of the lighting grid. Ask them if the building has any technical quirks and idiosyncrasies: most theatres do. Listen to

Lanterns in the grid of the Jerwood Vanbrugh Theatre, RADA. Note the tension wire grid that the electricians can walk on while rigging.

what they have to tell you, and respect their experience: they have probably lit hundreds of shows on the stage in their time, and will be invaluable allies in helping you to realize your design most effectively.

If there is no resident electrician, or you are working in a non-theatre space, you will need to find a qualified expert who can supervise the supply and control of an adequate power supply. Custom-built theatres have a two- or three-phase electricity supply installed to meet the demands of stage lighting, and a high degree of expertise is required to work with such levels of power safely.

Remember that electricity is dangerous and potentially lethal. This is definitely not an area for unsupervised amateurs to start learning.

If there is no grid, work out where you will be able to position the lights. Will you be able to rig scaffolding bars in the ceiling, or will they have to be fixed on stands?

CHANNELS AND LANTERNS

Once you have established the artistic requirements of the show and the physical limitations of the venue, you can start making decisions about what kind of lights (or 'lanterns') need to be positioned where, in order to best achieve the desired effects. In the USA, lanterns are referred to as 'units'.

There are various types of lantern, each of which offers different possibilities in the intensity, focus, shape and colour of the light beam produced. When cabled up, each lantern or group of lanterns is assigned to a specific lighting channel. The amount of power passed to each lantern – and hence its brightness – is controlled by a series of dimmers. Combinations of different lanterns and lighting levels can then be mixed through a control board to create a wide range of different lighting 'states'. Small theatres may have as few as sixteen channels, large ones a hundred or more.

If you are hiring a theatre there may well be a stock of lanterns that you can use as part of the rental agreement, but you may need to hire more to light a musical effectively. If you are not working in a conventional theatre, you will have to hire a lighting desk, a set of dimmers and cabling, as well as the lanterns themselves, and that will be expensive. Get the production manager to tell you how many lanterns the production is likely to be able to afford before drawing up a detailed plan.

Drawing Up the Plan

You will need to produce a detailed lighting plan to show the arrangement and position of various lanterns around the theatre. This is

149

also referred to as the lighting 'design', and is drawn out on a scale plan of the grid using

Types of Lantern

The main generic types of theatre lantern currently in use are as follows:

Flood	Wide spread of light. No focus. Good for providing large washes of light over large areas, including backcloths and cycloramas.
Fresnel	Soft focus. Beam is variable in size. Shape is controlled by external shutters known as 'barn doors'.
Pc spot	Soft focus. Beam is variable in size. Has a more efficient lens than the fresnel and provides a more precise, brighter light. Barn doors.
Profile	Hard or soft focus. Variable beam size, especially in zoom version. Size of beam can also be controlled by an iris. Internal shutters. Can be fitted with a gobo. Useful for defining specific areas of the stage.
Parcan	Fixed focus with a very bright beam. Good for saturated colour washes.
Follow spot	Modified profile spots with fitted sights with which an operator can follow actors and light them as they move around the stage. Flip-over colour changers. Regularly used in musicals to highlight solo performers during songs.

industry-standard stencils to indicate the types of lantern used. Nowadays designs are increasingly produced on computers using specialist software packages such as WYSIWYG or AUTOCAD.

There are no hard and fast rules about how to light a show: each production is different, and will have its own unique challenges and limitations. However, the designer should always be aware of the following considerations when drawing up their plan.

The Direction of Light

Actors lit by direct front light can be clearly seen, but their features flatten out and become inexpressive. Back-lighting will make the actor appear in silhouette, a striking and dramatic effect. Lighting from the side and above creates interesting shadows, and makes the actors appear more three-dimensional. A 'general cover' for a naturalistic scene would combine light from all three sources to give the most effective result. Remember, however, that in naturalistic states the light must appear to have an identifiable source.

Lighting from below gives actors a slightly macabre appearance and may cast unwanted

Follow-spot operator at work.

shadows on the cyclorama. Side-lighting from ground level illuminates the body rather than the face, and is used extensively for lighting dance. The effect of side-lighting can be extremely atmospheric – just check that actors will be able to get on and off the stage before filling the wings with lanterns on stands.

Follow-spots are extremely useful to focus on actors during musical numbers. A hard-focus, bright white follow-spot is the most unashamedly theatrical form of lighting, and is the very epitome of 'showbiz'.

The Colour of Light

Too much bright white light can be wearying on the eye, lacks atmosphere, and ultimately becomes extremely boring to look at. Light can be coloured with 'gels', translucent plastic filters that fit in frames in front of lanterns. These are sold in large sheets that can then be cut to size. Most theatres have supplies of the standard colour gels: ask if you can borrow theirs before buying a lot of your own.

Unobtrusive straw, yellow and pale blue gels are useful for creating naturalistic states. Of course, when lighting a musical you may wish to use vivid reds, purples, pinks and dark blues to create arresting and imaginative non-naturalistic stage images. Inventive lighting designers may put two thicknesses of gel in one lantern to intensify the colour, or create a new one.

Each gel colour has an identifying code number. Write the relevant number in front of each lantern on the lighting plan to show which gel will be used.

Follow-spots have a series of flip-over frames containing a variety of gels, so they can change colour from cue to cue. Gels in other lanterns cannot normally be changed once the curtain is up. Very occasionally gels are changed in the interval, but usually only as a last resort to solve a particularly knotty lighting problem.

Moving Lights

In recent years computerized lights – generically known in the industry as 'moving' or 'intelligent' lights – have developed, the forerunner (and thus the most commonly referred to) being the 'Vari*lite'. Fitted with three primary or secondary colour light sources, they can produce an infinite variety of colours and do not require gels. They can also be programmed to move during the performance, lighting different areas of the stage or producing dramatic sweeping effects. A carousel holding a dozen or more prismatic gobos offers yet more lighting design options.

Though expensive to hire and requiring a trained operator to use, they can be extremely useful in working in non-theatre spaces where options for hanging lanterns are severely limited.

The use of a colour wheel, or 'scroller', will give you a greater variety of colour choices. Four or five different gels may be fitted on a colour wheel, typically up to sixteen or more on a scroller, which can be selected from the lighting board during the performance. These devices are particularly useful if you have only a limited number of lanterns and/or circuits – though, as ever, hiring them will add to your expenditure.

The Shape of Light

Your selection of a particular type of lantern for a specific job may depend on how effectively the shape of the beam can be controlled. The beams of floodlights cannot be altered at all, except by moving the lantern so that it casts a larger or smaller beam onto an object. The beams from fresnels can be controlled by external shutters known as 'barn doors' and focused to differing sizes, but as

151

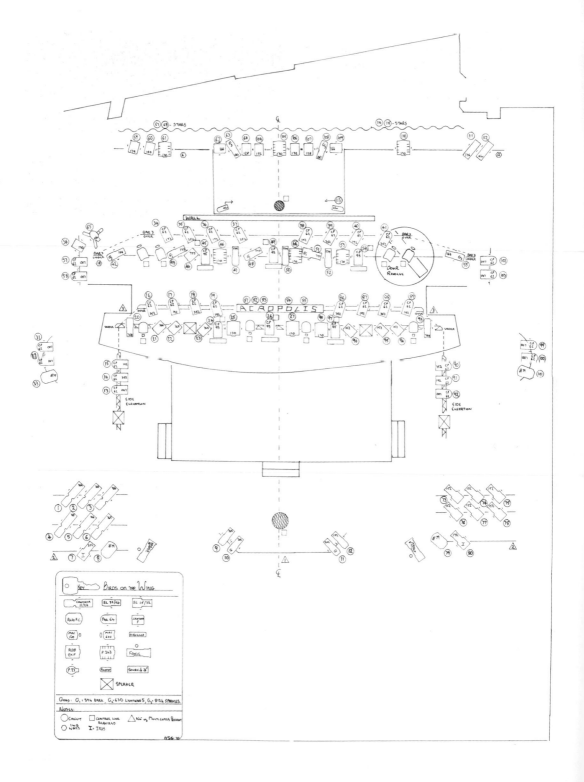

they are soft-focused they cannot be as effectively used to isolate areas of the stage. The shutters in profile lanterns, on the other hand, can be moved independently of each other, and can be focused to define a specific area without excess light spilling over on to the rest of the stage. They are particularly useful for lighting trucks and flown pieces, and for defining the limits of rooms.

Gobos

The shape and intensity of a lantern can further be changed by using 'gobos', metal or glass filters that break up the pure beam of light to create specific silhouettes and atmospheres. The theatre lighting department will have a copy of suppliers' catalogues if you are seeking a particular effect, or you can make your own out of heat-resistant metal.

A 'break-up' gobo can be used in soft focus to give the dappled effect of light coming through trees, while the sharply etched silhouette of a window or door can enhance the sense of the architecture of an imagined building.

Be aware that once a gobo is in a lantern, it is in there for the duration of the performance; also, it is unlikely that you will be able to use that lantern for anything but its single effect. A lantern such as this, that has only one function in the lighting design, is known as a 'special'.

OTHER EFFECTS

There are many other lighting devices and special effects that you may wish to include in your design, some very cheap, others extremely expensive.

*LEFT: **Neil Fraser's completed design for** Birds on the Wing **at the Playhouse Theatre, London.***

A selection of gobos and gel samples.

Musicals set in Manhattan cry out for the neon signs of Broadway, but they can be costly: a light box may provide an affordable alternative. Effects projectors can be used to project large-scale images such as clouds, snow and rain onto the cyclorama: just the thing for the wide-open skies of *Oklahoma!* Star cloths – backcloths covered in fairy lights or fibre optics – can provide the most romantic of skies, perfect for your romantic leads to sing beneath, especially if used in conjunction with a glass moon gobo. Mirror balls can be surprisingly effective in creating a sense of magic and wonder.

If you are designing a rock musical, you may wish to use a 'chaser', which will flash groups of lanterns off and on to give a sense of excitement and movement. Strobe lights are now used less frequently than in the seventies and eighties, but can still produce an extraordinary 'silent movie' effect. Be aware, though, that certain strobe speeds are illegal as they can provoke spasms and epileptic fits. If you use a strobe you must post warning signs in the auditorium.

Certain fabrics, paints and dyes fluoresce under ultraviolet (UV) light. Extraordinary magical transformations and gravity-defying effects can be achieved by the actors performing in specially treated costumes in front of a black frontcloth under UV light – though nowadays this technique is more generally used in pantomime and children's theatre than mainstream musicals.

Smoke, Dry Ice and Pyrotechnics

Smoke can be very effective in creating an atmosphere of mystery and danger. It can also add texture to the stage, revealing coloured beams of light in mid-air to breath-taking effect. Smoke machines heat up a special non-toxic fluid to produce a white vapour, which is then released under pressure. Some cheaper models may be unreliable and difficult to control; they may also emit a characteristic hiss that can be very distracting in quiet moments.

If you are feeling very ambitious you might consider using dry ice (liquid carbon dioxide); when this is put in water, dense white vapour is produced. Heavier than air, it flows across the stage to provide an unearthly effect; actors seem to float across the stage in moments of pure theatrical magic. However, it can be very expensive, and great care is required when storing it.

Pyrotechnics, flashes, fireworks and maroons also come under the lighting designer's control. Strict safety measures must be observed when using them, and you should discuss the theatre's policies with the resident stage manager or chief electrician before proceeding.

CUTTING BACK

Inevitably you will not be able to include everything you would like to have in your design: there are not enough circuits, not enough lanterns, and never, ever enough money.

Find ways of simplifying your lighting plan. If several lanterns are always going to be used together, group them together on one circuit.

Can lanterns that are used in the Act One general cover satisfactorily be used in Act Two? Will using scrollers enable you to cut down the total number of lanterns required? Can the number of specials be reduced or simplified? Can you create a moonlit night with a lit cyclorama and star gobos, rather than with a star cloth? Will one smoke machine do instead of two? Can you make do without the effects projector?

It is unpleasant to have to compromise, but you may have no option. Ask the director and designer to list their priorities, and brainstorm other possibilities with them. As so often in creative endeavour, the need to rethink issues may lead you to an alternative solution that is better than the original.

FINALIZING THE DESIGN

As rehearsals progress you should attend at least one run-through of the whole show. Rehearsal is an organic process, and the actors' blocking may change frequently. It is quite possible that the action at a run-through is very different from what the director described to you six weeks previously.

Before the production moves into the theatre, make up a lighting-cue synopsis, numbering all the cues, scene by scene, the time the cue will take to fade up or down to its completed state, the effect to be achieved and any other relevant notes. Give a copy of this to the stage manager and the DSM before plotting rehearsals begin.

Things will change. The lighting plan and cue synopsis represent the best guess you can make up to this point. When at long last you see the lights working in the theatre you will always want to make adjustments, move a lantern, change a gel, add an extra cue here, cut one there. So make sure that your completed lighting plan is comprehensive enough to meet all the forseeable requirements of the

PAGE	ACTION	LX Q	F/Spot Q	TIME	LIGHTING
	House open	1			Preset cosy candles on tables H/L
	Clearance	2			Build bring in foh rainy cold night outside H/L out
4	Safe the lights	3			Not so cosy maybe half light toppy
4	Start of cleo's song		1		F/Spot on cleo
5	End of Cleo's song		2		F/Spot out
7	Cleo finds tie pin	4		30	Cheat up light a bit on Rosabella and in center where action is happier bring in light from SR to catch R when she is near Cash desk
9	Cashier enters SR	5		3	LX 3 and SR light on Rosabella near cash desk dreaming
11	Rosabella sings		3		F/Spot Rosabella
11	Rosabella sings	6		15	Fade down lighting state
11	End of song	7		1	B/O
11	Start of scene 2 Music	8		4	Full stage bright and sunny
					F/spot Highlight Tony Marie steps into his light when she sings bring state down a bit

Lighting cue synopsis for The Most Happy Fella.

production, but allow yourself some room for manoeuvre so that you can accommodate new ideas.

Have a couple of options for tricky scenes. Keep two or three channels free, and make sure you order an extra profile lantern or two. You will inevitably find a use for them once you start plotting. Make sure you have some spare cables, plenty of extra gels, and a selection of gobos to hand, too. From the moment you start rigging the lights in the theatre, you will be working against the clock.

SOUND DESIGN

Over the last thirty-five years or so, no aspect of stage musicals has changed so significantly or been so influential in shaping modern ideas about production style as sound design.

Developments in micro-circuitry, recording, sound modification and digital audio technology have offered directors and producers a whole new range of opportunities for staging and choreography that were undreamed of in the Rodgers and Hammerstein era. Librettists and composers have responded by conceiving shows that push existing technology to the limit, leading in turn to yet more sophisticated technical developments. Despite this, however, sound design remains the most unappreciated and undervalued aspect of theatre production.

This is partly due to the fact that everybody is now used to the perfect sound quality of digitally reproduced music on CD, television and film. So when we attend a live performance of a musical, we automatically assume that we will be able to hear every word and that the audio balance of cast and orchestra, spoken

155

dialogue and song, will be flawless. While audiences will appreciate a stunning costume, a wonderful set or even a dazzling lighting effect, they will only be aware of the sound design when it is imperfect. Nobody leaves a theatre saying, 'Wasn't the sound great?' – but they *will* say, 'Wasn't that awful, I couldn't hear a word, my whole evening was ruined.'

The Principles of Sound Design

Any object that vibrates – a guitar string, a drum-head, a vocal cord – creates a sound wave. Individual sound waves combine with others to create complex patterns of varying pitch and volume. The human ear has an astonishing ability to capture and select these patterns, which are then interpreted by the brain as meaningful sounds.

When we watch actors speaking in a theatre with good acoustics, our brains take care of the sound design automatically. Sight and sound combine to provide us with a reassuring sense of reality. However, if there is the slightest inconsistency between the senses – say, if a door slams stage left then a character enters stage right – the brain is confused. We feel momentarily dislocated. The action on stage feels unnatural, and in some strange way fake.

In a straight play it is the director's job to make sure that the cast are speaking clearly and can be heard. The sound designer will then work to create a seamless balance between their voices and the volume and directionality of any sound effects or incidental music.

Musicals are far more complex. A vast range of sounds from a variety of sources – speaking

Calamity Jane belting out 'The Deadwood Stage'. No matter how strong a voice an actor may have, if the theatre is large and the band amplified, she will need some kind of microphone. GSA Conservatoire production at the Yvonne Arnaud Theatre, Guildford. Director, John Gardyne; designer, Janey Gardiner; lighting designer, Alex Rails. Photo: Mark Dean

and singing voices, acoustic instruments, electric instruments, pre-recorded sound effects, samplers – must be captured by microphones, balanced at a mixing desk, amplified and distributed through loudspeakers into the auditorium, so that the overall result is comprehensible and pleasing for all members of the audience.

It is the sound designer's responsibility to ensure that what members of the audience hear matches what they see.

MODERN SOUND DESIGN IN MUSICAL THEATRE

In the early days of the musical, the main consideration in casting lead roles was whether or not an actor could sing well enough to be heard over the orchestra. Large choruses beefed up the sound at relevant moments, and the conductor controlled the volume and musical dynamics from the podium. The staging of musical numbers had to be kept simple, as the actors spent most of their time downstage centre singing their hearts out.

Some rudimentary amplification began to appear in larger Broadway theatres after World War II. The 1960s saw the arrival of rock'n'roll, electric instruments and amplified pop groups. In the spirit of the age, musicals such as *Hair* and *Stomp* abandoned the traditional pit orchestra in favour of an on-stage rock band. The performers used hand-held microphones like pop singers, and the volume went up overnight.

Jesus Christ Superstar was originally released as a vinyl 'concept album', so when it was produced at London's Palace Theatre, audiences already had preconceptions about how it should sound. The production used both an on-stage rock group and a pit band, with the latter amplified to match the volume levels of the former. The sound was then mixed to reproduce the studio production of the album.

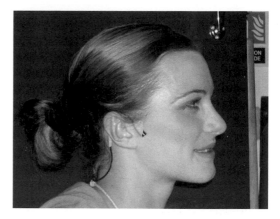

Actor fitted with a radio mic.

Again, the performers used hand-held microphones, which helped identify which character was singing at any one time.

Superstar also saw the early use of a rudimentary radio microphone, a cable-free device that allows an actor to go anywhere on stage – even to face upstage – without affecting the volume or quality of the sound heard by the audience. Radio mics started to be used more widely for leading performers, usually in conjunction with 'float' microphones on the stage and rifle microphones in the wings and/or at the front of the stage to amplify the chorus. At that time radio mics were extremely expensive and beyond the budgets of all but the richest theatre companies, and were technically unreliable.

However, the technology continued to improve, and when *Cats* opened in London in 1981 another landmark was reached: for the first time every member of the company was fitted with an individual radio mic – with a corresponding rise in overall volume.

The use of individual radio mics rapidly became the norm in professional productions, and a new world of possibility opened up for directors and choreographers. Within three years the cast of *Starlight Express* were roller-

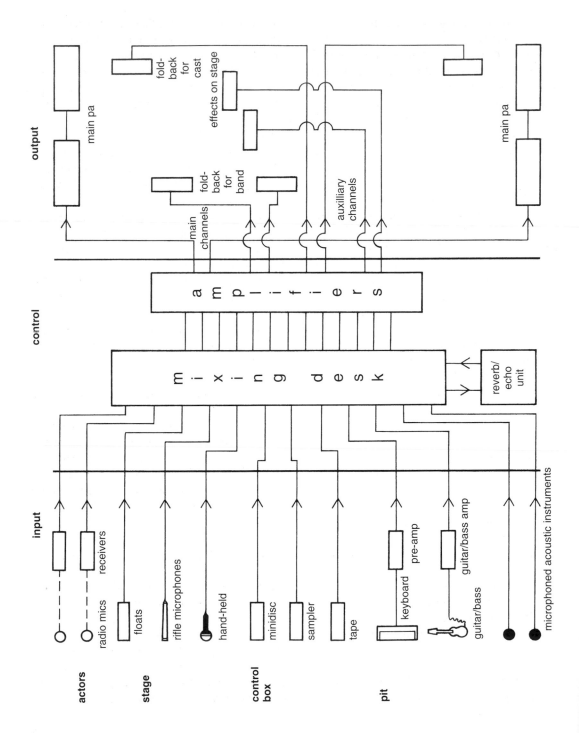

skating above, below and behind the audience as they acted and sang, with the sound balance unaffected.

Some theatre professionals – and some theatre-goers – feel that, as the sound of musicals has become more heavily controlled and amplified, the sound quality, paradoxically, has got worse. They argue that much of the richness, colour and subtlety of expression of which the human voice is capable has been sacrificed in favour of the crude sense of excitement produced by ever-increasing volume. They also claim that audiences have lost the ability to listen carefully, and are becoming passive recipients of bland walls of sound, rather than being active participants in a dramatic exchange with the performers; and that the performers, in turn, are losing the ability to articulate, project and communicate, skills that lie at the very heart of the actor's craft. The debate will no doubt continue.

However, in recent years, many leading designers have created increasingly subtle and unobtrusive sound designs in an attempt, ironically, to create the illusion of acoustic, unamplified speech and song – which is what we started off with in the first place.

Preparation

If you are designing the sound for a musical, the starting point, as ever, is the libretto. Read it carefully and make a list of the scenes and musical numbers. Listen to the soundtrack and get familiar with the style of the songs – though be aware that your production may not be using the orchestral arrangements that you hear on a CD – nor will you necessarily have such competent singers.

Talk to the director and other designers to get a sense of the scale of the production. Will

LEFT: Schematic diagram of the sound system required for an amplified musical.

there be five performers or fifty? A single piano or a twenty-piece band? A stage three metres wide, or thirty? An audience of fifty or five hundred? Look at the model box: is the set full of soft drapes and gauzes that will absorb sound, or does it have sculptural, hard-edged structures that it will bounce off?

Visiting the Theatre

As soon as you can, visit the theatre to get an idea of its acoustic quality. Take someone with you – preferably a friendly member of the cast – who can speak and sing on stage while you listen from various positions in the auditorium. Don't forget the circle and boxes, and pay particular attention to seats under overhanging balconies.

Try speaking on stage yourself. How does it feel? Does the sound of your voice disappear up into the flies? Get your companion to stand at the back and find out how much vocal effort you have to make so they can hear you clearly.

Some theatres have a Head of Sound; at others, this responsibility is shared between the resident technicians and the stage management team. Find out exactly what type of PA system and other equipment the theatre possesses. How many loudspeakers are there, and where are they distributed? How many other output channels are available? Do not assume that the existing equipment will be sufficient for your needs.

Ask a member of staff to play some music through the PA, then walk about the auditorium. Is the sound distributed equally throughout, or are there dead spots where it suddenly seems to disappear? Now go up on stage and listen: does it sound the same? Clearer? Louder? Fuzzier? (Be sure to take a cast recording of the show or something in a similar style with you to the theatre, otherwise you may end up listening to a CD by a technician's favourite heavy metal band!)

159

Pay particular attention to where the musicians will be: is there an orchestra pit? Or will you be taking out seats to accommodate them in the auditorium? Or maybe they will be in the wings? Or at the back of the stage? Will they be seen by the audience or not? The location of the band is probably the single most important factor you need to take into account when planning your sound design: ignore it at your peril.

All theatres are built with at least some thought given to their acoustics – though some are much better than others in this respect. No such thought will necessarily have gone into the design of a church hall, a barn or a gym – and certainly not a swimming pool. If you are performing in a non-theatre space, you may have to deal with an extremely unhelpful acoustic.

In that case you will have to source extra hardware – loudspeakers, amplifiers, microphones, a mixing desk, and cables. It will be expensive. Producers and directors sometimes expect sound designers to perform miracles and transform a building with a nightmarish acoustic totally unsuited to performance into Carnegie Hall – on a shoestring budget, of course.

Rifle microphones and lanterns rigged at the front of the stage.

Types and Direction of Microphone

Moving coil or dynamic microphones are most commonly used for live performance as they are sturdy, reliable, and respond well to the frequency range of the human voice.

Condenser and capacitor microphones employ a phantom power supply to boost their sensitivity. Rifle, float and radio microphones typically use this technology.

Ribbon microphones are more sensitive, but less robust than either of the above, and are usually only used for studio recording.

Omni-directional microphones pick up sounds coming from any direction.

Cardioid or uni-directional microphones are mainly sensitive to sounds from only one direction. They are useful for live performance as they do not pick up unwanted sounds from other performers or instruments.

Hyper-cardioid microphones are uni-directional, but also pick up a limited amount of sound from the opposite direction, adding a sense of atmosphere to the signal produced.

Bi-directional or figure-of-eight microphones are sensitive to sounds from two diametrically opposite sources, and are typically used for recording radio drama.

MICROPHONING THE STAGE

If you are performing in a small theatre and using a solo piano or small, mainly acoustic band, it is preferable not to use any amplification at all. However, if the band is louder, the theatre bigger, and – quite possibly – the singers less confident, you may feel it is necessary to use microphones to boost the sound levels. Be warned: once you start using amplification it is difficult to know where to stop.

It is increasingly the norm for principal actors to use radio mics. If you are working with limited resources you may wish to consider cheaper, less complex alternatives.

Attach several float microphones to the front of the stage to get a general cover of the downstage area. (They are essential for capturing the sound of tap dancers, too.) Rifle microphones, positioned in the flies or at the front of the stage, are more sensitive and can be aimed at specific points on the set – at the top of Dolly's staircase, say, or at the fiddler on the roof. They are particularly useful for amplifying upstage areas where inexperienced singers may find it difficult to project their voices from.

Used with sensitivity and care, a combination of float and rifle microphones can achieve highly effective results, though they cannot offer the same sophisticated level of control as radio mics.

MICROPHONING PERFORMERS

Hand-held microphones are essential props for rock showmanship and cabaret. However, although used briefly in the rock musicals of the late 1960s and 1970s, they are intrusive in most dramatic settings. You may wish to use one to give the impression of a public meeting or an on-stage performance, but otherwise their use in musicals is limited. Of course you may need to have a microphone in the wings – either handheld or on a stand – for the disembodied voice of Aurora in *Kiss of the Spiderwoman*, or Audrey II in *Little Shop of Horrors*.

If the chorus get short of breath and find it difficult to create enough volume during energetic dance routines, extra actors singing into an offstage microphone can be used to boost and balance the sound. 'Booth singers', who may not even appear on stage at all, are frequently used in large-scale professional productions in this way.

Radio Microphones

Nowadays many professional performers will not even contemplate performing in a musical without a radio mic, so amateurs can hardly be blamed for feeling the same way.

The microphones themselves are the size of a small bead, and can be concealed in the hairline, by the ear, or clipped to the front of a costume. They are powered by battery packs the size of a cigarette packet, which are attached to the actors' bodies in a sweat-resistant pouch. Each radio mic produces a signal at a specific frequency that is then picked up by aerials on a series of receivers connected directly to the mixing desk.

Make sure that the wardrobe department know which actors will be using radio mics, as this may have implications for costume changes and the styling of the their hair, hats and wigs.

You can cut down on hire costs by sharing radio mics between actors. A character who appears for only one scene in the second half will be able to use the same mic as a character who disappears at the end of Act One. Draw up a microphone plot showing the route that each mic will take during the show, allowing a realistic amount of time for the changeover. Principal characters should always stay on one mic channel throughout, or matters may get very complicated for the sound operator during performance. Don't overdo mic doubling – it may prove counter-productive. Swapping tiny mics in poorly lit, crowded wings during the performance can be a fiddly and distracting business for the performers, and increases the likelihood of technical failure.

Once you get into the theatre you will need to appoint a microphone runner to be responsible for making sure the right person gets the right mic at the right time.

Radio mic plot for Honk!, showing how six mics can be shared between thirteen characters.

Mic No.	Ii — Poultry Tale	Joy of Mother-hood	Diff-erent	Hold Your Head	Look At Him	Iii — Diff-erent	Play With Your Food	Elegy	Iiii — Goose March	Finale	Ii — Takes All Sorts	Hold Your Head	To-gether	Iii — Coll-age	Now I've Seen You	Iiii — Warts And All	Snow	Iiv — Awak-ening	Finale	Curtain Call
1	Ugly	–	–	Ugly	Ugly	Ugly	Ugly	–	Ugly	Ugly	Ugly	Ugly	Ugly	–	Ugly	Ugly	Ugly	Ugly	Ugly	Ugly
2	Drake	–	–	–	Drake	–	–	–	–	–	–	–	–	Drake	–	–	–	–	Drake	Drake
3	Maureen	Maureen	–	–	Maureen	–	–	–	Greylag	–	Queenie	Queenie	Queenie	–	–	Bullfrog	–	–	Grace	Grace
4	Turkey	–	–	–	Turkey	–	–	–	Dot	–	Lowbutt	Lowbutt	Lowbutt	–	–	–	–	Penny	Penny	Penny
5	Cat	–	–	–	Cat	–	Cat	–	Cat	–	–	–	Cat	–	–	–	Cat	Cat	–	Cat
6	Ida	Ida	Ida	Ida	Ida	–	–	Ida	–	Ida	–	–	–	Ida	–	–	Ida	Ida	Ida	Ida

Transmission Frequency Licensing

Radio mics were bedevilled with technical glitches when they first appeared, not least because of the confusion over on which frequencies they should transmit. Radio messages from passing taxis and police cars would suddenly boom out of theatre PA systems in the middle of tender love scenes. On the press night of *Starlight Express* radio mic frequencies were severely disrupted by a TV outside broadcast covering the event.

That led to a major rethink of the problem, and in the UK the Radio Communications Agency was set up to organize matters. However, laws governing which frequencies are, and are not available for transmission in the UK are extremely complex, and subject to local legislation.

Up-to-date information on the use and licensing of wireless transmission equipment in the UK can be found on the web site of the Joint Frequencies Management Group Ltd at www.jfmg.co.uk

Unless you have a huge budget it will be impractical to fit radio mics on all your actors. Use general stage mics for the chorus, radio mics for the leads, and aim to mix an acceptable balance of the two during performance. This is not as easy as it sounds. Live mixing requires a good ear, lots of concentration and great sensitivity to the interplay of music, lyrics and dialogue.

MICROPHONING MUSICIANS

The extent to which you microphone the musicians will depend on the size of band, the nature of the instruments and the style of music being played. The orchestra for *The Pirates of Penzance* will present different problems from the band for *Tommy*.

Arrange a meeting with the MD and find out how the band will be arranged on the night. Most MDs like to have the strings to their left, woodwind in the middle, and brass to their right with the drums behind, though personal preferences vary.

Acoustic instruments – the strings, woodwind, brass and possibly percussion – will need to be amplified through microphones, either individually or as a group. Electric keyboards and guitars require amplifiers to boost or distort the signal they produce, and these are then connected to the mixing desk by a direct input or 'DI'.

You may need to use acoustic screens to keep the sounds of the individual instruments separate and discreet. The drums are always the loudest things in the pit and may threaten to overwhelm the other instruments; a drummer who can play softly is a great asset. If you are in a tiny theatre but the musical arrangement includes drums, you might consider using drum synthesizer pads, which create no

Amplified orchestra pit. Note the acoustic screen in the foreground.

163

An extensive selection of sound-effect CDs in the sound studio at RADA.

acoustic sound and whose volume can be controlled through the mixing desk.

THE MIXING DESK

When the sound system is installed in the theatre, cables from the various sound sources – microphones, radio mic receivers, electric instruments plus tape or mini-disc players for recorded sound effects (*see below*) – are plugged into the input channels of the mixing desk.

During each performance the sound designer or their assistant will use the desk to equalize, or 'EQ', the signals from the input channels so the sound mix remains rich and clear. Echo and reverberation may also be used to intercept the signal and modify it further.

Needless to say, computerized desks with highly sophisticated software are increasingly commonplace. Sound technology changes rapidly, and the layman may find it difficult to keep up with the latest developments. Aura Sound Design Ltd provides up-to-date information at its web site www.aurasound.co.uk.

Outputting the Sound

The sound is output from the desk to a series of amplifiers, and then to various loudspeakers around the theatre. The number and location of these will depend on the size of the venue, the complexity of the sound design, the technical capacity of the mixing desk and the number of amplifiers available.

The source of the sound should always appear to be the action on stage, so speakers carrying the main stereo output should be placed above or to the side of it. Large loudspeakers can be visually intrusive, especially if the show is set in an historical period, and you should discuss the aesthetic considerations with the set designer. Speakers can be concealed behind black gauze without affecting their sound quality.

In larger theatres you may need to install speakers behind and to the side of the audience to distribute the sound evenly throughout the auditorium. Digital sound-delay machines can be used to delay the arrival of the output signal to speakers by fractions of a millisecond, so that the sound is synchronized with stage action and does not have the disorientating effect of appearing to originate from behind the audience.

Auxiliary outputs can be used for monitor or 'foldback' speakers in the orchestra pit so the MD can hear the actors properly. Monitor speakers may also be needed behind the stage or in the wings so that the cast, in turn, can hear the band. You may also have to conceal speakers in the set and on the stage if you are using sound effects that need to originate from a specific source – say a radio, a child's crib, or an on-stage musical instrument.

CUTTING BACK

Like the lighting designer, the sound designer always wants more – more microphones, more speakers, more effects, a bigger mixing desk – than the budget will allow. Cuts have to be made and compromises reached: these are frustrating, but inevitable.

It is worth remembering that the 'perfect' sound design is impossible to achieve. Even if you employed the most skilful technicians, spent a fortune on all the latest equipment and used literally hundreds of speakers and microphones, there would always be room for some tiny improvement somewhere. Console yourself with that thought as the production manager slashes your budget for the third time.

SOUND EFFECTS

The sound designer is also responsible for providing any sound effects or ambient background noise that the production may require. As you read through the libretto, note any specific sound effects that are mentioned in the dialogue or stage directions – gunshots, telephones, thunder, doorbells and so on. Keep an eye on the rehearsal reports to make

sure that you are aware of any new ones that get added. The DSM should make a note if the effects are required to last for a specific duration of time, and if they are to be created live in the wings, or need to be pre-recorded.

You may consider using ambient sound under scenes to give a specific sense of place and atmosphere: birds singing in the trees, the crash of waves on the seashore, traffic on a busy city street. Some productions of straight plays use ambient sound virtually throughout. However, in musicals this extra auditory colour is sometimes provided by the orchestra – birdsong may be suggested by flutes, sirens by saxophones, thunder by timpani. Check this with the director and MD before starting working through the night on multi-layered background tracks.

Most large music shops have a section devoted to special effects CDs, and recordings are often organized into categories such as 'machines', 'animals', 'weather' – even 'death and horror'. The BBC has produced a series of disks specifically intended for amateur use that are widely available. Effects can also be downloaded via the internet from sound libraries, but these are primarily intended for professional use and can be very expensive. Check out sites such as www.sound-ideas.com, www.hollywoodedge.com, www.dewolfemusic.co.uk and www.sound-dogs.com to find out more.

Many sound designers take great pride and pleasure in creating and recording their own sound effects, and you may find that it is more satisfying – and much cheaper – to do so too. The widespread availability of samplers, digital recording and audio-editing software on PCs provides affordable opportunities for stunning and innovative work. Don't get too carried away, though: the director will certainly cut any sound cues that could distract the audience from the musical score, and your efforts may be wasted.

DAMES AT SEA

SOUND CUES

ACT 1

CUE	PAGE		DURATION
1	Pre Show	The buzz of an audience filling the theatre	10 mins.
2	7	Offstage demolition fx. – jackhammer or pneumatic drill	5 secs.
3	23	Offstage – wall falling over	
4	23	Offstage – loud crash	
5	23	Offstage – louder crash	
6	29	Offstage – demolition crash	
7	29	Offstage – louder demolition crash	
8	30	Offstage – much louder demolition fx. and crash	
9	31	Offstage – whole theatre is demolished and crashes down	

N.B. You can hear the crashes etc. building in the last number on side one of the cassette.

ACT 2

CUE	PAGE		DURATION
10	31	New York harbour track – hooters, ships horns, engines, dockside fx. etc., 1930s (This may also be played while the audience comes back in)	5 mins.
11	37	Rain fx. – steady, heavy rain (Possibly only – not yet certain	2 mins.
12	40–42	Harbour fx. (as Q 10) (Again, not yet set)	5 mins.
13	46–47	Audience reaction to show in progress (Heard offstage) Coming from show relay, crackly, with calls, taped music and applause etc. – in response to an Adagio Act (or similar)	1 min.
14	47–48	Applause cues – several and building in intensity	
15	49–51	Loud applause – huge standing ovation	2 mins.

Plugs and Cables

If you are hiring sound equipment, make sure that you order the right cables, and particularly the right plugs, for the hardware. While lighting equipment is generally manufactured to a single standard, audio equipment is supplied with a baffling range of plugs, sockets and connectors that are all incompatible with each other.

It is frustrating in the extreme to arrive at the theatre and find that none of the components of your sound system will fit together.

If you are asked to produce a certain effect – a barking dog for instance, or a distant church bell – record several alternatives, play them through to the director, and decide between you which is the most effective. Cues may need to be lengthened or shortened, edited, slowed down or speeded up. If ambient sound is to be played under a scene, find out how long it runs in rehearsal, and record double that amount. You can then be sure it will not run out during a performance when the leading man is late for his entrance and the scene proceeds at a leaden pace.

Making up a Sound Disk or Tape

As the production week nears, you need to make a master recording of all the sound effects, in order. Only a few years ago these had to be recorded onto reel-to-reel tape and the various sections spliced together manually with lengths of leader tape. Sound designers huddled over their desks with razor blades and lengths of coloured leader all around them. Today, most theatres are equipped with mini-disc players, and these have removed much of this fiddly and time-consuming work.

If effects are to be played simultaneously – an explosion occurring during a rainstorm, for instance – they will need to be recorded on separate discs, and several mini-disc players may be required. Some theatres use samplers to provide simultaneous effects; others have the capacity to record sound effects directly onto the hard drive of a PC, offering greater flexibility and more sophisticated control of the sound. No doubt this will become standard practice in due course.

Attending Rehearsals

If sound effects need to be synchronized with stage action, it will be a great help if you give the DSM a copy of the disc so the actors hear it in rehearsal.

Make sure you drop into rehearsals from time to time. On the night, both actors and musicians will be relying on you to make the show sound as good as possible, so the more of an understanding you have of their work and abilities, the better.

Attending a run-through in the final week will provide you with invaluable information. Inevitably, blocking will have changed, and you may find that Annie is singing 'Tomorrow' from a completely different position than you were told. You may also find that five extra people have been added to a song you thought was a duet.

LEFT: *Sound cue synopsis for* **Dames at Sea.**

12 PRODUCTION WEEK

Most theatre rentals run on a weekly basis from Sunday to Saturday. If you are hiring a venue, you will get access to the building either on Sunday or early Monday morning. Depending on how many hours you are allowed to be in the theatre, your show may then open on Tuesday, Wednesday or Thursday night. Even if you are planning to run for months, the week you get into the theatre and open is known as 'production week'. The process of installing a new production in a theatre is referred to as the 'get-in'.

Production week is a stressful time for all concerned. There is a huge amount of work to get done in a limited amount of time, lots of people are involved, everybody has their own agenda and tempers can fray. Scheduling and prioritizing the work is the responsibility of the production manager, and careful planning is essential if things are to run smoothly.

Of course, if you have access to your performance space earlier, the pressure of time will not be so great, and your production 'week' can be spread out over a longer period.

RIGHT: Production schedule for **The Most Happy Fella.** *The theatre is available from 9am Sunday morning, and the first performance is scheduled for 7:30pm on Wednesday evening.*

Production Schedule

Between getting into the theatre and the opening night, the following jobs have to be completed:

- Rigging: hanging, cabling and connecting the lighting and sound equipment.
- Fitting up: assembling all the elements of the set, building them on stage, then hanging them in the flies and storing them in the wings as appropriate.
- Focusing: ensuring that the lanterns are correctly focused, shaped and coloured.
- Plotting: building and recording the lighting states, and fixing their exact timing and cue points. Sound effect cues also need to be plotted.
- Technical rehearsal: running through all lighting, sound and stage cues with technicians and cast in costume.
- Sound check/band rehearsal: checking the acoustic or amplified sound balance between cast and orchestra.
- First dress rehearsal: a complete run-through of the show as per performance, usually done without the orchestra.
- Final dress rehearsal: a complete run-through of the show as per performance with full orchestra.

PRODUCTION SCHEDULE

THE MOST HAPPY FELLA

DATE	TIME	EVENT	CALLED
Sun 28/10	9–1	LX Rig	JT; MH; AP; JF; JL; SMOY x2
	10am	Load Van – Kadek	JG; SH; RM; JB; DW; RS; DB
	11.30am	Unload set – Mill	
	12pm	Fit up commences	NH to join
	1–2	Lunch	
	2–6	Rig and fit up continue	
	6–7	Supper break	
	7–11	LX Focus	
		Fit up and set dressing continue	
	11pm	Call ends	
Mon 29/10	9am	Prep for plotting	JT; JG; MH; Show crew
	10am	LX Plot commences	GT to join
	1–2	Lunch	
	2–5.30	LX Plot continues	
	5.30–6.30	Supper	
	6pm	Cast called	Full cast
	7pm	Technical rehearsal commences	Full company
	10.30pm	Call ends	
Tues 30/10	9am	Company call for tech	Full company
	10–1	Technical continues	GT to join
	1–2	Lunch	
	2–6	Technical continues	
	6–7	Supper break	
	6.55pm	Half-Hour call	Full company
	7.30pm	Dress Rehearsal 1	
	10.30pm	Call ends	
Wed 31/10	AM	Stage free for technical work	As called
	1.55pm	Half Hour Call	Full company
	2.30pm	Dress Rehearsal 2 followed by notes	
	6.55pm	Half Hour Call	Full company
	7.30pm	Performance 2	
Fri 2/11	1pm	Crew call to set back	Show crew
	1.55pm	Half Hour call	Full company
	2.30pm	Performance 3	
	6.55pm	Half Hour call	Full company
	7.30pm	Performance 4	
Sat 3/11	1pm	Crew call to set back	Show crew
	1.55pm	Half Hour call	Full company
	2.30pm	Performance 5	
	6.55pm	Half Hour call	Full company
	7.30pm	Performance 6	
		FOLLOWED BY STRIKE	

Even so, you will still need to draw up a detailed schedule to ensure that all the necessary work gets done in time for opening night.

The production manager and stage manager will have been planning the move into the theatre since the first production meeting. A draft schedule should be prepared well in advance, and modified if necessary. Once it is agreed with the director and creative team, print it and distribute copies to all departments. It is important that everybody understands the time constraints their colleagues are working under.

WORKING IN THE THEATRE

Theatres are dangerous places. People are working both at height and in cramped conditions; they use power tools and electrical equipment; hours are long, and they may get tired and careless.

Working conditions and practices for professional technicians are now strictly regulated by union agreements. In addition, every theatre has a health and safety policy that must be adhered to by law. The production manager should become familiar with this, and ensure that anyone who comes into the building to work, whether amateur or professional, is fully aware of the risks and safety regulations.

Particular care should be taken when working up ladders, lifting heavy weights, and working with any electrical equipment. Lanterns can heat up very quickly, so protective gloves should always be worn when working with them. If anything is thrown – or drops – onto the stage from the flies the normal warning cry is 'Heads'. 'Going dark' means that the electricians are about to turn off the lights and plunge the stage into darkness.

There is a lot of hefting and carrying to do during production week, and extra manpower will be needed. Recruiting the crew is another of the production manager's responsibilities.

The theatre staff will be able to put you in touch with 'casuals', temporary employees who work on get-ins regularly, but you will have to pay them the going rate. If you are relying on volunteers, make sure they appreciate exactly when and for how long they will be expected to work.

In professional theatres the lighting, sound, stage and props departments usually have their own dedicated crew members. If you are working with amateurs, assign people to specific departments for efficiency. Appoint a dedicated flyman, who should stay up on the fly floor whenever equipment is being rigged on stage. It can waste a lot of time to have someone running up and down a ladder every time a bar needs to be flown in or out.

Before the get-in begins, the stage manager should ensure that the stage is clean, and that all remains of the previous production have been removed. A temporary set of steps or 'treads' from stage to auditorium may be useful. Make sure these are safe and secure.

The crew will need refreshment: supply tea, coffee and water, plus plenty of cups, and ashtrays for smoking areas. Get-ins generate vast amounts of rubbish, so bring plenty of bin bags, too.

You should always plan to finish work half an hour before lock-up time to allow for clearing up at the end of the day. Give the caretaker, the stage-door keeper or whoever is responsible for locking up the building a copy of the schedule so they know what is going on. Always be polite and friendly to them: you may need their co-operation later on.

Some venues and/or some production teams issue 'passes', laminated tags that indicate the department you are working for, and the areas that you are allowed to access. Other venues may require a list of names to be allowed entrance at the stage door. The production manager should make sure that all security procedures are adhered to.

RIGGING

If you are hiring sound and light equipment, the production manager should fix a specific time for delivery and have the crew ready and waiting for its arrival. The hardware will arrive in bulky metal flight cases, and you will have to make sure that there is somewhere these can be stored.

Unload the equipment, lay it out on the stage, and check that nothing is missing. It is much easier for the electricians to see what they are doing if they have plenty of room to work in, so try and keep the stage free of bits of set and props.

Always make sure that the lighting power supply is turned off before you start rigging.

Rig lights on fly bars first, as you will then leave the stage free for other departments as quickly as possible. Fly in each bar that is being used down to stage level, remove any lanterns that are already on it, and replace them with the lanterns as per the lighting design. Each lantern should be checked on a live circuit to make sure it is working properly before moving on to the next one. Only fly in as many bars as you can easily work around at any one time, and fly them out as soon as you have finished with them.

A series of cables is then taped along the bar, one for each lantern; in Britain the resulting thick mass of cables is known as 'tripe'. The individual cables are numbered at each end, so you can make a record of which cable is connected to which lantern. A manufactured device known as a 'multi-core', which is easier to manage, may be used as an alternative in some theatres.

Fit any gobos, gels or shutters that are specified on the plan. Each cable is then plugged into one of the input circuits of the theatre's lighting system, with each lantern or group of

Unpacking hired lanterns. Note the large flight cases they have been delivered in: these will have to be stored somewhere.

lanterns having a dedicated circuit number. The lighting designer or chief electrician should normally specify where each lantern should be plugged in on the plan; if this has not been done, mark up the circuit numbers as you go. Each circuit is then assigned to a dimmer, a device that controls the flow of electricity to each lantern.

If you have the time, leave the bar flown in until all the lanterns have been cabled to dimmers, and then check to see if everything is working properly. It is much easier to track down a faulty cable while the bar is still at working height. When you are done, fly the bar out carefully and move on to the next one.

Front-of-house lighting may be hung from scaffolding mounted on either side of the auditorium or under balconies, and connected to the dimmers in the same way. Many theatres now have lighting bridges spanning the width of the auditorium, which make access for rigging and focusing much easier.

Leave rigging lanterns in the wings and on stands to the end, as they may get in the way, or get damaged, during the fit-up. Obviously no on-stage lighting should be rigged until the set is complete.

A bar flown in to ground level for rigging.

Rigging Sound Equipment

Rig loudspeakers in the auditorium, and on the front of the stage or in the wings as per the sound designer's plan, and make sure they are fixed securely. If you are hanging microphones or speakers in the flies, liaise with the lighting department to avoid too much doubling up on flying. Set up microphone stands and foldback speakers in the pit or band area. You will not be able to rig on-stage microphones and speakers until the fit-up is completed, but you should identify and test in advance the circuits and equipment that will be used.

It is essential that whoever mixes the live sound hears the show in exactly the same way as the audience – that is, not through the thick plate-glass window of the lighting box. Unless there is a specially designed sound box, set up the mixing desk as centrally as possible at the rear of the auditorium. Rig the amplifiers, radio mic receivers, sound control devices and mini-disc players in racks beside it, so the operator can access all the equipment easily.

Cables should be kept well away from the lighting dimmer racks, as these will interfere with the sound signal when operating. Use gaffer or duct tape to keep cables out of the way and as far as possible off the floor.

Once the sound system is cabled up, test each microphone and speaker individually, and make sure the radio mics are operating on the appropriate frequencies. Never tap a mic to test it is on, always speak into it. When you are satisfied that everything is working, detach the microphones from their cables and lock them away in a safe place. Don't leave mics lying around during the fit-up or between rehearsals and performances; they are delicate and expensive, and may get damaged, lost, or even stolen.

THE FIT-UP

Even if you have had unlimited access to the stage for some time, at least some of the components of the set are likely to have been built and painted in a workshop elsewhere. The production manager needs to ensure that the set is transported to the venue and delivered according to the schedule. You will need to borrow or hire a van for this, preferably big enough to transport everything in two or three trips – any more will be time-consuming and frustrating. When loading up the van at the workshop, work out which components of the set you are going to need first, and pack the van accordingly in reverse order.

To save time at the fit-up, the set components should be as large and complete as possible, without being impossible to transport or fit through the dock doors. It is always amazing how pieces that seemed gigantic in the workshop shrink in size when they arrive in the theatre.

As with the lighting, get the flying done first, starting with the extreme upstage bar. Once a backcloth or gauze has been attached to the bar, fly it out until the bottom is just touching the stage floor. The flyman should mark this as the cloth's 'in dead'. Then fly the piece up to a point where it is no longer visible from the auditorium, and mark this as the 'out dead'.

Guildford School of Acting

Cabaret

Final Hanging Bar list

House Tabs

1	LX
2	Border
3	LX
4	Carriage backing
5	Hall Lamp
6	
7	Cliffs light
8	
9	Border
10	LX
11	DLC
12	Full blacks
13	Cliffs Window
14	Gauze
15	LX
16	
17	Hall light
18	
19	Border
20	
21	LX
22	
23	
24	
25	Border
26	
27	LX
28	Crystal drop
29	
30	Crystal drop
31	Star cloth

Final version 20/6/02

Final hanging bar list for **Cabaret** *at the Yvonne Arnaud Theatre. Both staging and lighting departments will need a copy of this document.*

The 'in dead' for smaller flown pieces is an aesthetic consideration, and should be decided by the set designer.

Assembling the Set

If backstage space is limited, you may find it easiest to assemble trucks, periaktoi, or any other large movable pieces on the stage before moving them into position. The set designer needs to be on hand to double-check the position of any permanent structures such as rostra, walls, doorways and staircases before they are finally assembled.

The stage manager should liaise with the production manager to organize the transportation of props and furniture to the venue. As the actors will almost certainly still be rehearsing elsewhere during the fit-up, don't worry about small hand props until after the final run-through in the rehearsal room. Keep fragile props out of the way during the fit-up, especially valuable ones.

The designer and/or scenic artists will probably want to touch up the set once it is in place on stage. Schedule a paint call, and keep it separate from any other stage activity. Paint calls are often done late in the evening when there are fewer people around to get in the way. If the floor has to be painted, do it last and leave it to dry overnight.

Ideally all painting should be completed – and dry – before plotting begins, but shortage of time may make this impossible.

Monitoring the Work

The production manager needs to supervise and monitor the progress of the fit-up throughout. Make sure that the work is constantly moving forward, and that crew members are completing one job before moving on to the next. Schedule refreshment and meal breaks, and stick to them. The crew will not work efficiently if they are hungry, thirsty and exhausted.

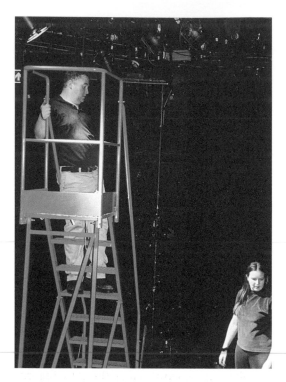

An electrician focusing a lantern while the ASM looks on. Photo: Charlotte Cunningham

Crew members stapling black serge to a masking flat at the fit-up.

If time runs short, prioritize the work so that all the major set elements are assembled in time for the focusing session, even if they still need further work: better four assembled but unfinished trucks, than one beautifully finished and painted and three in pieces in the wings.

Focusing

Once the set is in place, the lighting department need time to focus their lanterns. While they do this, the stage will be dimly lit and occasionally plunged into darkness. Ideally, other work should not be done on the stage during the focusing session, on safety grounds. In practice, however, it often is, so be very careful.

The focusing session is run by the lighting designer, who looks at the effect of each lantern in turn, and directs an electrician on the lighting bridge or up a ladder to adjust it as necessary. The level of each lighting channel is brought up and down by the board operator. (Note that, if you are using hired equipment, or the operator is unfamiliar with the theatre's lighting board, take a few minutes to run through its features and programming techniques before you start.)

You will also need a skeleton stage crew to move set and furniture into position, including a flyman if required. An ASM or two should be on hand to 'walk' (meaning to stand in for actors at various points on the set), steady ladders and run errands.

The show, the set design, and the position and accessibility of lanterns will dictate the sequence in which lanterns are focused. It may be easier to get a complete stage set in position, focus all the lanterns that are used to light it, then repeat the process with the next set; alternatively you can focus each lantern in sequence and bring items of set and furniture on and off as required.

The procedure for focusing is as follows: the electrician focuses it down to its narrowest beam, and aims it as directed by the lighting designer at the appropriate point on the stage or set. The lantern is then fixed in position and its focus widened as required. If necessary, the shape of the beam is altered or controlled by shutters and barn doors. The electrician then checks that any gobos, gels, colour wheels or scrollers are correctly fitted and working properly, and moves on to the next lantern.

If you come across a technical problem that cannot be fixed instantly – a lantern that is not working, or is incorrectly gelled, for instance – make a note of it and move on. As with all the stages of production week, it is essential to finish the job in the time allocated; go back and sort out minor problems later.

PREPARING FOR THE PLOTTING REHEARSAL

The stage manager should put a long table in a position affording the best view of the stage, probably the centre stalls. This is the 'production desk', and it should be left in place until after the final dress rehearsal. Place two or three anglepoise lamps on the desk so the director, DSM and lighting designer will be able to see their notes. A blue gel helps reduce distracting glare.

Most theatres have a series of headsets called 'cans', over which technicians can communicate with backstage, the control box, the fly floor and the production desk. Make sure they are working properly before you start plotting.

During the plotting session the board op brings up combinations of channels at various levels as instructed by the designer, and gradually each lighting state is 'built'. Some lighting designers like to have the lighting board moved down to the production desk for plotting, as they can communicate with the board operator more easily. Definitely do this if your board op is inexperienced and likely to need assistance.

As for the focusing session, you will also need a skeleton stage screw, a flyman, at least one ASM to 'walk', and the follow-spot operators.

Marking Up the Prompt Copy

During the plotting session the DSM needs to mark specific points for each lighting cue in the prompt copy. Bring plenty of pencils, a rubber, and a pad of post-it notes, as these will change repeatedly over the next few days.

Lighting cues are marked in the right-hand column of the interleaved sheets of the prompt copy. They are always referred to as 'LX' cues, to distinguish them from cues for other departments. 'Cue' is usually written as 'Q'. Cue points are *always* specific, and must relate to a word or note in the music. As the director and lighting designer agree upon each one, draw a line across to the relevant point in the script or music.

Time can be saved in the plotting session if the lighting designer runs through the cue synopsis with the DSM in advance, giving rough points for each cue ('Cue seventeen: start of Angela's song'). The cue numbers on the synopsis should always match up with the cue numbers in the prompt copy.

THE PLOTTING REHEARSAL

The plotting rehearsal can be nerve-racking for lighting designers, because this is when they find out whether what they worked out in theory will work in practice.

The designer experiments with balancing levels and intensity, colours and shadows, until the state is satisfactory. There is inevitably a degree of trial and error, especially in setting levels. Levels are always expressed as percentages ('Channel six at 80 per cent'). Avoid plotting lanterns at 100 per cent, as this increases the possibility of the bulb blowing.

Discuss the state with the director, and modify it as required. Ask the ASM to walk the stage so you can check there are no unwanted shadows or underlit areas. Always have someone to walk each state, otherwise you may end up lighting the floor rather than the actors' bodies and faces.

Once the state has been agreed on, set the time over which it is to establish itself. Of course, the exact timing is sometimes impossible to judge, as it may need to synchronize with the actors or orchestra. In that case set a rough time – say, three seconds – and move on: that can easily be fixed later.

The process of switching from one state to another is known as cross-fading. Each cue has a 'down time' (the speed of the previous cue fading out) and an 'up time' (the speed of the new cue coming in); for a smooth transition keep the down time a couple of seconds longer than the up time. Instant or 'snap' cues can be very dramatic, but should be used sparingly.

The first state to be plotted is usually the 'preset' – that is, the light the audience will see when they first enter the theatre. If you are in a traditional proscenium-arch theatre with red front curtains or 'tabs' it is traditional to front-light them at a low level; this is known as 'tab-warming'. If you are not using tabs, you can create a sense of atmosphere and anticipation by using a few lights at a low level to highlight elements of the set.

Inevitably, the director and designer will have new ideas when they see the stage lit for the first time, and will want to modify and add to the design. As far as possible stick to the cue synopsis numbering. A new cue added after LX cue 12 should be numbered 12.5, not cue 13, as this will allow further cues to be added before (12.1, 12.2) or after it (12.6, 12.7) if they are required.

In addition to the cue points themselves, the DSM should mark 'stand-by' cues in the

Follow Spots

Follow-spot operators are responsible for turning their lanterns on and off, focusing, gelling and moving them during performance. If there is more than one follow spot, assign them an identifying number; don't confuse their cues with the board operator's: they should be designated clearly as, say, 'follow spot Q3'. In Britain, follow spots are sometimes known as 'limes', a reference to early models that burnt lime to produce a beam: hence 'limelight'.

The follow-spot operators should write up their own cue synopses as they go, showing the technical nature of each cue, the required gel and focus, and which actor they are following.

prompt copy, which will be called to let the operators know that a cue is coming up. Stand-bys should be given thirty seconds to a minute before the actual cue. If the rehearsal is moving very quickly, put a post-it note at the stand-by points, and mark them in properly later.

Plotting rehearsals may take two or three sessions, depending on the complexity of the show and the experience of the crew. They usually speed up as they go along, as certain states and cue patterns are repeated. An Act Two scene set in Higgins' office may use exactly the same state as an earlier scene in Act One.

If you are using smoke, give the stage manager a cue point and duration for firing the smoke machine ('Smoke cue 3: four seconds'). Smoke is affected by temperature and humidity, and may behave in unpredictable ways. Also, be aware that once the stage is full of moving actors it will dispel more quickly.

The production manager needs to make sure that the director and designer keep the plotting rehearsal moving. Sitting in a quiet, darkened theatre staring at different coloured lights has a hypnotic effect, and the hours can slip away.

If you start to run out of time when plotting, get the cue points into the prompt copy and agree a rough state for each cue. There will be time in the technical rehearsals to refine the remaining states. Just make sure you get to the end of the show.

Note that, as the director is not available to rehearse with the cast during plotting, this is a good time for the MD and choreographer to run through numbers and routines with the cast in the rehearsal room to refine details that may have got lost during the run-throughs.

Preparing the Theatre for the Cast

Before the cast arrive at the theatre, the stage manager should check all the dressing rooms and make sure they are clean and tidy. When assigning dressing rooms, keep men separate from women, and adults from children. Principals are usually given separate dressing rooms to the chorus, but in some cases this may not be appropriate. Put the names of the relevant actors on each door, and post a list at the stage door showing who is in which room.

In the professional theatre there is tremendous kudos in being assigned the 'star' dressing room. Depending on how many rooms you have available, the size of your cast and the temperament of your leading actors, you may require tact and diplomacy.

Ensure that the routes from the dressing rooms to the stage, fire exits and green room are clear. As ever, keep the green room supplied with tea, coffee and water. Pin up a signing-in sheet at the stage door, so that you can see at a glance who is in the building at any time – and more importantly, if anyone is missing.

Sound Plotting

Cue points for any recorded effects and music also need to be set and marked in the prompt copy in the same way as the light. They are usually identified as 'Sound Q 15', or whatever. However, unless your production is using a large number of recorded sound cues, it will probably not be worth scheduling a separate sound plotting rehearsal. Wait until the technical rehearsal to set the output volume levels, when they can be more easily balanced with the actors' voices.

The wings need to be thoroughly tidied and swept before the technical rehearsal can begin. Photo: Tina Bicât

The Wardrobe

The production manager needs to liaise with the wardrobe department, and organize the delivery of the costumes to the theatre. The stage manager should assign a wardrobe room for final fittings, adjustments, alterations, maintenance, and any last-minute jobs that have not yet been completed. During the run there will also be washing to be done, and most theatres have a laundry room equipped with washing machines and dryers.

The wardrobe mistress should check through all the costumes, then hang them in the relevant dressing rooms with the name of the actor, character and scene clearly labelled on the coathanger; for example: 'Miss Jones. Julie Jordan. Act 1 scene 3.' Personal accessories, jewellery, handkerchiefs and so on should be sorted for each actor, and kept together in a plastic bag on the hanger. Shoes go underneath, labelled on the inside. Wigs should be set on a wig block.

THE SOUND BALANCE REHEARSAL

If you are microphoning the stage and/or using radio mics, you should schedule a separate sound balance rehearsal. Ideally this should be done with the full cast and band, so that the MD can practise conducting, and consolidate lines of communication with the singers on stage and the musicians in the pit. This rehearsal also gives the sound designer and operator the opportunity to set gain levels for each input channel, EQ the various voices and instruments, and experiment with refining the overall mix. Depending on the availability of people and equipment, this rehearsal, also known as the sound check, may be scheduled before or after the technical rehearsal.

The more people who are singing, the harder it will be to achieve a successful balance, especially if you are using a mixture of radio, float and rifle microphones. If time is pressing, do the big numbers first and work your way through to the solos at the end – there is no need to run the show in order.

It is also important that the actors on stage get used to the sound of the band. The sound operator should set the output level of stage foldback speakers high enough so that the cast can hear the orchestra even at the loudest moments on stage.

Actors need not be in costume for this rehearsal, unless there are costume elements – women's corsets, for instance – that may affect their singing. Nor do you need stage lighting. Scenery that may affect the sound balance, such as heavy drapes, front cloths and gauzes, should be set as per performance.

Don't be afraid of repeating a number if you are unsure, but keep an eye on the clock. At this stage it is far more important to cover everything in the show once, than to spend hours perfecting one solo.

It is an unfortunate fact that this vital rehearsal is often given a low priority, and is frequently truncated or rushed. As the first performance gets ever closer it is easy to see the jobs that still have to be done on the stage; but improving the condition of something invisible and intangible such as the sound balance seems less important, and may be considered, wrongly, to be a luxury.

It is also frequently the case that, for financial reasons, the orchestra is not called until the final dress rehearsal, and this is therefore the first opportunity the sound technicians get to balance the overall mix.

PREPARING FOR THE TECHNICAL REHEARSAL

Once the rigging, fit-up, focusing and plotting are completed, the stage management team need to prepare the stage for the technical rehearsal (the 'tech'). Clear the wings of any left-over building material, tools, odd bits of fabric, spare lanterns, cables, empty tea cups and anything else left over from the get-in. If time and space are limited, you can put stuff in the auditorium for now.

You may need to create one or more small screened-off or curtained-off areas so that actors can perform quick changes in the wings with a degree of privacy. Make sure it is in the most convenient location for the actor(s) concerned.

Set up a props table in each wing, or by each stage entrance if you are not working in a pros-arch theatre. Cover them in white paper, put each prop in place according to the setting lists, and mark out an appropriately sized area for each one in thick pen or tape. Write a description of the prop, and the name of the character who uses it inside each area. You will then be able to see at a glance if a prop is missing. Actors should never leave props lying about; always return them to an ASM, or replace them on the props table after use.

Running lights (dim-coloured lights illuminating the prop tables, wings, fly floor and cross-over areas) are usually the responsibility of the electrics department and must be in place before this rehearsal begins. In many situations the stage manager may cue the fly-men, conductor and sound operator via cue lights instead of cans, so these, too, must be in place before the rehearsal begins.

Even if the sound check is not scheduled to take place until later on, radio mics should be used throughout the tech, as it provides an opportunity to check the operation of the equipment, and is useful practice for the mic runner. Be sure to have plenty of batteries available for the radio mics, and keep them charged up. In most professional shows the batteries are changed at least every rehearsal or performance, and sometimes in the interval, too.

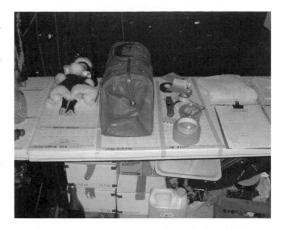

Section of the props table for **Annie.** *The stage manager can see at a glance that the 'oval office jug' is missing.*

Note that, as technical rehearsals invariably only use a piano, they are of limited use to the musical director and the sound designer and operator.

THE TECHNICAL REHEARSAL

At the technical rehearsal – or 'tech' – all the staging departments come together with each other and the cast for the first time. It is the rehearsal where the individual elements of the production are co-ordinated, and where the director and creative team catch a first glimpse of the combined scale and quality of their work.

Even in the most meticulously planned production, things will change at the technical. Ideas may be scrapped, re-invented and re-applied in minutes. Problems have to be solved and compromises made, everybody is under intense time pressure, and a mild sense of panic may hang in the air.

Technical rehearsals are fragmented, constantly stopping and starting, and tend to proceed at a snail's pace. There is also inevitably a

Technical rehearsals involve a lot of waiting around. Tell your actors to bring a good book.

The production desk during the tech. Note the DSM in the foreground marking up the prompt copy.

lot of hanging about, especially for the cast, and boredom can set in. Techs can therefore be extremely stressful, and everyone needs to be at their most alert and co-operative.

On the day of the tech, the cast and crew should be called to the theatre an hour before it is due to start: the technicians to check their equipment, the stage management team to set up the stage as per performance, and the actors to get into costume. If there are lots of complex costumes and/or quick changes, you may need a team of dressers, and they should attend this and all subsequent rehearsals. Make-up is not usually required at techs unless there are quick changes involved. Wigs should be checked but need not be worn once the designer has approved them. Do not call the band to the tech: it will be a complete waste of their time and – if they are being paid – your money.

When all departments are ready to begin, the stage manager should call the company to the stage and welcome them. Run through any safety routines and fire regulations, and point out potential dangers. Remember this may

well be the first time they have been inside the theatre. Go through the geography of the building; it may be worth taking them on a guided tour, as backstage can be a perplexing place.

The director should emphasize that this rehearsal is primarily for the technicians. There is no need to go for an all-out knock-'em-down-in-the-aisles performance: it is more important to be careful, safe and accurate. Remind them to be especially careful of their costumes: there should be no eating or drinking in costume except bottled water.

Technical rehearsals are notoriously difficult to get started: there are so many different elements and departments coming together that it is difficult to co-ordinate them. Just getting the house lights off and the curtain up can take an age.

During the tech the creative team sit in the auditorium at the production desk, with the stage manager in charge of running all the activity on stage. If the director or DSM wishes to halt the tech – and they will, frequently – they should contact the stage manager on cans.

Start at the top of the show, with the DSM calling all sound, lighting, flying and staging cues. Unless there is an accident or a significant safety risk, the cast should keep going until they hear the call to halt. The director should stop the tech when necessary to re-run scene changes, tidy up cueing, check special effects and deal with technical problems encountered by the cast. Avoid the temptation to stop for every little thing. If a scene change starts to go wrong, it may be as well to let the crew complete it as best they can before re-running it. Discover where the problems lie, then make clear, positive decisions to solve them.

The stage manager should always appoint jobs to specific crew members and ASMs. For instance, don't say 'Take the chair off, someone'; say, 'Robert, take that chair off upstage left and watch out for the chorus in the wings.' Ensure that the stage action is safe, and then re-run the sequence. If it works, carry on to the next cue; if not, run it again.

Remember that at the tech the DSM will be under considerable pressure, as this is the first opportunity to call the show. Allow time to make sure that everything gets marked down in the prompt copy accurately before moving on, or you may have to re-tech sequences later on.

Meanwhile, the production manager, set designer and costume designer should make notes on details of scenery, costume and staging that need to be fixed, altered or completed. The lighting designer may modify lighting states and cues as the tech proceeds, as long as this does not interfere with cueing sequences.

A production of a naturalistic play may have five, ten, even twenty-minute sections in which there are no technical cues. It is therefore common practice to 'top and tail' such scenes, jumping ahead to the point of the next technical standby.

Actors need to know how to find the light on stage: find it and stay in it.

'Finding the Light'

Inexperienced performers sometimes assume that they can be properly seen on stage as long as they can see the audience. That is not the case.

When a stage is partially or dimly lit, or a special is being used, it is important that actors know exactly which lantern in the rig has been plotted to light them at that moment, so they can get themselves into the optimum position. This is known as 'finding the light'.

If asked to 'find the light', do not look down at the floor to see if you are standing in its beam, or look directly up into the grid: move forwards slowly until you feel it like a warm glow on your face. Some actors close their eyes to intensify the sensation. Remember: the audience will only see you properly when your head is lit.

Of course, if you are being lit by a follow-spot, the light will find you.

Anna Rising

Cabaret

Act 1

FOLLOW SPOT 'Q' SHEET ①

FSQ	LXQ	COL	IRIS	ACTION	NOTES
2 In	5	OPEN White	Waste	Cabaret Girls one bye/ one and Shimi	Cabaret Girls SHIMI Slash Curter
2 A	6	/	/	Fade Out	
3 I	7	OPEN WHITE	White small	Boys	Boys
3 A	8	/	/	Fade Out	
5 In	17	OPEN Frost Whit	Waste	Cliff's Table	Cliff's Table SR
5 A	19	/	/	Fade Out	
6 In	20	OPEN White	Head Sholder	Stage left table in Auditorium Spot Her	Caroline Wheeler
6 A	21	/	/	Fade Out	
8 In	23	OPEN White	Waste	Sally through the Slash and DSC Chair	Sally
	24			Still on Sally but Smaller	Sally
∨	25			It's a vissule for OUT	∨
8 A	26			Fade Out	
4 IN	27	OPEN White	Big	Still on Sally	Sally
4 A	29	/	/	Snap Out	
10 IN	30	OPEN White Frost	Waste	Sally DSC Cliff's Table	Sally
10 A	31	/	/	Fade Out	
11 in	33	OPEN White	Waste up	On to Shimi	Shimi

Cue sheet for follow-spot operator, giving cue numbers, colour, focusing and operational instructions.

This is unlikely to be the case in a musical, however, where cues and music come thick and fast; so don't be tempted to cut ahead for even just a page or two of dialogue. Stopping and re-starting can be surprisingly time-consuming, and it may be quicker to let the action run continuously.

Always run through musical numbers, as this will allow the follow-spot operators to practise. The soloists will also appreciate the

It can take actors time to get used to wearing their costumes, especially if they are elaborate. Don't expect flawless performances at the first dress rehearsal. Photo: Robin Cottrell

opportunity to try out their voices in the theatre for the first time, even if they are not singing full out.

Above all, the director needs to stay focused, and to concentrate on the technical aspects of the show. Many of your artistic decisions can suddenly seem unsatisfactory once you see the action unfolding on the stage. Make minor adjustments by all means, but don't start re-blocking whole scenes. Instead, make a list of scenes you want to work on, and prioritize them later.

The production manager needs to keep an eye on the clock and keep the tech moving; it is easy to get behind. However, make sure you call a fifteen-minute refreshment break every couple of hours, and take proper breaks for meals. Techs are hard enough anyway, without everybody getting hungry and dehydrated.

After the Tech

At the end of the tech you may feel overwhelmed, even depressed. Everybody is exhausted, yet there is a huge list of jobs to do, and it feels as if there is no time left to do them in.

The production manager should always schedule some time in the theatre between the end of the tech and the start of the dress rehearsal for work to be completed. Immediately after the tech finishes, get together with the stage manager, the heads of the technical departments and the director, and assess what still has to be done. Everyone will, of course, have a very good reason why it is essential that they should be given priority.

The production manager then has the ticklish job of drawing up a mini-schedule for the time remaining. Use your judgement and be fair. Assign specific time on stage to each head of department, including the director, who may wish to re-work some sections with the cast on the set. But make it very clear that the schedule must be respected and adhered to by everyone.

THE FIRST DRESS REHEARSAL

Professional productions usually have two dress rehearsals, one on the night before the opening, and one on the afternoon before the first night.

Ideally you should follow this practice, then if things go seriously awry during the get-in, you can cancel the first dress and use that time to complete the tech. Showbiz lore is littered with tales of shows that opened to huge acclaim without a proper dress rehearsal: do not, however, rely on this.

The purpose of the first dress rehearsal is to see if you can get from the top of the show to the final curtain safely, efficiently, and without stopping. In theory, every individual element of the show should now be in place and have been rehearsed at least once. In practice, something new always arrives just in time for the dress – a wig, a complex prop, a special effect, a new paint finish on the floor.

Set a definite time for the dress rehearsal as per the technical schedule. Call the actors at least an hour before it is due to start, so there is time to run a vocal and dance warm-up on the stage. Make it clear that if there is an accident, or a serious safety issue arises, they or the stage manager should stop the show, but otherwise they should keep going: this is not the time to stop and say, 'Sorry, I fluffed my line, can I just do that again?' If the stage is suddenly

The view from the production desk. Annie at the Yvonne Arnaud Theatre, set by Roger Ness. GSA Conservatoire production directed by Gerry Tebbutt.

plunged into darkness, the actors should keep focused, and wait until light is restored before continuing.

The cast should wear make-up at the dress rehearsal. If a specific 'look' is required – for the Red Indians in *Annie Get Your Gun* or the animals in *Honk!*, say – the make-up should be designed and supervised by the costume designer or someone working closely with them.

As for the tech, the lighting and sound departments should check that all circuits are fully operational: it has been known for electricians to forget to turn on the dimmer racks. The stage management team should set

Backstage and Font of House Calls

Although the exact wording may alter slightly, the DSM should always give the following backstage and front-of-house calls:

Thirty-five minutes before curtain up, call 'the half':
Backstage: 'Ladies and gentlemen of the cast and crew of ——, this is your half-hour call, you have half an hour. Thank you.'

On receipt of front-of-house clearance:
Front of house: 'Ladies and gentlemen, welcome to the —— theatre. The house is now open. Please take your seats for tonight's performance of ——. Thank you.'
Backstage: 'Ladies and gentlemen of the cast and crew of ——, the house is now open, the house is now open. Thank you.'

Twenty minutes before curtain up, call 'the quarter':
Backstage: 'Ladies and gentlemen of the cast and crew of ——, this is your fifteen-minute call, you have fifteen minutes. Thank you.'

Ten minutes before curtain up, call 'the five':
Backstage: 'Ladies and gentlemen of the cast and crew of ——, this is your five-minute call, you have five minutes. Thank you.'

Five minutes before curtain up, call 'beginners':
Backstage: 'Ladies and gentlemen of the cast and crew of ——, this is your Act One beginners' call. Miss ——, Mrs —— and Mr —— to the stage, please. Miss/Mr —— (conductor) and ladies and gentlemen of the orchestra to the pit, please.'

Three minutes before curtain up:
Front of house: 'Ladies and gentlemen, tonight's performance of —— will begin in three minutes. In three minutes. Will you please take your seats. Thank you.'

Two minutes before curtain up:
Front of house: 'Ladies and gentlemen, tonight's performance of —— will begin in two minutes. In two minutes. Will you please take your seats. Thank you.'

One minute before curtain up:
Front of house: 'Ladies and gentlemen, tonight's performance of —— is about to commence. Will you please take your seats. Thank you.'

Repeat after fifteen seconds.

In the interval:
Give an Act Two five minute and beginners' call backstage. Repeat the front of house calls, but say that the performance will 'Continue' or 'Re-commence'.

After the show, give the 'goodnight' call:
Backstage: 'Ladies and gentlemen of the cast and crew of ——, thank you for tonight's performance. Your next call is at ——am/pm tomorrow/on Monday. Thank you, and good night.'

Director Ian Watt-Smith giving notes to the cast of The Secret Garden *before the final dress rehearsal. The Arts Educational School, London.*

up backstage exactly as they would for a performance.

Front-of-house calls welcome the audience to the theatre, and warn them that the show will begin; backstage calls warn actors that their appearance on the stage is coming up. It is another of the DSM's responsibilities to give these calls from their desk. Making front-of-house calls can be strangely intimidating for non-actors, and the first dress is a good time for the DSM to practise.

Again, all members of the creative team and the production manager should watch the dress. Do not always watch from the production desk: move about the theatre. How does the show look from the front row, the back, the balcony? You may be surprised, and not always pleasantly.

Again, everybody makes notes. The director in particular needs to watch the show like a hawk. If there is an assistant director, get them to write down notes as you dictate them, so you do not have to take your eyes off the stage. No matter what happens, resist the temptation to leap on the stage and start manhandling and moving actors about. Take a fifteen- or twenty-minute interval so that everyone gets used to the amount of time they will have to re-set the stage on the night.

The first dress rehearsal is everybody's first attempt to do the show, and inevitably things go wrong. Lighting cues go beserk, microphones fail, props disappear, and set changes take an eternity. The cast have numerous new factors to deal with, they lose focus, frustration mounts and performances suffer.

By the time you reach the finale, a mood of gloom and despondency may have settled over the theatre. This is often the point at which the director's inspirational and leadership qualities come into their own.

Let the cast get out of costume while you make a plan with the production manager and stage manager. There will still be technical tasks to be completed, so again the staging departments need to negotiate time for work on stage. The time of the second dress will have been set, so work backwards from that point as you make up the new schedule, allowing sufficient time for stage management to reset the stage.

After the First Dress

Some directors like to get the actors in a circle

Curtain Calls

There is a theatrical tradition that it is bad luck to rehearse the curtain call until after the last dress rehearsal. Ignore this when staging a musical. The curtain call for a play with a cast of three can be worked out in minutes, and has no technical requirement beyond an extra lighting state at the end of the play. By contrast, the curtain call for a musical will typically involve a large number of performers and the reprise of music, songs and possibly choreography from earlier in the show.

Traditionally the chorus take their bows first, then cameo roles, second leads, and finally the leading couple. Leading ladies are usually afforded the last bow. There may then be further bows for the whole company, and a final chorus. Make sure you agree a moment for the cast to acknowledge the MD and orchestra.

Nothing looks worse than a chaotic curtain call, so make sure it is fully rehearsed and teched in time for the final dress rehearsal.

immediately after the dress rehearsal for a lengthy notes session. Others – including the author – prefer to wait till the next day, when the cast are fresher and more receptive to ideas, and the director has had a chance to check through what has been scribbled down and to decide how to deal with any particularly sensitive issues that have arisen during the dress.

Remember that the actors have just done the show for the first time, and inevitably their movement around the set, interplay and timing will not have been as slick as it was in the rehearsal room. But they will have learned from the experience, and most will automatically make adjustments and improvements.

Giving an actor a note on every tiny less-than-perfect moment may appear patronizing and can be counter-productive.

On the other hand, if some actors are still messing up a scene or number because they are still unsure of their lines or blocking, don't be afraid to note 'em, and note 'em hard.

PRODUCTION PHOTOGRAPHS

At some point you will probably want a photographer to take some production shots of the show. The first dress is a good time for this, as the set, lighting and costumes should (should!) be largely complete, and the cast will be wearing make-up.

A friendly amateur photographer may want to come and watch a run-through in the rehearsal room, so they have some idea of the show before they shoot it. Professional photographers are unlikely to do this, so you should alert them to any particularly visually striking moments before the curtain goes up.

You may wish to set up and re-run specific scenes for the photographer's benefit after the dress. Make sure the wardrobe department know you are doing this so the correct costumes are available, and keep the photo session brief.

If there are two or more teams of children in the cast, make sure that both teams appear in the photographs or there will be tears and angry parents to contend with.

PREPARATION FOR THE FINAL DRESS REHEARSAL

Call cast and crew in good time for the final dress. The stage management and the technicians may well have been working in the theatre since early morning anyway, and most actors will want to arrive early.

The director should run through actors' notes in the green room to maximize available

Making up for the final dress rehearsal.

stage time for the staging departments. Be as positive and upbeat as you can about the first dress, especially if it did not go particularly well. If you have lots of individual notes for particular actors it may be best to speak to them privately rather than holding up a general notes session.

Some producers and directors like to invite an audience of friends and families to the final dress rehearsal. Actors usually have mixed feelings about this. On the one hand it is good to get a sense of a living, breathing audience out there in the auditorium, if only because they will laugh at the jokes: it is amazing how dreary lines that you have been saying for weeks can suddenly spring back to life, witty and dazzling, once the audience are there to respond to them. It is also useful for the sound engineer to find out how the presence of the audience alters the acoustic of the auditorium. And front-of-house staff may well appreciate having a dry run of getting an audience in and out of the theatre.

On the other hand, the presence of an audience, especially a large one, can put extra pressure on the dress rehearsal and make it feel like a first night.

THE FINAL DRESS REHEARSAL

Get the actors on stage forty-five minutes to an hour before curtain up for a full vocal and physical warm-up. Run a big company number to get people focused and in the mood. The arrival of the band adds to the excitement of the final dress, and the cast are usually dying to get on with it.

The stage manager may stop the final dress rehearsal, but should only do so in the most extreme circumstances. If you do have to stop, solve the problem quickly, re-set and carry on. It is disconcerting in the extreme to stop the final dress, especially if you have an invited audience.

Run Act One, have an interval, then run Act Two and the curtain call. The director may have a few final notes to give, a cue may be changed, the sound balance tweaked. But those aside, that is it.

Next time, it's for real.

13 THE FIRST NIGHT AND BEYOND

The extent to which the members of the audience enjoy their evening at the theatre is not solely limited to the quality of the performance on stage. Numerous other factors contribute to the overall experience, from the ease with which they can find a parking space to the range of drinks available in the interval. The more forethought and planning that are put into these aspects of the show, the more enjoyable and fulfilling the evening will be for everybody.

LOOKING AFTER THE AUDIENCE

Front-of-House Manager

Appoint a front-of-house manager, to take responsibility for dealing with the public and all aspects of the theatre operation that may affect them. These include: ensuring that the box office runs smoothly; organizing the sale of refreshments, programmes and merchandise; welcoming the audience to the theatre and moving them in and out of the auditorium safely and efficiently; looking after critics and VIPs; sorting out difficulties in ticketing; and dealing with any latecomers.

Accessibility

Remember that the audience have to find their way to the venue. How easy is it to get to? Where is the nearest station or bus stop? Is a

Make sure the audience can find their way to the theatre. You may need to buy some signs, or make your own.

car park or on-street parking available? How well are the approaches lit? Most theatres are well signposted, but if you are performing in a school or non-theatre venue you may need to make your own. In particular, don't underestimate how confusing – and threatening – large college campuses can be to those unfamiliar with their layout, especially after dark.

Make sure there is no doubt about where the performance is taking place by keeping the exterior of the building as bright as possible. If you have a strong branded image, blow it up on a poster or banner as large as you can afford, and stick it up outside.

Production shots of The Ballad of Little Jo *on display in the foyer of the Bridewell Theatre.*

If you are organizing your own car park, ensure that there are plenty of signs showing drivers where to go, and appoint a couple of marshals to direct traffic.

The front-of-house manager and staff should also make themselves familiar with the venue's disabled or wheelchair access facilities, and ensure that the keys for any elevators or chair lifts are available.

The Foyer

During the get-in, the front-of-house manager should make sure that all audience areas are clean and tidy. Don't forget the toilets (ah, the glamour of show business...!).

A pleasant and welcoming foyer sets the tone for the evening, so decorate it with posters, production photographs and head-shots of the cast. Photographs of the show in rehearsal are always extremely interesting; and presenting these on wall-mounted or free-standing display boards will always look better than pinning or taping them to the wall.

Arrange for any newspaper articles that have appeared to be photocopied, blown up and prominently displayed. Once the show has opened, do the same with good reviews: they are a key marketing tool, and should be exploited shamelessly to boost your ticket sales. If you have commercial sponsors, don't forget to use any promotional or advertising material that they have supplied.

The Programme or Playbill

Buying a programme is an essential part of the theatre-going experience for many people. Some like to build up a collection over the years, to keep a record of all the shows they have seen.

In America, programmes (or 'playbills' as they are known) are usually supplied to the audience free of charge. In most other countries they are sold, and can provide an important additional source of revenue for the production.

Programmes can range from a single sheet of paper to elaborate full-colour glossy publications full of spectacular photographs and pull-outs. The producer should decide at an early stage how elaborate or simple the programme will be, and how much time and effort will be expended on it. Producing even a comparatively modest programme is like publishing a magazine, and may require a dedicated editor to organize the content, layout and design, and a business manager to manage production costs, some of which may be offset by attracting advertisers.

Compile a draft layout of the programme on a PC or Mac. The stage manager should then

Programme Content

At a minimum the programme should contain:

- the cast list;
- names of the creative and production teams;
- synopsis of scenes;
- a list of musical numbers and the names of the characters who perform them;
- some information about the show, the writers, and where and when it was first performed;
- thanks and acknowledgements to individuals, organizations and businesses who have contributed goods or services to the production.

You may also choose to include:

- a piece by the director on the approach or style of this production;
- background information on the socio-economic and historical background to the show;
- rehearsal and/or production photographs;
- information about your organization, including future plans and membership details;
- professional theatre programmes also contain short biographies of the performers and creative teams, listing their previous work. These are usually inappropriate for school, college and amateur productions.

circulate this to the creative team and cast to ensure that everyone is credited as they wish to be, and that names are spelled correctly. Biographies if used should be submitted by the individuals concerned, but give a strict upper limit to the number of words required.

The usual considerations of economy of scale, turn-around time and run-on cost apply to the production of the programme. The printer you used for your posters and flyers may not necessarily be able to tool and produce a programme, so once you have finalized the content and layout, shop around for quotes. Above all, make sure that the printer can guarantee delivery in time for the first performance.

Programme Sales and Merchandizing

Programme sellers should stand in the foyer, and by each main entrance to the auditorium. Never sell programmes at a price that will require dealing with large amounts of change; it is easier and quicker for people to pay £1 than 80p, and somehow they seem psychologically more willing to do so. Don't forget to have programmes on sale in the interval and also after the show.

Ever since *The Beggar's Opera* became a hit in 1728, successful shows have provided scope for lucrative merchandizing opportunities, and the sales of branded clothes, souvenirs and gifts provide a significant proportion of the gross income of many West End and Broadway shows. Follow their example: if you have spare T-shirts and posters, set up a stall in the foyer and sell them. Every little bit of income helps to balance the budget.

Box Office

Queuing for tickets can be an irritating start to the evening, and the front-of-house manager needs to set up an efficient system for collection and payment to keep this to a minimum.

Set up two outlets, one for pre-paid ticket collection, the other for new sales. Pre-paid tickets should be sorted out in advance and stored alphabetically by the name of the person who booked them. If you are using a computerized box office, print out pre-paid tickets in advance to save time later.

Make sure that you brief box-office staff about payment methods. If you have set up your own box office, you probably will not be able to accept credit or debit cards. In that case it should be stated clearly on all publicity that payment is by cash or cheque only, and put up a sign to this effect as well to avoid hold-ups.

Ticket sales are the single largest source of income for the production, and the viability of the whole enterprise depends upon that income being generated and protected. As a result, most theatres now reserve the right not to re-sell unwanted tickets bought and paid for in advance, and it is common practice only to accept tickets for re-sale once all others have been sold.

Be prepared to sell off any remaining tickets as 'standbys' at a reduced price just before curtain up. Each performance is a unique revenue opportunity that will never be repeated, and it is always better to get *some* money for unsold tickets and fill up the seats, rather than perform to a half-empty theatre.

Decide on a policy for standby and reserve tickets, inform the box-office staff what it is, and stick with it. If you are selling tickets at concessionary rates to the unwaged, to senior citizens, students and other groups, ask to see proof of their status. Refer complaints to the front-of-house manager to avoid long arguments at the head of the queue.

Expect a rush at the box office ten minutes before curtain up. Audience members arriving then will be anxious about missing the opening of the show, and the front-of-house manager should be on hand to provide reassurance and assistance to hard-pressed box-office staff. And at the end of the evening people may be worried about catching last trains, relieving babysitters and so on, so put up a notice stating at what time the show is due to finish.

It is a good idea to keep a few good 'house seats' unsold until the last minute. Under the terms of your performing licence, you are committed to provide two tickets per performance should the publisher, writer or their representatives attend, and in theory they could turn up at any time. House seats are also useful for accommodating an unexpected VIP or friend of the producer who arrives just as the curtain is about to rise.

Refreshments

In most theatres the catering facilities and bar will be stocked and run by the management as a profit-making operation. If you are bringing in a very large audience you may be able to swing some sort of deal on bar profits if you are persuasive enough.

If there is no permanent bar or catering, boost your income by selling ice creams, tea, coffee and cold drinks before the show and in the interval. Make sure that you have enough supplies and sufficient volunteers to cover each performance.

Actor signing in at the stage door for the first performance.

There are strict laws controlling the sale of alcoholic drinks, and if you intend to run a bar you should apply to the local authority for further information. Many licensed catering companies are experienced in setting up and running temporary bars, and some local authorities offer this service, too. If you choose to use one of them, remember that they will be turning a profit themselves, so negotiate the best deal you can.

BACKSTAGE PREPARATIONS

In the professional theatre, shows often have several previews before the official press night. These enable the cast to get used to playing in front of a living, breathing audience, and the creative team to assess and fine-tune their work. On a new show, of course, that may mean a period of frenzied rewriting, brutal cuts and endless re-rehearsing. Whether the actual first performance in front of an audience is a preview or the press night, it is an experience like no other.

After the final dress rehearsal the die is cast. There may be time for the director to give a few notes, the MD to run through some tricky harmonies and the choreographer to check some positions on stage, but this is little more than nervous tinkering. For better or worse, the show is now fundamentally complete.

If the first performance is immediately after the final dress rehearsal, at least give the cast and crew time to grab a sandwich before preparing for the show. If it is on the following day, the actors will usually be unable to keep away from the theatre, and may start drifting in to the building hours before curtain up.

The production manager should organize whatever stage time remains effectively. The piano may need to be tuned, so make sure there is an opportunity for the tuner to do this without interruption. Final adjustments to lighting states and cues may need to be done with a particular set or scenic element on stage. The stage manager should remove the production desk and clear up any remnants of the get-in. Leave the DSM alone to work through the prompt copy and make any final amendments. The auditorium should be cleaned and vacuumed, either by the theatre's resident staff or the front-of-house team.

During the course of the day good luck cards and bouquets of flowers from well-wishers arrive at the stage door. A strange expectant calm hangs over the theatre. It feels a bit like Christmas Eve.

If the cast have not already done a dress rehearsal that afternoon – or even if they have – call them on stage at least an hour before curtain up for a thorough physical and vocal warm-up, ending with a big song and dance number. The director should say a few last words of thanks and encouragement. If there have been technical foul-ups at the final dress, reassure everybody that they have been dealt with, and wish everybody good luck. Make sure that all warm-ups are completed by the 'half' to allow the cast plenty of time to get into costume and make-up.

Encourage your actors to maintain a professional attitude. Once the half has been called they should not go into the foyer or any areas where they may meet the public, and certainly not in costume.

The DSM should give the cast warning of the 'quarter' (twenty minutes before curtain up) and the 'five' (ten minutes). With five minutes to go the DSM calls 'Beginners', the cue for all cast members in the opening scene to go to the stage, and for the musicians to go to the pit. The DSM then makes a series of front-of-house announcements warning the audience that the performance will begin shortly. The final announcement should be that 'Tonight's performance is about to begin.'

The DSM should then check that all the production crew, lighting and sound operators,

DSM at the prompt desk ready to cue the show.

flymen, follow-spot operators and musicians are standing by. The stage manager checks that the relevant actors are on stage or in the wings.

Now it is only the audience that you are waiting for.

ORGANIZING THE AUDIENCE

When all backstage checks are complete, the stage manager should inform the front-of-house manager, who can then open the auditorium to the public. Theoretically this should happen just after the half, but last-minute work often means it is later, especially on the first night. The DSM should then make an announcement to both backstage and front of house that the house is now open.

On press night the front-of-house manager needs to keep an eye out for VIPs and critics. Usher them to a private room or small roped-off area, where the press and publicity officer should be on hand to greet them and give them a complimentary drink and a programme. Unless reduced to a quivering nervous wreck by this stage, the producer should also be present.

Once the auditorium is open the audience will start to drift in. If seating is unreserved, keep a few seats near an entrance for late-comers. The front-of-house manager needs to check with the director via the stage manager when the best time to admit late-comers will be; this is usually after the first musical number, or at the first major scene change.

When the front-of-house manager is satisfied that the audience are seated, give the stage manager 'front-of-house clearance' – that is, permission to start the show.

Over the last few years it has become common practice for the front-of-house manager to request that the audience turn off their mobile phones before the performance begins. If an actor is indisposed and an understudy is performing, announce this, too.

Then the DSM calls the first cue, the orchestra starts to play, and the house lights dim.

THE FIRST PERFORMANCE

During the first performance the creative team usually huddle together at the back of the auditorium, and most directors experience a strange feeling of powerlessness. After weeks or months of preparing the show, they can now only sit back and watch it.

W.S. Gilbert, who directed all the original productions of the Savoy Operas that he wrote with Arthur Sullivan, would leave the theatre as the overture started on opening night, only to return in time for the curtain call. Few producers and directors can match his *sang froid*.

During production week it is easy to forget just how impressive the show will be to the audience when they see if for the first time. GSA Conservatoire production of **Once upon a Mattress.** *Director, Jonathan Best; designer, Janey Gardiner; lighting designer, Paul Franklin.* Photo: Mark Dean

For the cast, first performances usually go past in a blur. Everyone is pumped up with adrenalin, and the presence of an audience – usually a full house – adds a unique air of excitement to the proceedings. Audiences are unpredictable, and cannot be second-guessed. There may be an unexpected gale of laughter at a line that has always seemed utterly flat and prosaic, while moments that have seemed hilarious in rehearsal pass in glum silence.

Give the audience time to applaud at the end of numbers. As the applause starts to subside –

but before it finishes – speak the next line and move the action on. Keep moving the performance forwards, and before you know it, the interval will have arrived.

Note that in proscenium arch theatres it is a legal requirement to raise and lower the safety curtain in the audience's presence. This is usually done in the interval.

The front-of-house team should prepare for a flurry of activity during the interval. Have the hot-water urn ready for tea and coffee, and pour any pre-ordered drinks at the bar.

Live sound mixing during the performance.

The press and publicity officer should round up the critics and other VIPS and take them back to their private room or area for another drink. Be polite and positive to the critics, but don't pester them or ask them if they are enjoying the show: they will volunteer as much information as they want you to know.

The director should resist the temptation to go backstage and give notes: leave the actors to get on with it. Meanwhile, the stage manager supervises the crew as they re-set the stage for the second half. If the re-set runs into technical problems, tell the DSM to delay the front-of-house calls announcing the start of Act Two, but sort the problem out as quickly as you possibly can and get the show re-started.

Act Two begins, and in a flash the cast are taking their curtain call. Even if you feel the performance has not gone well, smile and take your ovation with pride. You've earned it.

The director, producer and creative team will often rush backstage after the show to congratulate the cast. This is a heady moment, the culmination of months, maybe even years

of work, and you should enjoy it to the full. If a member of the cast has made a significant error during the show, this is not the time for recriminations: they will feel bad enough as it is. Encourage them to put it behind them and to join in the celebrations, no matter how little they may feel like doing so. Tomorrow is another day.

While cast and crew are still in the theatre, the DSM should make a final 'Goodnight' call, thanking everybody for their contribution and giving the call for the next day. Then the cast get changed, the crew tidy up, and everybody goes out to mingle with the audience, usually in the nearest pub.

Note that the stage manager should make sure that children do not get forgotten in the euphoria, and that parents or guardians arrive to take them home safely.

Show Reports

The first night audience is usually full of friends and relatives of the cast and production teams. Amidst the welter of their congratulations, the

SHOW REPORT: PROMISES PROMISES

<u>DATE</u> 6th December 2001: 2nd performance

<u>CURTAIN UP TIME</u> 7.34 p.m.

<u>INTERVAL</u> 8.45 p.m. - 9.03 p.m.

<u>CURTAIN DOWN TIME</u> 10.08 p.m.

<u>RUNNING TIME</u> 1st Act 1 hr 11 min; 2nd Act 1 hr 5 min

<u>HOUSE PERCENTAGE</u> 68 %

<u>TECHNICAL OBSEVATIONS</u>

Telephone sound cue on p.41 didn't go: Sound Op had wrong disk in

DSM went slightly late on LXQ82, misjudging the piano music cue

The scene change p.79: crew still leaving stage as Mr Underwood began to cross stage and speak, forcing DSM to bring lights up on him: perhaps change was too slow, or perhaps actor should not have spoken until he had light?

Problem with the scrollers: colours didn't match

<u>PERFORMANCE OBSERVATIONS</u>

Four lines of dialogue skipped on p.26 by Mr Hornigold & Miss Ainsworth

Line on page 48 skipped by Miss Ainsworth (reference to picture frame)

One of Miss Ainsworth's lines cut off by Mr Underwood p.62 ("A hundred dollars is the going rate for me these days")

Thankyou
Laura Farrell
DSM

Distribution: PM, Director, Lx Designer, Jacqueline George, James Thompson, SM, 3 ASMs, Prod. Lx, Light Op, Sound Op

Show report for Promises Promises *prepared by the DSM, giving performance timings, audience information, and technical and performance observations.*

celebrations and the popping of champagne corks, it is often impossible to judge the true quality of the performance. The objective facts of the first night – and of every subsequent performance – are recorded in the show report prepared by the DSM.

During the course of the performance the DSM should note any errors in cueing, lighting, flying or stage management, any costume, prop or microphone problems, and any major loss of lines or inadvertent cutting by members of the cast. These are then listed in

Beware 'Second Night Syndrome'

The first night is fuelled with adrenalin and the thrill of the unknown. It is the culmination of several days of frenetic activity in the theatre, which have been a race against time. Everybody is intensely focused, and concentration levels are high.

The second night is inevitably an anti-climax. What seemed an impossible feat less than twenty-four hours ago is now routine. 'What were we all worrying about?' everybody asks, 'It wasn't so hard after all!' The theatre is usually packed with well-wishers on the first night: on the second it may be half full.

Professionals often speak of 'second night syndrome', when concentration levels drop, lines get lost, cues are forgotten, and problems with props, scenery, costumes – and indeed the entire physical universe – conspire to create chaos on stage.

Beware!

the report, along with the times of curtain up, interval and curtain down, and the running time of each act. The DSM should also mark down any particularly positive elements of the show, such as the receptiveness of the audience and the length of the ovations the cast received.

Show reports are usually written up immediately after the show and distributed to the producer, creative team, theatre management and stage management the next day.

PREPARING FOR THE SECOND PERFORMANCE

The first night is an education for everybody. The audience's response is the only unre-hearsed and therefore the only truly spontaneous element of the performance, and director and cast must be prepared to learn from it. The first public preview of a new musical marks the start of a massive rewriting process that may continue for months on tour prior to a West End or Broadway opening. The acid test for each revised version is always the reaction of the audience.

Before the second performance the director should run through any technical notes with the stage manager and the relevant departments heads. Frequently cue points need to be changed, or their uptimes and downtimes modified. Talk to the sound department about the balance, particularly if it seemed erratic or uneven.

Get together with the company, the MD and the choreographer well before the 'half', and run through any notes. Unless the first night went disastrously wrong there is usually a relaxed atmosphere at this session. The air is filled with a palpable sense of achievement that may verge on smugness. Encourage the actors to stay on their toes, and warn them not to fall prey to 'second night syndrome'.

You may wish to re-block and re-rehearse some sequences on stage. That is fine, but don't get carried away and try to do too much. Actors like to feel that the work is secure, and too many changes at this point can be disconcerting for the amateur. If you have a brilliant new idea for a scene halfway through the second act, introduce it by all means, as long as it does not involve re-blocking the next twenty minutes of the show and requires five new costumes. If you are making any cuts or re-assigning lines, use tact and discretion.

Make sure that the actors feel they can discuss specific concerns with you. A loved one or a critic may have made a specific criticism about an actor that has undermined their confidence. It is not unknown for actors to radically alter aspects of their performance or

Choreographer Aidan Treays warms up the cast of **The Secret Garden** *before a performance. Arts Educational School, London.*

appearance due to a casual remark from a friend. This is highly unprofessional and unsettling for their fellow actors, not to mention the director.

The director needs to be aware if actors have any such anxieties. Be open: maybe they have a point. After all, a fresh eye may have spotted something that you have missed. If an actor voices a specific concern and you think it may be valid, tell them to stick with their original performance but assure them that you will watch it carefully, critically and objectively. Make it clear, though, that your decision will be final. Be prepared to stick to your guns, or you may find more of the cast starting to make their own 'improvements', and the fabric of the production will come apart at the seams.

REVIEWS

Even the smallest review of the production in the humblest local paper can have an overwhelming effect on your cast's morale. Particular words or phrases may haunt actors for decades, long after the production has been forgotten and the reviewer has forgotten they ever saw the show.

Some strong-willed actors claim never to read their reviews, or at least to wait until the run is over. Good reviews appear on the company noticeboard in a flash, whereas the merest suggestion of a bad one circulates backstage like a virus. While everyone loves a good review, dealing with a negative one is difficult. Try and shrug it off. Tell yourself, if the vast majority of the audience seem to be enjoying themselves, why should you worry what one or two killjoys think?

It can still be very hard, though.

Into the Run

The second performance is followed by the third, the fourth, the fifth. As the cast grow in confidence, the pace of the show will speed up, and the dance numbers get slicker. Quick costume changes that seemed impossible at the tech are now achieved with time to spare; scene changes speed up; the sound balance improves. If you are only running for a week, the cast and crew may feel that they are only just beginning to get to grips with the show and give of their best when the curtain falls for the last time.

In professional productions, all the creative team except the MD are usually paid off after the press night. Their work is done, and

Wardrobe mistress mending a costume that has been damaged during a performance.

ownership of the show passes from them to the cast, the production team and the audience.

Every director finds leaving a show a strange, bittersweet experience, especially if rehearsals have been positive and enjoyable. They change overnight from being ever-present, all-powerful controllers at the heart of the production, to peripheral figures with no specific function.

Commercial managements may pay the director a small retainer (or a negotiable percentage of the gross receipts) to watch the production once a week or so, and to ensure that its artistic integrity is main-

tained. It is amazing how performances can change over the course of a week, sometimes for better, sometimes for worse. Encourage cast members to continue with new ideas that are working well and enriching the show; on the other hand, be clear about those that are not, and give the appropriate note.

Large-scale West End and Broadway shows employ associate directors to keep the show on track, rehearse new cast members and understudies, and in some cases take it on tour, while the original director may not see it again for months, or even years.

Costumes have to be washed after each performance: the glamour of show business!

Keeping the Show Polished

If your show is only running for a week or so, it is unlikely that cast and crew will get bored and start doing their work in a slapdash fashion. On longer runs, especially if the director is not present, this is a real danger, and steps need to be taken to ensure that the quality of the show does not deteriorate.

If the MD is playing and/or conducting throughout the run, they will be able to monitor the musical quality of the show, and call additional individual or group rehearsals as required. Maintaining the standard of the choreography is the responsibility of the dance captain, and they may call company rehearsals once a week or so to recap routines, tighten up on timing, and check the spacing on stage. Fights should always be rehearsed every night at the 'half': actors can get blasé about them, and that is when accidents occur.

Even if the production is only running for a week, each staging department must check and maintain materials and equipment on a daily basis. A wardrobe mistress needs to be appointed to take charge of costume cleaning and maintenance, keeping an eye out for split seams and missing buttons, and doing running repairs as required. Wigs should be checked daily, and re-dressed when necessary.

Lighting and sound-board operators must check all circuits and equipment before each show, and replace any blown fuses or bulbs. The mic runner needs to check that the radio mics have not been damaged during the previous performance, and that battery packs are fully charged. The ASM checks that the props are working properly, and that supplies of any consumable items such as food or drink are replenished.

UNDERSTUDIES, CHILDREN AND DEPUTIES

In theory, understudies should be sufficiently rehearsed to go on stage from the first performance. In practice, the rush of last-minute activity in production week means they become a low priority – unless the leading lady breaks her leg, of course, and then rehearsing her understudy suddenly becomes the number one priority!

Once the show has opened, the assistant director or stage manager should rehearse the understudies on the set. The MD or his assistant should give them individual coaching on their music, and the dance captain work with them on choreography. If you are running for several weeks, give them the opportunity to rehearse and sing on stage at least once a week. Understudies for large-scale professional shows are frequently allowed to play the role at mid-week matinées, to give them performance experience and give the principal actors a break.

If an understudy has to go on, it may be at very short notice. They will inevitably be nervous, so if time permits, you should let them walk through the role on stage. Make sure that any fights, dances, slapstick business or kisses have been rehearsed with the relevant members of the cast, if only in the green room or in the wings. At the 'half', the DSM should inform the company that the understudy will be performing. If the understudy is a chorus member, make sure that any business they do in the show – be it setting chairs or firing a fatal shot – will be covered by someone else.

Understudying can be a terrifying business, and most casts will do their utmost to help the understudy get through the show. It is not uncommon for the rest of the cast to applaud an understudy at the curtain call: they have deserved it. Plus, of course – as in *42nd Street* – a star may be born overnight.

Stage performances by children are controlled by law, and most countries now impose limits on how many performances a child may give within a week, and/or over

Save your reviews, especially the good ones. They are vital for maintaining interest in the show and keeping up ticket sales once you have opened.

a period of months. Even a short run will probably require two teams of children to cover all the performances, and longer runs may need many more. Responsibility for rehearsing in a new team of children may be shared between the assistant director and the MD, or the assistant director, the dance captain and the stage manager.

Instrumentalists frequently cannot attend all performances, and in these cases a deputy, or 'dep', must be found. It is usually the responsibility of the individual musician in question to recruit – and, if appropriate, to pay – a deputy who is capable of playing the score on sight, as often there will be no time for them to rehearse.

MAINTAINING TICKET SALES

Ticket sales are the lifeblood of any production. In the professional world, the moment a show's weekly sales' income is no longer sufficient to cover its running costs, it will almost certainly close.

A production in a school or college has a captive market of parents and students, and a short run may well sell out quickly. If you are not in this situation, do not let your marketing regime fizzle out after the first night. Commercial producers have ongoing publicity budgets, and often spend vast amounts of money on print and press advertising to keep the public aware that their show is on.

If you are going on tour, on whatever scale, make sure you remember to take everything with you. Photo: Tina Bicât

You can do the same without spending a fortune. Make sure that good reviews are posted up in front of the theatre. Reprint your flyers and/or posters with selective quotations from the press, and distribute them as widely as you can. Post them on your web site, along with booking details, times and prices. Make sure the production continues to appear in listings magazines and local newspapers.

If sales start to slide, try offering two-for-the-price-of-one deals. Give out handbills in the street. Don't be proud: do anything and everything you can to keep ticket sales going.

GOING ON TOUR

If the show is going on tour to another town or city, advance publicity is essential. The press and publicity officer should visit the theatre or theatres you are going to well in advance, and ensure that they have an adequate supply of your promotional material. Liaise with their publicity departments to identify opportunities in local newspapers, radio or even television.

The key to successful touring is good planning. The tour manager – a role often undertaken by the production manager – is responsible for liaising with the technical managers of the theatres on the tour, and ensuring that the technical requirements of the show are fully understood and can be accommodated in each building. Transportation of the set and any additional technical hardware needs to be organized, and a schedule agreed for the fit-up, rigging, focusing, technical rehearsal and dress rehearsal if required.

When a large cast goes on tour there is usually a dedicated company manager to organize their transport and accommodation. On smaller tours this responsibility is undertaken by the stage manager. If the cast travel independently of the crew and equipment vehicles, make sure they know when they are required to attend, and that

Strange Theatres, Strange Towns

No two theatres have exactly the same lay-out backstage, so when actors perform in a new venue the most familiar place is on the set. The stage manager should make sure they take time to learn the routes to and from their dressing rooms, the green room and the stage. Meanwhile the company manager should scout around and produce a map of supermarkets, cafés and restaurants in the area.

A short tour can be an exhilarating and exhausting experience for an amateur company. It generates enormous esprit de corps and can feel like a thrilling, extraordinary holiday. Longer tours can be more of a strain. Some professional actors love touring, but many others find the endless days hanging around in strange towns, far from family, friends and loved ones, an ordeal.

they allow a realistic amount of time for the journey.

Professional artists on tour are awarded a daily allowance, or 'per diem', to cover their accommodation and living costs while they are away from home. The company manager should provide a list of local hotels or 'digs', but it is usually advisable to let the actors choose their own accommodation and book it themselves.

Block bookings should be made for large school and college casts. Be aware that children under the age of sixteen require a licensed chaperone or parent or guardian to travel with them.

THE END OF THE RUN

Eventually, always, whether it has lasted for a few days or many years, the run comes to an end. Professional actors usually take a san-guine attitude to the final performance: for many it means unemployment; others are already planning to move on to the next job. Either way, they need to look to the future, not dwell on an experience that is already in the past.

The last performance of an amateur production can have a similar bittersweet air of anti-climax. Suddenly the whole experience is over, and the common purpose that bound a disparate group of people together, and which was the focus of their work, enthusiasm and energy over weeks or months, has suddenly disappeared. The company spirit may last a few hours longer if there is a 'last night' party, but by the next day people have begun to go their separate ways and the experience is over, never to be repeated.

THE LAST PERFORMANCE

On the day of the final performance there is a general wish to get things done quickly. The work begins as soon as the curtain has gone up for the last time.

As costumes are no longer needed, the wardrobe department should gather them up and start to sort them on rails depending on whether they are to be returned to hire companies, stored or thrown away. Act One trucks may be dismantled in the wings during the interval, and loaded into a van to be salvaged or dumped.

The stage manager should start collecting up scores and libretti from the cast a few days before the end of the run, returning deposits as appropriate. Getting the actors to erase any pencil marks will save you a lot of tedious work. Gather up the band parts and the MD's score as soon as the final encore has been played.

When the final curtain has fallen, the 'strike' begins: this is the get-in, in reverse, at high speed. Great care should be taken during the strike: it takes place late in the evening,

Lighting on tour. Notice that the flight case is being used as a stand for the board.

everybody wants to get it done as quickly as possible, and accidents can easily happen.

Make sure the lighting power supply is turned off before starting the strike.

If the strike is to run quickly and efficiently it needs to be planned. Assign crew members to specific departments as you did at the get-in, and make sure the transportation is ready and waiting. If you are using a professional crew be aware that you may have to pay them double or triple time after midnight. That should act as an incentive, if nothing else does.

As final performances usually take place on a Saturday night most of the hired and borrowed equipment cannot be returned until Monday morning. You may be allowed to leave some equipment in the theatre for the remainder of the weekend, but be sure to clear the stage for the next production coming in.

Hired lanterns, loudspeakers, microphones and other hardware need to be unplugged, de-rigged, sorted and packed up in flight cases. Backcloths and gauzes need to be detached

*RIGHT: Final production report on **The Frogs**. Send this information to everyone who supported the production financially or in kind: especially if you are planning on asking them for money for another project.*

PRODUCTION REPORT - THE FROGS

"The wittiest and most original musical in London... a triumph" (The Guardian); "One of the most unusual and entrancing shows I've ever been to... quite brilliant" (Financial Times); "Why can't real opera be as inventive, original, flamboyant and unpretentious?" (The Observer).

This was the press response to COEX's production of Stephen Sondheim's THE FROGS, which was performed at - and in - Old Brentford Swimming Pool from July 24th - August 4th 1990, by a largely amateur local cast of 40.

The project was over a year in the making, and the company had to overcome massive logistical, financial and bureaucratic hurdles to bring it to fruition. Apart from the obvious difficulties involved in mounting a production in a swimming pool - designing and building floating stages, choreographing singing swimmers, coping with strange acoustics, meeting rigorous safety requirements etc etc - there were many other unforeseen problems. Building delays at Acton Pool - the original venue - led first to a postponement of several months, and subsequently to a shift of venue; the change in political control at Ealing Council meant that our grant from them was frozen pending review at a critical juncture; and a last minute safety review of the pool meant a reduction in our projected audience capacity.

However, with financial support from the London Borough Grants Authority, the London Borough of Ealing and Cameron Mackintosh, and with the co-operation of Hounslow Council, the staff of the pool, the Rushmore synchronised swimming team and over 100 volunteers, the show opened on time.

The first night was covered by BBC TV, Channel 4 and BSB, and by Radio 4's Kaleidescope and LBC's Artbeat. Features about the production also appeared in The Times, The Independent, The New York Times and the American magazine Theatre Week.

The response from our audiences was very enthusiastic and we were completely sold out by the second performance - before the newspaper reviews came out! Audience members included Stephen Sondheim, James Lapine, Julia MacKenzie, the Mayor of Hounslow, plus a gentleman who had travelled from Hamburg especially to see the show.

Thanks to our success at the box office - and some astute merchandising - the production made a small profit (see attached accounts). Although COEX have no plans to mount a production in 1991, the Management Committee have decided to keep the company bank accounts open, pending plans for 1992 and beyond.

John Gardyne - Director

from the flies and packed away. Props need to be gathered up and sorted for return.

How much of the set is thrown away, and how much is kept will depend upon the nature of your organization and the amount of storage space available. Rostra, treads, large flats and doorframes can always be salvaged and used in future sets. It is usually the set pieces that were made specifically for the show – the most lovingly designed, the most carefully painted and built, and the most striking on stage – that will never be used again.

If you are throwing away a lot of material, hire a skip or organize a big enough van for a run to the dump. Old sets make good materials for bonfires, too.

The stage manager is, as usual, the last person out of the building. Double check all the dressing rooms, the green room, and all backstage areas before you go. Something always gets left behind.

It is traditional to leave a good luck note for the next company in the green room or the largest dressing room. Then turn off the lights, and tell the stage-door keeper that you have finished.

BALANCING THE BOOKS

Over the next week or so the production manager should make sure that all the production departments have submitted their final accounts and returned any petty cash that has not been spent. These records should then be handed on to the producer.

The box-office manager will supply the producer with final audience figures for each performance, the number of seats sold, whether standard price, concessionary, standby or complimentary, and of course, the takings. The income from ticket sales is used to calculate the final rights payment due to the licensing agent, and is normally due within thirty days of the final performance. Scores, libretti and band parts should be returned as soon as possible.

The producer should prepare a final report for backers and funding bodies. This should include a global balance sheet for the production, showing a final breakdown of all income and expenditure, plus statistics of ticket sales and a report on popular and critical reactions to the show, exposure in the media and so on.

Put a selection of good production shots, press coverage and publicity materials into a binder. Theatre is written in sand, and you need to keep a tangible record of your achievement; as people's memories fade, this will become the only true record of the production.

Making a video of the production can be a violation of your performance licence, so check with the agent before doing so. Be aware also that lighting for the stage is very different from lighting for film. An amateur video of a performance, filmed from the back of the stalls with the sound picked up by its internal microphone, can be at best disappointing, at worst positively distressing.

Musicals are expensive. The vast majority of commercial productions never recoup their original investment, and yours may end up losing money. You may be able to recoup losses by selling off materials and costumes. Try posting information about what you've got on offer, and see what happens: there must be someone out there who is looking for a well-made Audrey II or a complete set of costumes for *Into the Woods*.

You can continue with fund-raising activities – car boot sales, sponsored parachute jumps, benefit nights and so on – but it is always difficult to motivate people to partake in these once the production is in the past. Or you could, of course, start thinking about producing another show...

What is a musical without a big finish? The finale of The Wizard of Oz *at the Hong Kong Academy for Performing Arts. Photo: by courtesy of HKAPA*

STARTING AGAIN

The producer is the person who lives longest with the show, who works hardest at it, who expends the most blood, sweat and tears on it, and who is the last to leave it.

By the time you have been through this process once, you will have learned an immeasurable amount. You will have sharpened your organizational and negotiating skills, honed your business acumen, created working relationships with numerous artists, made many new friends with whom you have shared an extraordinary journey, and created an unforgettable, unique and enriching experience for your audience.

Remember: the first time is the hardest. Once you have one successful and memorable show under your belt, producing a second one will be easier; and a third will be easier still.

Producers are a rare breed: without them, theatre would not exist. Bear that in mind as you walk away from the theatre after the final performance, the applause still ringing in your ears. You may even feel like jotting down a few thoughts on the back of an envelope about what you might do next year.

Just make sure you take a holiday first.

GLOSSARY

Acapella   Unaccompanied singing.

Angel   A private individual who invests in a production for a share in the profits.

Apron   Extension of the stage beyond the proscenium arch.

Aria   A solo song in an opera.

ASM   Assistant stage manager, the most junior member of the stage management team.

Backcloth   A painted cloth suspended from the flies at the rear of the stage.

Backlight   Light that comes from behind the actors, used to sculpt and shape their bodies.

Band parts   The music for each instrumentalist.

Bar   *see* Flying bar.

Barn doors   External shutters on a lantern used to control the spread of its beam.

Barre   A horizontal rail used by dancers for support when exercising.

Batten   A length of timber used to build and reinforce scenery.

Beginners   (1) Actors who are onstage or ready in the wings at the beginning of each act. (2) The warning call given by the DSM five minutes before each act begins.

Black   A large black cloth, usually serge, that can be flown in to cover the whole height and width of the stage.

Blacks   A complete set of black clothes worn by the crew and stage management so they are less obtrusive during scene changes.

Bleed through   The effect of lighting a gauze from behind, so that whatever is behind it gradually becomes visible.

Blocking   The actors' entrances, exits and movement round the stage, recorded in the prompt copy by the DSM.

Board   Control unit for mixing and controlling sound and light equipment.

Boards   The stage – hence 'to tread the boards'.

Book   (1) The script of a musical. (2) The prompt copy prepared by the DSM.

Box office split   Business arrangement between a production company and a theatre under which income from ticket sales is split between them at a previously agreed percentage rate.

Box set   A set consisting of three walls and sometimes a ceiling piece. The proscenium arch is the 'fourth wall'.

Break down   (1) To add extra splashes of colour to a painted flat to give it a richer texture when lit. (2) To distress a costume or prop to make it look old or well-worn.

Bridge   (1) A musical link between two other passages. (2) A gallery above the stage or auditorium used for access and rigging lights.

Build   (1) To increase in level. (2) To add lanterns one by one into a lighting state until the desired effect is achieved.

Business   The actions performed by an actor during a performance.

Busy   Distracting, containing too many disparate elements. A performance, costume or set can be 'busy'.

Call   (1) Notification of the time an actor, musician or crew member is required at rehearsal; for example, 'a ten o'clock call'. Also the length of a single working session: 'The call lasted three hours.' (2) Tannoy announcement made to backstage or front of house. (3) The curtain call.

Calling the show   The DSM's main function during a performance. To run a show from the prompt copy by giving cues to the staging and technical departments.

Cans   Headsets used by stage management and technical departments to communicate during rehearsals in the theatre and in performance.

Carrying the show   A role or performance that is so large and significant that it is the overwhelmingly predominant feature of the production. Tevye 'carries' *Fiddler on the Roof*.

Casuals   Temporary staff – usually crew members – who work on the show for a few days during the get-in and the strike.

Choreographer   The member of the creative team responsible for creating and rehearsing all dance elements.

Clearance   (1) Confirmation from front-of-house staff that the audience are seated and the performance can begin. (2) The distance between one flying piece and the next.

Cloth   A canvas sheet, large enough to cover the whole height and width of the stage which has been painted or treated to give a certain scenic effect and is flown in when required.

Company call   A rehearsal session at which all performers are required.

Control box   The closed-off area at the back of the theatre where the lighting board operator (and sometimes the DSM) sits while running a performance.

Comps   Complimentaries, i.e. free tickets.

Creative team   The team of people – director, musical director, choreographer and set, costume, lighting and sound designers, and others – who between them conceive and plan the entire production.

Crew   Stage technicians who fit up and operate all the technical aspects of the show during performance.

Crossfade To move from one lighting or sound cue to the next with no gap between them.

Crossover A route from one side of the stage to the other – usually extreme upstage – which the actors can use without being seen by the audience.

Cue (1) Actor's signal to speak their line or perform some action on stage. (2) Point at which a staging, sound or light effect takes place.

Cue light A light used to give a cue that cannot be given verbally, such as to the conductor to start the show.

Cue sheet Numeric list of effects carried out by each specific stage or technical department.

Cue to cue Running the whole show but cutting sequences in which there are no technical effects or cues. Often done at the technical rehearsal.

Curtain call Bows at the end of the performance.

Curtain up The start of the show: 'Five minutes to curtain up.'

Cyclorama ('Cyc') A large white or light blue cloth at the back of the stage that gives an impression of light and space. Sometimes referred to as a 'skycloth'.

Dance captain Choreographer's assistant, responsible for leading dance warm-ups and running brush-up dance rehearsals once the show has opened.

Dark A theatre that is temporarily or permanently closed.

Dead (1) The exact position of a flown piece when it is either in view ('in dead') or out of view ('out dead'). (2) Redundant: 'The throne is dead in Act Two.'

Desk The lighting board or sound mixing control. The 'production desk' is the table the creative team and board operators sit at during technical and dress rehearsals.

Dimmer Device that controls the amount of electricity passed to a lantern.

Director Person in overall control of all artistic and creative elements of the show.

Dress To add decoration or objects to the set to make it look more authentic.

Dresser Member of the wardrobe department who assists the actors with their costume changes and wigs during a performance.

Dry To forget lines during rehearsal or performance.

DSM Deputy stage manager, responsible for recording all elements of the production in the prompt copy and running the show during performance.

Earned income Income from sales of tickets, programmes, refreshments, programmes and so on.

Electrics ('LX') The lighting department, or the technicians who work within it: 'Can you tell LX that this bulb has blown.'

Equalization ('EQ') Series of controls on a sound mixer used to adjust and balance tonal quality.

Feedback   High-pitched squeal caused when a microphone picks up sound from a loud-speaker to which it is connected electronically. Sometimes known as 'howlround'.

Fit-up   (1) To assemble and install all elements of the set on stage. (2) The period of time allocated for this job.

Flies   The area above the stage that holds suspended scenery and lighting.

Float microphone   Microphone fixed at the edge of the stage.

Flood   Simple lantern giving a fixed spread of light.

Floor cloth   Heavy-duty cloth which may be painted as part of the design.

Fluff   To muddle up or miss out lines during a rehearsal or performance.

Flying bar   A long metal tube hung or flown horizontally in the flies, from which scenery, lighting and other equipment can be suspended. Known in the USA as a 'pipe'.

Fly floor   A raised platform in the wings running the whole depth of the stage from which the theatre's flying system is operated.

Flyman   Specialist crew member who operates the flying system.

Foldback   Loudspeakers in the orchestra pit or at the back/sides of the stage, that let the band and cast hear each other clearly.

Follow spot   Lantern that can be moved to follow performers as they move round the stage.

Fresnel   Type of stage lantern.

Frontcloth   A cloth painted as part of the design, hung as far downstage as possible to allow scene changes to happen behind it.

Front of House (FOH)   (1) The area of the theatre that is open to the public. (2) The department responsible for all aspects of this area, including the audience.

Frost   Diffusing filter used to soften the beam from a lantern.

Gauze   Stage cloth made from open-weave fabric that becomes transparent when lit from behind. Known as 'scrim' in the USA.

Gel   Translucent plastic filter placed in a lantern to colour the light beam.

Get-in   The process of moving all the elements and equipment for the show into the theatre.

Get-out   The reverse of the 'get in': dismantling and removing all the show's elements and equipment from the theatre.

Gobos   Metal or glass filters used to break up or shape the beam of light produced by a lantern.

Green room   Actors' common room and rest area.

Grid   Wooden or metal framework that supports the flying and lighting system.

Ground plan   Scale plan of the set showing the positions of scenic elements and furniture.

Ground row   (1) Row of lanterns set on the stage floor, usually used to light the bottom half of the cyclorama. (2) Low-level piece of scenery running across the width of the stage to mask its back edge and give a sense of perspective. Often used to conceal lanterns fixed on the stage.

Half   The half-hour call, given thirty-five minutes before curtain up.

Hanging plot   List of all flying bars showing what equipment is attached to each one.

'Heads'   Warning given to alert people on stage that equipment is being lowered (or has been dropped!) from the flies.

HODs   Heads of staging departments, working under the production manager.

House   (1) The auditorium. (2) The audience ('We had a good house tonight').

House tabs   The heavy velvet curtains that separate the stage from the auditorium.

Howlround   *see* Feedback.

In the round   Form of theatre where the audience sit on all four sides of the acting area.

Instrument   Alternative term for a stage lantern, especially used in America.

Iris   Adjustable circular diaphragm used to alter the beam size produced by a profile lantern.

Iron   Safety curtain used to separate the auditorium from the stage in the event of a fire. Must be lowered and raised once during the course of each performance, usually in the interval.

Lantern   A single stage light of whatever type.

Lead   A principal actor, usually the largest or most important part in the show.

Legs   Vertical strips of fabric, usually used for masking.

Libretto   Printed script of all dialogue and lyrics.

Limes   Follow spots, sometimes follow-spot operators.

Line run   A run through without moves, action or dance to ensure that everybody knows their words.

LX   Abbreviated term for 'Electrics'.

Marking   To sing, dance or act with limited volume or commitment to conserve energy in rehearsal.

Mark out   To stick coloured tapes to the rehearsal room floor or stage to indicate the correct position of furniture and props.

Masking   Neutral material or scenery – usually black – which defines the limits of the stage area and conceals backstage.

MD   Musical director.

Not-for-profit   An organization with no shareholders that is solely concerned with covering its operating costs.

Notebash   Initial teaching and learning of vocal lines.

Notices   Alternative term for newspaper reviews.

Offstage   In the wings or out of the audience's view.

Pack   A radio mic transmitter.

Paintframe   Structure in which stage cloths are suspended for painting.

Palette   The colour-scheme chosen by the designers for set, costume and lighting.

Paper the house   To ensure a full house for a particular performance by giving away large numbers of complimentary tickets.

Parcan   Type of lantern.

Pass door   Door that leads from backstage to the auditorium.

Performance licence   Licence that gives permission for a public performance to take place within a building.

Performing rights   Permission granted by writers or their agents to a producer or organization, allowing them to stage their show for an agreed number of performances.

Periaktoi   Triangular truck with painted flats mounted on each side, particularly useful for achieving quick scene changes in theatres that have no flying equipment.

Personal prop   A small item such as a wallet, purse or cigarette packet that a certain actor wears or carries on stage.

Pipe   American term for flying bar.

Practical   A prop, light or set item (such as a door) that has to work during the performance.

Preset   Anything that is positioned in advance, such as props set on stage before the action begins.

Press night   Official first performance of a show, to which reviewers and critics are invited.

Preview   Public performance held before the official first night.

Profile   Type of lantern.

Promenade   Style of performance in which the actors and audience mingle together, and the action moves from place to place.

Prompt copy   Definitive, annotated copy of the score/libretto used by the DSM to run the show.

Prompt desk   DSM's control desk incorporating all cue lights, relays and communications facilities.

Proscenium arch   Traditional form of theatre where the audience sit in a single block and are separated from the stage by some kind of 'picture frame'.

Pyrotechnics   Bangs, flashes, maroons and so on, usually fired electronically.

Q   Shorthand form of 'cue'.

Quarter   The fifteen-minute call, given twenty minutes before curtain up.

Répétiteur   Music and singing coach, assistant to the MD. This term is used especially in opera.

Resumé   Professional performer's CV, giving personal details and a list of previous engagements. Especially used in America.

Rig   The entire disposition of all lanterns, microphones and speakers for a performance.

Run   (1) All the performances from opening to closing night: 'a five-week run'. (2) A rehearsal at which the action is not stopped or interrupted: 'There will be a run on Monday.'

Safety curtain   *see* Iron.

Scrim   *see* Gauze.

Segue   Musical term meaning 'to follow on immediately without any break'.

Setting list   List of where all props must be placed on stage and in the wings before curtain up.

Sightlines   The limits of the audience's vision into the wings and flies.

Sitzprobe   Rehearsal at which the cast sing along with the orchestra but do not act or dance.

Skycloth   · *see* Cyclorama.

Slash curtain   Shiny foil strips hanging from a bar which give the impression of a single metallic sheet.

SM   Stage manager.

Spill   Stray light outside the main beam of a spotlight.

Standby   Warning given to an operator or performer that a cue is about to be given.

Strike   To remove an item from the stage when it is no longer needed: 'strike that chair'.

Swatch   A sample of fabric.

Swing   Performer who can understudy any chorus role. This term is especially used of dancers.

Tallescope   An adjustable ladder on wheels with a platform on top, used when adjusting lanterns and other equipment in the flies.

TBC   To be confirmed.

Throw   The distance between a lantern and the object or person it is lighting.

Topping and tailing   *see* Cue to cue.

Tormentors   Narrow masking flats set at right angles to the proscenium arch.

Traveller   Stage cloth that runs horizontally across the stage.

Traverse   Form of theatre where the audience sit on two opposite sides of the acting area.

Treads   Stairs.

Tripe   Mass of several cables taped together on a flying bar.

Triple threat performer   A performer who is equally adept at acting, singing and dancing – and who is therefore highly employable.

Truck   Castored platform on which set elements may be constructed.

Underdress To wear several costumes at once, one over another, to allow for quick changes.

Underscoring Music played under dialogue scenes.

Unearned income Income from grants, donations, investment and so on.

UV Ultraviolet light, used to light treated materials to give a fluorescent effect on a darkened stage.

Vari*lite Type of computerized, programmable lantern.

Vocal selections Sheet music of selected songs from a show.

Walk the lights To stand on or move around the stage during the focusing or lighting session so that the position of lanterns can be fixed.

Walkdown Extended curtain call in a pantomime.

Wings (1) Space at the side of the stage. (2) Painted flats or black masking that define the limits of the acting area.

Working lights Theatre lights that are independent from the stage lights, and used during rehearsals and fitting up.

FURTHER READING

REFERENCE

Bell, M. *Backstage on Broadway – Musicals and their Makers* (Nick Hern Books 1994).

Bordman, G. *American Musical Theatre – A Chronicle* (OUP 2001).

Bordman, G. *The Oxford Companion to American Theatre* (OUP 1984).

Bullock, G. *Enchanted Evenings: The Broadway Musical from Showboat to Sondheim* (OUP 1997).

Bunnett, R. *Guide to Musicals*, 2nd edition (Harper Collins 2001).

Citron, S. *The Musical from the Inside Out* (Hodder and Stoughton 1991).

Gänzl, K. *Gänzl's Book of the Broadway Musical: 75 Favorite Shows from HMS Pinafore (1879) to Sunset Boulevard (1995)* (Schirmer Books 1995).

Gänzl, K. *Musicals – The Complete Story* (Bloomsbury 1995).

Gänzl, K. *The Encyclopedia of the Musical Theatre* (3 volumes) (Scirmer Books 2001).

Green, S. (revised Green, K.) *Broadway Musicals Show by Show* (Hal Leonard 1996).

Harris, A. *Broadway Theatre* (Routledge 1993).

Larkin, C. *Virgin Encyclopedia of Stage and Film Musicals* (Virgin Books 1999).

Mandelbaum, K. *Not Since Carrie: Forty Years of Broadway Musical Flops* (St Martin's Press 1992).

Sheward, D. *It's a Hit – The Backstage Book of Longest Running Broadway Shows 1984 to the Present* (Backstage/Watson-Guptill Publications 1994).

Steyn, M. *Broadway Babies Say Goodnight* (Faber 1997).

Wilmeth, D. and Miller, T. *The Cambridge Guide to American Theatre* (CUP 1993).

PRODUCTION AND INDIVIDUAL THEATRE ARTS

Aronson, A. *American Set Design* (Theatre Communications Group 1985).

Berkson, R. *Musical Theatre Choreography* (A.&C. Black 1990).

Burnett, K. and Ruthven Hall, P. *Make Space* (Society of British Theatre Designers 1994).

Campbell, D. *Technical Theatre for Non-Technical People* (Allworth Press 1998).

Craig, D. *A Performer Prepares* (Applause 1993).

Craig, D. *On Singing on Stage* (Applause 1993).

Filichia, P. *Let's Put On a Musical* (Backstage Books 1993).

Fraser, N. *Lighting and Sound* (Phaidon 1988).

Goodwin, J. (ed.) *British Theatre Design – The Modern Age* (Weidenfield & Nicholson 1989).

Govier, J. *Create Your Own Stage Props* (A.&C. Black 1984).

Hoare, W. *The Musical Director in the Amateur Theatre* (J. Garnett Miller 1993).

Kelly, T. *The Back Stage Guide to Stage Management* (2nd edition) (Backstage Books 1999).

Leonard, J. *Theatre Sound* (A.&C. Black 2001).

Pilbrow, R. *Stage Lighting* (Nick Hern Books, revised edition 1979).

Reid, F. *Discovering Stage Lighting* (Focal Press 1993).

Reid, F. *The Staging Handbook* (A.&C. Black 1983).

Spencer, P. *Musicals – The Guide to Amateur Production* (J. Garnett Miller 1983).

Sunderland, M. and Pickering K. *Choreographing the Stage Musical* (J. G. Miller 1989).

Young, D. *How to Direct a Musical – Broadway Your Way* (Routledge 1995).

OTHER BOOKS IN THIS SERIES

Baldwin, C. *Stage Directing – A Practical Guide* (Crowood 2003).

Bicât, T. *Making Stage Costumes – A Practical Guide* (Crowood 2001).

Bicât, T. *Period Costume for the Stage – A Practical Guide* (Crowood 2003).

Ed. Bicât, T. and Baldwin, C. *Devised and Collaborative Theatre – A Practical Guide* (Crowood 2002).

Blaikie, T. and Troubridge, E. *Scenic Art and Construction – A Practical Guide* (Crowood 2002).

Copley, S. and Killner, P. *Stage Management – A Practical Guide* (Crowood 2001).

Dean, P. *Production Management: Making Shows Happen – A Practical Guide* (Crowood 2002).

Doyle, R. *Staging Youth Theatre – A Practical Guide* (Crowood 2003).

Fraser, N. *Stage Lighting Design – A Practical Guide* (Crowood 1999).

Fraser, N. *Stage Lighting Explained – A Practical Guide* (Crowood 2002).

Perry, J. *The Rehearsal Handbook for Actors and Directors – A Practical Guide* (Crowood 2001).

Taylor, V. *Stage Writing – A Practical Guide* (Crowood 2002).

Thorne, G. *Designing Stage Costumes – A Practical Guide* (Crowood 2001).

Thorne, G. *Stage Design – A Practical Guide* (Crowood 1999).

Wilson, A. *Making Stage Props – A Practical Guide* (Crowood 2003).

INDEX